Men Without Country

MEN WITHOUT COUNTRY

The true story of exploration and
rebellion in the South Seas

Harrison Christian

ultimo
press

Published in 2021 by Ultimo Press,
an imprint of Hardie Grant Publishing

Ultimo Press
Gadigal Country
7, 45 Jones Street
Ultimo, NSW 2007
ultimopress.com.au

Ultimo Press (London)
5th & 6th Floors
52–54 Southwark Street
London SE1 1UN

Men Without Country
ISBN 978 1 76115 070 8

10 9 8 7 6 5 4 3 2 1

Cover design and illustration
Jessica Cruickshank / The Jacky Winter Group
Text design
Kirby Jones | Typeset in 13/19 pt Adobe Garamond Pro
Copyeditor
Deonie Fiford
Proofreader
Pamela Dunne

Printed and bound in Great Britain by Clays Ltd, Elcograf S.p.A.

Ultimo Press acknowledges the Traditional Owners of the country on which we work, the Gadigal people of the Eora nation and the Wurundjeri people of the Kulin nation, and recognises their continuing connection to the land, waters and culture. We pay our respects to their Elders past, present and emerging.

For my family

CONTENTS

Author's Note

Fletcher Christian led a mutiny on the British naval ship *Bounty* in April 1789; that much we know for sure. We have no want for facts about the mutiny itself, because a court martial pored over every physical detail. We know roughly what orders, insults and meaningful looks passed between the sailors, where they stood on the decks of the ship, and who among them carried muskets or cutlasses. A jury of captains in wigs and blue coats listened to the evidence and condemned three men to death by hanging. That was supposed to be the end of an interesting and obscure episode in naval history.

But the public interest in the story was only beginning. There was a sense the true drama of the *Bounty* voyage had been suppressed. The court martial revealed little in the way of cause or circumstance; it was only interested in sorting the mutineers from the innocents. William Bligh's baffled account of the mutiny did not ring true, and Christian remained an enigma, because he was never caught. Adding to that, the setting of his escape was ripe for myth and mystery. To Europeans, the Pacific was still alive with the shapes and forms of some atavistic dream, a place of incredible torments and delights where tethers to the Old World wore thin. Bligh crossed the threshold of that legendary world and returned with a strange tale. Fletcher Christian remained behind in it forever. Or did he?

Elusive as he was, Christian's descendants are scattered around the globe. He left three children on Pitcairn Island, including Charles Christian, my fifth great-grandfather. A Tahitian baby girl who arrived at Pitcairn Island with the mutineers on the *Bounty*, eleven months old at the time, grew up to be a woman known as Sully, my fifth great-grandmother. Among the migrants from Pitcairn Island to Norfolk Island in 1856 was my fourth great-grandfather Isaac Christian. My grandfather John Garton Christian was born on Norfolk Island and migrated to New Zealand as a young boy in the shadow of World War II. My father Brett Stephen Christian was born and raised in Auckland.

When I was growing up, my father told me I was a direct descendant of Fletcher Christian. I heard how Christian overthrew Bligh in the world's most famous mutiny. How he cast the lieutenant adrift, sailed the *Bounty* off the map and stranded himself on an island in the Pacific. I saw Christian and Bligh portrayed by actors like Marlon Brando and Anthony Hopkins. It was thrilling to think I was descended from such a man, and still is. But as I grew older, I realised the movies were works of fiction. The real story was unfinished, full of unanswered questions.

Men Without Country is my personal quest to know the *Bounty* characters and the world they lived in. My relation to Fletcher has no doubt coloured the contents of these pages, but I hope it hasn't disqualified me from writing a balanced account. My trade is journalism, and I have applied a journalistic method to the story. All quotes are taken from journals, letters, court proceedings, and other documents from the time. For smoother reading and easier comprehension, I have replaced archaic place names with their modern ones, and corrected misspellings and capitalisations, except where I think those spelling errors reveal something about a character.

Harrison Christian

Like one, that on a lonesome road

Doth walk in fear and dread,

And having once turned round walks on,

And turns no more his head;

Because he knows, a frightful fiend

Doth close behind him tread.

Samuel Taylor Coleridge, 'The Rime of the Ancient Mariner'

Introduction

On the evening of 15 January 1790, a gang of fugitives on the Royal Navy ship *Bounty*, searching the Pacific for a hideout from the law, raised an island that was remarkably well suited to their purposes. It was a high volcanic rock, thousands of miles from any continent, in a part of the world that was still poorly mapped and understood. The island's shoreline had all the qualities of a natural fortress, rising in sheer cliffs out of a lather of heavy surf, and allowing no anchorage for passing ships. No white man had ever set foot on it, but petroglyphs and stone figures recalled an outpost of Polynesians who had since perished or moved on. Despite its puny size (it was not much larger than New York's Central Park, with an area of just two square miles), the island was blessed with all the necessities of life. A freshwater stream ran down from the mountains, and fertile soils supported wild crops of bananas, breadfruit and yams.

According to British common law, the sailors on the *Bounty* were pirates, robbers and mutineers deserving of hanging. Their leader, 25-year-old Fletcher Christian, had rebelled against the ship's commander, Lieutenant William Bligh, and cast him adrift in a small boat with a huddle of loyalists in the Tongan islands. In the eight and a half months since, Christian and his supporters had ranged across the Pacific intending to start a secret colony, beyond the reach of Royal Navy ships that would inevitably come to hunt them. They had skirted disaster, narrowly avoiding other European ships and running into conflict with Polynesian tribes. Their attempt to settle another island, Tubuai in present-day French Polynesia, was a bloody failure. They were probably the first Europeans to lay eyes on Rarotonga, where the local populace remembered their ship for generations thereafter as a floating island that came bearing iron and oranges.

HMS *Bounty* was a leaky shell of the small but well-turned-out navy vessel that had sailed from Spithead years earlier. Her crew had jettisoned spars, sails and anchors while her timbers warped and shrunk in the tropical sun. Seawater would have rained through her decks onto the weary heads of her crew as they worked the bilge pumps. Before they raised their island, the *Bounty* mutineers had not seen land for two months. Morale was fading as Christian carried his followers east against the trade winds, poring over the books in Bligh's library and working to solve an old riddle before patience ran out.

Pitcairn Island's true location was unknown to the world. The British commander Philip Carteret had charted it decades earlier, but his recorded longitude was off by about three degrees, putting the island two hundred miles west of its actual position. Carteret did not have access to the latest gadgetry and he resorted to dead reckoning, a guesswork based on his vessel's speed, drift and compass heading. In the eighteenth century, islands could still outwit their discoverers and spend years dancing across the map, expanding into continents, shrinking into rocks and fogbanks, or simply vanishing altogether. Pitcairn was such an island. Even the great Captain James Cook had failed to find it again.

Christian had read Carteret's description of the island in Bligh's library and pinned his faith on it. When he reached the erroneous coordinates and found nothing but open sea, he correctly guessed that the longitude was a mistake, while the latitude, a much easier calculation, was probably correct. The *Bounty* zigzagged east, along the line of latitude, until Pitcairn's towering form appeared out of the heat haze in mid-January. The seas around the island were so violent that Christian had to wait three days before he could go ashore with a scouting party. A couple of days later he returned with a 'joyful expression such as we had not seen on him for a long time past'.* Pitcairn fulfilled all his requirements and crucially, it seemed devoid of inhabitants. He decided to settle the island, though not all the members of his company shared his resolve. While Christian was ashore, John Mills, the forty-year-old gunner's mate, tried and failed to persuade the others to leave their leader behind and run for Tahiti.

The mutineers ran the *Bounty* up on the rocks in an area they generously named 'Bounty Bay', little more than a slight indentation in the island's northern shoreline. In the shadow of cliffs of dark basaltic lava, they ferried their supplies ashore in jumbled parcels.

Together they formed a motley-looking group, an unlikely crew of outlaws and captives. Christian and the other Englishmen had been sailors in the Royal Navy, but they were no longer officers or men the Admiralty would recognise. Their slops had long since rotted off their backs; instead they wore makeshift jackets made from spare sails. On their heads were crazy hats made from leaves in the Tahitian fashion. Their hair hung loose about their shoulders, and their skin was tanned and tattooed from more than a year in the South Seas.

The *Bounty* also carried a cohort of Polynesians from the islands she had called at over the past several months. This heterogeneous group comprised six men, twelve

---

* Ford, *Pitcairn Island as a Port of Call*, p. 7.

women and a baby girl. They were clad in cloth bark ponchos, skirts and loincloths. They ranged in social rank from chiefs to commoners, spoke different languages, and had different ideas about the *Bounty*'s voyage. Some were willing passengers, like Christian's partner Mauatua, a tall and commanding woman from the chiefly class in Tahiti. Also among Christian's intrepid followers were two chiefs, one from Tubuai and another from the Polynesian holy land of Raiatea, as well as three Tahitian men who were discovered as stowaways and allowed to remain aboard. Other Tahitians were less agreeable to the voyage, and had not been aware, when the *Bounty* departed Tahiti, that they were leaving their homes forever to settle a foreign land.

All told, nine Europeans and nineteen Polynesians came ashore on Pitcairn Island that summer evening. Also proceeding from the ship were pigs, goats, chickens, cats and dogs, bucking in the surf on a raft made from the ship's hatches. Then came muskets, sails, grog and bushels of tropical fruit plants. The raft went to and fro all day. From the rocks, the crew carried the supplies up a steep slope, grasping at vines and fussing in the undergrowth, until they reached a small plateau overlooking the shore below. Reeling in the heat, they looked down at the *Bounty* and quarrelled over what to do with her. Christian wanted to save the ship, at least for a time, but some mutineers feared she would advertise their presence to other vessels. 'We shall be discovered,' was the argument from Matthew Quintal, one of the more unruly men among Christian's followers.[*]

Three days after the *Bounty* ran aground, not nearly enough time to bring everything useful ashore, three mutineers climbed into the ship and set fire to her in the forecastle. The rest of the settlers wept as they watched their only link to civilisation engulfed in flames.[†] Some of the mutineers regretted not confining Bligh in the *Bounty* and simply returning to England to give their reasons to a court martial. That night they slept under the firmament in the heat and quiet. Next day they were building temporary shelters behind a screen of trees.

In cautious forays, the white men confirmed the island was abandoned. The Tahitians, for their part, saw everywhere the ghosts and demons of the original settlers, lost to famine, civil war or some other remote doom. Before long it seemed the island's ancient curse had passed to the *Bounty* settlers. This was not a safe haven but a special kind of prison. Two decades of total isolation followed, enough time for the men to murder each other to the last, and for the women to carry out their own intrigues of murder and escape. The fate of Fletcher Christian, the mutinous lieutenant who hoped to live out his days in peaceful hiding, would never be known for sure.

---

[*] Teehuteatuaonoa (Jenny) interview, *Sydney Gazette and New South Wales Advertiser*, 1819.

[†] Teehuteatuaonoa (Jenny) interview, *United Service Journal*, 1829.

This book follows the men of the *Bounty* from England to Tahiti. It describes the mutiny that set them on divergent paths across the Pacific, and the assorted fates and fortunes of each group. The mutineers who settled Pitcairn Island constitute one thread of the story; a separate group of rebels were captured by the Royal Navy in Tahiti and brought back to England for trial. Another thread is the strange life of Lieutenant Bligh, who made a remarkable voyage to safety after his overthrow, only to be haunted by Christian and his pirates for the rest of his career.

Understanding the whole *Bounty* story requires a before-and-after that is seldom given. The events in this book are not presented in a historical vacuum, but as episodes in the human history of the Pacific Ocean. That means starting at the beginning; not in 1790 but many years earlier, with a violent meeting of cultures across the seas.

CHAPTER ONE

'The Peaceful Sea'

Europeans were driven into the Pacific by a combination of crusading Christian zeal and a hungry desire for new trade routes to Asia's spice lands. For centuries the world spice trade was a predominantly Islamic enterprise. Arab merchants bore the spices across the Indian Ocean from Asia to the Near East. From there, the cargo travelled overland to the Mediterranean and the colourful warehouses of rich city-states like Venice. When a sack of saffron reached Western Europe, its vibrant colour and aroma only hinted at some distant and magical wellspring of the world. Spices were luxuries, medicines and currency. Landlords accepted peppercorns in lieu of coins, while the heady smells of ginger, turmeric and cinnamon filled European courts as symbols of wealth and worldliness. The Arabs kept the source of the spices a secret, warding off prying customers with tales of pepper trees full of poisonous snakes, or giant birds that built their nests out of cinnamon sticks.

Portugal began testing the Venetian and Arab hold on the spice trade at the turn of the fifteenth century. Crescent-shaped carracks sailed forth from Lisbon with red crosses emblazoned on their sails, probing the African coast for a new sea route to Asia. In 1488 the Portuguese rounded the Cape of Good Hope, the south-western limit of the African continent.

Ten years later they reached the black pepper–filled emporiums of eastern India, where Arab merchants were amazed to see them: 'May the devil take you! What brought you here?'

'Christians and spices,' was the sailors' reply.

The Portuguese were relying on scientific instruments like the astrolabe to cross the ocean, but they still believed in a mythical Christian king named Prester John hidden somewhere in the Orient, and their maps were still populated with medieval sea monsters. In another decade they arrived at the Spice or Maluku Islands in Indonesia, the sole producer of nutmeg and cloves.

The Spanish, neighbours and sea rivals of the Portuguese, sent Christopher Columbus west rather than east. Columbus hoped to reach the Spice Islands across the Atlantic, a proposal dismissed as far-fetched even in those years. The Italian navigator understood the earth was spherical, but grossly underestimated its size, and the westerly distance of Asia from Europe. When he landed in the Caribbean Islands, he believed he had reached East Asia, not anticipating the existence of the Americas or the Pacific beyond it. He fancied the lush coasts of Cuba and Haiti might be those of China and Japan, but when he returned to Europe, spices were conspicuously absent from his cargo.

Shortly thereafter, Spain and Portugal signed a treaty carving the world in half along a demarcation line in the Atlantic. Portugal laid claim to the east, throwing out a chain of forts and factories that spanned the coasts of Brazil, Africa, India and China. Spain ruled everything to the west, including her discoveries in the Caribbean and any new lands beyond. The gold wealth waiting in lands such as Mexico would propel her ahead of Portugal as the great power of the sixteenth century.

In 1513 the Spanish conquistador Balboa, having heard local talk of an 'other sea', climbed a jungle-covered range in Panama and became the first European to lay eyes on the Pacific. In 1519 Spain sent five ships under Ferdinand Magellan to sail through or around South America and continue west in search of the Spice Islands. Magellan found a strait through southern Chile and emerged into the Pacific, naming it *Mar Pacifico*, Peaceful Sea, because it seemed a calm reprieve from the treacherous waters behind him. Like Columbus, he believed Asia to be much closer than it was, and expected to reach the Spice Islands in a matter of days.

Europeans were about to be brutally undeceived of the notion among Christian cartographers that the earth was seven parts land and only one part sea. The Pacific is a gigantic body of water that occupies one-third of the earth's surface. Magellan's voyage took nearly four months, and his ill-equipped company was forced to subsist on rats and sawdust before they reached Guam and the Philippines. Only eighteen of the expedition's two hundred and seventy men returned to Europe, completing the first circumnavigation of the globe. Magellan himself died in the Philippines, killed by a poison arrow in a skirmish with Filipino warriors. But he had secured for Spain a western gateway to Asia.

An oval-shaped trade route sprang up between Mexico and the Philippines, arcing south on the outward voyage and north on the inward in sync with a gyre of wind. Bulbous galleons left Acapulco carrying silver, chocolate and tobacco and returned from Manila eight months later stuffed with spices and porcelain. Their tracks across the Pacific were mere highways through a vast wilderness. The Spaniards charted a handful of Pacific Islands and remained oblivious to whole empires of Polynesians, skilled voyagers and navigators in their own right. The Hawaiian Islands, for example, lay hidden in the centre of their circular trade route. European pirates, when they did venture into the Pacific, tended to hug the western coast of South America in their search for Spanish plunder. To strike off into the blue expanse beyond the New World usually meant scurvy, starvation and death.

By the late eighteenth century the Pacific remained a dangerous and uncharted domain in the minds of the most learned Europeans. King George III ascended to the British throne in 1760: the 22-year-old was inquisitive and clever, the first English monarch to study physics, chemistry and astronomy. In those years he betrayed no hint of the mysterious illness that turned him permanently insane later in life. A lover of precision who dated his letters to the minute, King George never left southern England, but explored the world through the maps hung on mahogany frames about his residence. In hand-drawn detail he observed how his grip on the American colonies was slipping, and how coasts and islands in the Pacific were starting into history like shapes in a brightening light.

Nobody knew how far the Pacific reached to the west, what land bounded it on that side, or what connection it had with the jigsaw pieces of coastline charted by the Dutch. Australia was only half-mapped, the great sweep of its eastern, northern and southern coasts trailing off into a blank mass, perhaps connected to New Guinea and Tasmania, perhaps not. The mapped part of New Zealand, a short portion of western coastline, was an even bigger riddle, believed to represent the tip of a mythical southern continent. Europeans had long entertained the notion of *Terra Australis*, a gold-filled continent in the southern hemisphere thought to counterbalance the land in the north. Another asset the Pacific might yet hold was the Strait of Anian, a hypothetical route to Asia through the waters north of North America. These were mythical concepts akin to the Fountain of Youth that Europeans drew on early maps and struggled to part with.

Britain had secured mastery of the seas in victories over Spain and France in the Seven Years' War, and the ongoing search for the southern continent now became a British project. King George sent Captain Samuel Wallis to the Pacific in the *Dolphin* under secret orders to find *Terra Australis*. The orders expressed 'reason to believe that lands or islands of great extent, hitherto unvisited by any European power, may be found in the southern hemisphere between Cape Horn and New Zealand, in latitudes convenient for navigation, and in climates adapted to the produce of commodities useful in commerce'.[*] Wallis, sighting the green mountains of Tahiti on 18 June 1767, assumed he had reached his goal. On reflection he realised his mistake, but he was still delighted to find land, because at least thirty of his men were suffering from scurvy, languishing near-death in their hammocks with bleeding gums, loosening teeth and foul-smelling breath. Even so, relief in Tahiti was not guaranteed. Her shores were crowded with thousands of ambivalent islanders, and Wallis feared whether he would be able to stop for provisions at all. If not, he would have to limp to the Spanish outpost of Tinian in the Mariana Islands, thousands of miles to the north-west.

Tahiti consisted of two old volcanoes connected by a narrow isthmus. The island lay within a perimeter of coral

---

[*] Robertson, *The Discovery of Tahiti*, p. 7.

reefs and thunderous surf, which gave way to calm lagoons and black, palm-lined beaches. The volcanoes towered upward in jagged green ridges and glinting waterfalls, their uppermost reaches disappearing into misty clouds. It looked like a sort of fairyland, and the Europeans were incredulous that such a place could exist on earth. So rich was the island with flowering plants that a perfumed fragrance reached their noses over the lagoons.

The Tahitians were an Austronesian people whose origins lay on the coast of southern China. Starting about 1600 BCE, their ancestors trekked across the Pacific in double-outrigger sailing canoes, the greatest seafarers among Neolithic peoples. In the west, their forays reached Madagascar; in the east, they struck out against the prevailing trade winds, gradually colonising every habitable speck of land in the world's largest ocean. Ultimately, their dispersal covered more than half the globe. Around 300 CE, they had reached Tahiti from Tonga and Samoa, and they proceeded north to Hawaii, south to New Zealand and east to Easter Island. They must have reached the western coast of South America, because the sweet potato, a crop native to the Americas, quickly rolled back through the Pacific and became an island staple. The plant's Polynesian name, *kumara*, is strikingly similar to its Quechuan name in Peru, *kumar*.

Polynesian voyages were undertaken in large canoes with central platforms that supported dozens of men and women. They carried tropical crops like coconuts, breadfruit and yams, as well as pigs, dogs, chickens and rats. Tahiti's first settlers were farmers, raising fruit and vegetable crops in the island's volcanic soil. They lacked writing, and in time the history of their Asian origins melted into legend, their voyaging methods retained as guild secrets among priests and navigators.

The crew of the *Dolphin*, desperate for fresh food, began sounding the bays around Tahiti for a suitable anchorage. On the fine and clear morning of 24 June, six days after the ship's arrival, an estimated four thousand Tahitians surrounded her in hundreds of canoes. The armada must have looked and sounded like a floating carnival, carrying a pitched noise of flutes, drums, conches and singing. The sea around the ship became a rippling mat of plantain fronds thrown from the canoes in offering. The canoes nearest the ship came bearing chickens, fruit and squealing pigs, which were exchanged for nails. (The Tahitians instantly appreciated the value of iron.) The canoes were also full of young women, who exposed their bodies and drew the *Dolphin*'s sex-starved crew to the gunwales. If this was a ploy to distract the sailors it had the desired effect. The whites were caught completely off-guard when one of the chiefs in the larger boats gave a signal and a hail of stones hit the ship from all sides.

The two parties exchanged volleys of musketry and stones before the Europeans took to their 'great guns', using a combination of round shot (iron cannonballs) and grapeshot (a cluster of smaller rounds that had the effect of a giant shotgun). The acrid smoke and boom of the guns must have seemed to the Tahitians a terrible magic. Some of their canoes were smashed to pieces and untold numbers of people were killed and wounded as they retreated back to shore, slaking the sand with their blood, the body of a local woman left strewn across the ship's bow. George Robertson, the master of the *Dolphin*, described the scene in his journal:

> While this skirmish lasted, all the bay and tops of the hills round was full of men, women and children to behold the onset, and I dare say in great hopes of sharing all our nails and toys, besides the pleasure of calling our great canoe their own, and having all of us at their mercy, to ill or well use us as they thought most proper: but in place of that, when they came all running down to receive their victorious friends, how terrible must they be shocked, to see their nearest and dearest of friends dead, and torn to pieces in such a manner as I am certain they never beheld before.[*]

By noon the bay was quiet, not a canoe left in the water. On 26 June, the whites went ashore and claimed the island for King George with a pennant on a pole. The pennant was red, which happened to be the colour the Tahitians associated with their deity of fertility and war, 'Oro.

Watched through spyglasses, the islanders seemed to look on the flag with reverence, and to run away in fear when it flapped in the wind. Next day, the Tahitians again gathered

---

[*] Robertson, *The Discovery of Tahiti*, p. 43.

by the thousands; and the sailors, noticing piles of stones on the shore, feared a renewed attack. The ship's guns opened fire, dispersing the crowds and driving them into the wooded hills surrounding the bay. The ship kept up a withering fire on the hills, splintering trees and throwing up earth, while her crew went ashore and hacked up some eighty of the islanders' canoes, undoing years of hard labour. Some of those vessels were fifty feet long with a capacity for more than thirty people. It was a devastating blow, and the Tahitians didn't dare collect any more stones.

It's unknown why the Tahitians attacked the first white men they ever saw. It seems they interpreted the arrival of Wallis and the *Dolphin* as a religious event. The ceremony of their armada, the sacrifice of plantain leaves into the sea and the sensual gestures of the women, were consistent with offerings to the war god 'Oro. The British, then, were gods, not in the Western but in the Tahitian sense, flawed and human-like gods who could be seduced and challenged, who had come to demand sacrifice and tribute, and might yet remain to colonise the land.

In any case, when the Tahitians saw that their visitors could use a combination of fire and smoke to cause mayhem at incredible range, there was a rapid shift in relations. They surrendered their weapons and showered their visitors with pigs, fruits and many more plantain leaves. Practically overnight, all hostilities towards the white men ceased, replaced with an endless stream of island goods. An old woman in red cloth, whose husband and three sons had been killed in the sea skirmish, tearfully gave the *Dolphin*'s crew two pigs, refusing anything in return.

Wallis became so confident that he sent small bands of men up into the country to gather supplies, and they were warmly received in distant villages. A female chieftain, when she saw that Wallis was weak with illness, led him to her property, making her people kiss his hand along the way. Beneath the thatched roof of her large house, she had four young girls give Wallis a massage, a local form of medicine that did the captain 'much service'.* Wallis designated this chieftain, Purea, the 'queen of Tahiti', and when he told her he was leaving the island, she famously burst into tears. The captain's crew was quickly on the mend from scurvy, and began trading nails for sex with Tahitian women. Soon the ship was so stripped of nails that there were few left to hang the hammocks, and most of the men were sleeping on the decks.†

Western civilisation had slammed violently into Tahiti, and the islanders had little time to regroup. The *Dolphin*'s month-long visit was only the beginning of a long train of Europeans who would call at the island with increasing frequency. Tahiti was not part of the southern continent as Wallis had hoped, and it wasn't teeming with gold or silver. But the island's strategic and commercial value to an empire with designs on the Pacific was obvious. It was an oasis of fresh provisions and

---

* Robertson, *The Discovery of Tahiti*, p. 94.
† Robertson, *The Discovery of Tahiti*, p. 43.

lovely women that made future runs across the ocean more feasible. Within five years, Tahiti had been claimed by three separate European powers, named 'King George the Third's Island' by Wallis, 'Nouvelle Cythere' by the French and 'Isla de Amat' by the Spanish. None of those powers seemed to care about the island's previous contacts. And the Tahitians, caught in the centre of competing colonial forces, faced the greatest upheaval they had ever known.

James Cook arrived at Tahiti in the *Endeavour* in 1769, during the first of three voyages to the Pacific. He was under Admiralty orders to observe the transit of Venus in the clear, day-time skies of Tahiti, an exercise that could help establish the earth's distance from the sun. But he was also under secret instructions, once his astronomical side-project was finished, to continue the hunt for the southern continent. Cook would finish what the Dutch had started in the Pacific, charting the rest of Australia and New Zealand. He would run down into Antarctic waters, farther south than any human had ever been, to finally dispel the myth of *Terra Australis*. The farm boy from Yorkshire sailed thousands of miles through uncharted waters, producing charts on a scale and level of detail never seen before from Western European explorers, and gathering thousands of biological and botanical specimens to carry back to England. He was a physically intimidating man, standing more than six feet tall, with bushy eyebrows, high cheekbones and a long, straight nose. A contemporary portrait depicts him wearing a powdered wig over his brown hair. His gaze is sharp and discerning, and his prominent nose and well-set eyes lend him a bird-like appearance.

In many ways, Cook left his mark on seafaring. With a novel interest in the health of his sailors, he fed them concoctions of malt, sauerkraut and portable soup to ward off scurvy. During his first voyage, he did not lose a single man to the disease that had wreaked havoc with other expeditions. On his second and third voyages, his ships carried a chronometer, a large watch-like device built to keep Greenwich Mean Time through salty air, temperature changes and rough seas. Cook took to calling the gadget his 'trusty guide the watch'.* To calculate longitude he had only to compare Greenwich Mean Time with local time and multiply the difference by fifteen, a much faster and more reliable method than lunar observations or dead reckoning. The device, suspended on gimbals to keep it horizontal no matter the inclination of the ship, was his tether to civilisation in the wastes of the Pacific.

British explorers in those years were under orders to make detailed records of the 'genius, temper and inclinations' of the people they met, and to 'endeavour by all proper means to cultivate a friendship and alliance with them'.† Cook's ships were loaded with gifts that served as tokens of civilisation, and he sprinkled them liberally everywhere he went: looking glasses, axes, linen shirts, iron nails, horses, cows, goats and

---

* Cook, *A Voyage Towards the South Pole and Round the World* (Vol. 2), ch. 10.
† Frost, *Mutiny, Mayhem, Mythology*, ch. 4.

geese. He expected his men to treat Polynesians with kindness and respect, and enforced his expectations through flogging.

For his time, Cook was sophisticated in his thinking about Indigenous peoples. He was troubled by the changes he saw in Polynesian societies as a result of European contact, such as the spread of venereal disease and the practice of trading sex for iron. During his second voyage he lamented in his journal that new diseases and goods had disturbed the 'happy tranquility' of New Zealand Māori. 'If anyone denies the truth of this assertion,' he added, 'let him tell me what the natives of the whole extent of America have gained by the commerce they have had with Europeans.'* When he heard that a party of sailors from his sister ship had been killed and eaten in New Zealand, he thought the sailors were probably responsible for their own deaths, reflecting that he had always found Māori a 'brave, noble, open and benevolent' people who did not suffer insults easily.† He also broke from a tradition of disparaging remarks about Indigenous Australians, describing them as 'far happier than we Europeans' and better off without European conveniences.‡

But Cook could be cruel and petty with his island hosts, qualities that worsened later in his career and shocked even his own men. He once had a Tahitian man's ears chopped off for raiding a European-style garden; in another incident,

---

* Edwards, *The Journals of Captain Cook*, Journal of the Second Voyage 1772–1775.
† Edwards, *The Journals of Captain Cook*, Journal of the Second Voyage 1772–1775.
‡ Cook, *Captain Cook's Journal During the First Voyage Round the World*, ch. 8.

he sent an armed force of thirty-five men to burn houses and canoes in a search for stolen goats. He clearly thought himself qualified to exact his own forms of justice on Polynesians as their civilisational superior. He always tried to make peace through gift-giving, but opened fire with guns at the first sign of aggression. The people he made first contact with often attacked him, and he responded with brutal force, before hostilities gave way to an uneasy or sometimes cordial truce. In this way, Cook and other European navigators left a trail of dead and wounded Indigenous people across the Pacific.

Soon after the *Endeavour* anchored in Tahiti in 1769, the sailors shot an islander dead after he wrestled a musket from them and ran off with it. Later, two crew members deserted the ship, hoping to take up lives with Tahitian women, and Cook held the local chiefs to ransom until the islanders brought them back. This kind of ransom would lead to his killing in Hawaii years later.

CHAPTER TWO

A Botanical Mission

Lumped in among the rarefied spices that trickled into Europe before the Age of Discovery was sugar. The sweet crystal from the Far East was much sought after, and only began arriving in commercial quantities when the Portuguese set up sugarcane plantations in Brazil. Before long, sugar had a drug-like hold on the British public. By the eighteenth century it had grown from luxury to necessity, served in the most exclusive coffee houses and poorest farmhouses alike; the blackened teeth from overindulgence no longer the preserve of monarchs like Queen Elizabeth I.

Britain followed the blueprint laid down by Portugal and Spain for sugar-producing gulags in the New World. Her supply came from slave plantations in a faraway realm that Britons knew as the West Indies, British-owned islands in the

Caribbean. Those islands formed one corner of a triangular trade route spanning the Atlantic. Merchants sailed from Europe laden with rum, guns and textiles, which they exchanged for African slaves on the west coast of Africa. Next they ran across the Atlantic and traded the slaves for sugar in the Caribbean before returning home. In this feedback loop of human suffering, more guns for West African warlords meant more slaves to market, and more slaves for the sugar planters meant more sugar.

The American Revolution in the late eighteenth century was a blow to British influence in the entire Western hemisphere. The Caribbean planters fretted over how to feed their slaves cheaply as they were in the compromised position of relying on the revolutionary American colonies for corn. The gentleman botanist Joseph Banks persuaded King George, and then the prime minister and his government, that the breadfruit plant from the South Seas was the solution. Breadfruit was a staple on the surf-fringed islands of the Pacific, where Britain's imperial ambitions had led a number of explorers. On islands like Tahiti, the explorers wrote glowing reports about the fruit as they gorged on it to ward off scurvy. Its flesh was said to taste like freshly baked bread when cooked, and it seemed to grow in prodigious quantities without any cultivation. They were reminded of the potato, another hardy and prolific crop that had already proved its usefulness to the Old World, supplying the calories for population booms across Europe.

Banks had tasted the breadfruit years earlier on a voyage to the South Seas with Cook; now aged in his forties, he had made himself an establishment figure and a long-time friend and adviser to the king. He argued the Royal Navy should transport a cargo of breadfruit plants from Tahiti to the Caribbean, relieving the planters of their reliance on American corn. The king not only agreed, but gave Banks oversight of the expedition. The botanist set to work in his London townhouse, a private museum of exotic curiosities and plants (Indian cannabis included). The navy purchased a merchant vessel and modified her according to Banks's specifications. She was christened the *Bounty*, a reference to Tahiti's natural abundance, but with an added royal flavour. The ship would be carrying the king's bounty, a gift from King George to his Caribbean subjects.

The man appointed to command this ostensibly high-minded mission was Lieutenant William Bligh. A skilled and ambitious navigator, Bligh had, at twenty-one years old, served as sailing master on the *Resolution*, the flagship for James Cook's third voyage to the Pacific. He was short in stature, about five feet tall, with jet black hair and a distinctive pallor that never changed in the tropics. His face was small and pixie-like, with a dimpled chin and a noticeable boyhood scar across one of his cheeks. His father, trying to turn a horse in an orchard, had thrown a hatchet and hit him in the face.

Bligh's voyage with Cook was the first European expedition to discover the Hawaiian archipelago. Here Cook, approving of the young master's performance, gave Bligh the task of charting the islands. Nothing about the *Resolution*'s initial reception in Hawaii suggested Cook would soon be murdered. The ship had happened to land at one of the most important ceremonial sites in Hawaii during a festival celebrating Lono, god of fertility. It seemed the Hawaiians thought Cook was Lono, heralded by his messenger, Bligh, who was sent ahead in a small boat.* As the *Endeavour* nosed into the harbour, tens of thousands of Hawaiians welcomed her from the cliff edges. They swam or paddled out to the ship and climbed aboard, before cheerfully leaping from her gunwales when the decks became too crowded for the whites to perform their duties.

But while Cook was feted, the islanders were less sure about his shipmates. The sailors ate much of the island's pork and fruit supply and invited women into their tents on the shore, violating the sacredness of the precinct where they were camped. By the time Cook's expedition set sail to chart the rest of the islands in the archipelago, the Europeans and Hawaiians were 'reciprocally tired of each other',† as one crew member observed. The islanders had begun patting the bellies of the sailors and suggesting it was time for them to leave. Yet, when the *Resolution*'s foremast was damaged in a storm, Cook was forced to return to the same bay two days later.

The festival was over, and Cook was no longer in character as Lono; his embarrassing return to the island was largely

---

*   Salmond, *Bligh: William Bligh in the South Seas*, ch. 1.
†   Salmond, *Bligh: William Bligh in the South Seas*, ch. 1.

ignored. An atmosphere of mutual suspicion developed as Cook smarted at his cool reception and the Hawaiians worried the whites had returned for good. The sailors loaded their muskets and cannon, while the islanders made ready their clubs, stones and newly acquired iron daggers. The Hawaiians stole one of Cook's small boats, and the captain tried to ransom a high priest to get it back. He was on a beach crowded with thousands of warriors, attempting to get the priest into a boat and take him out to the *Resolution*, when the warriors and marines began exchanging stones and musket fire. Overwhelmed, the marines dropped their muskets and ran into the sea, leaving Cook, who couldn't swim, alone on the beach. The warriors hit him in the back of the head with a club and stabbed him in the base of the neck with an iron dagger.

William Bligh watched all this unfold from a small boat in the bay. Cook fell face-first into the water. The Hawaiians hauled his body onto the rocks, pulverising it with stones and clubs, then dragged it up into the hills and out of sight. Bligh came under attack himself when he was sent to guard the *Resolution*'s mast, which was still being repaired on the island. Meanwhile, the Hawaiians baked Cook's body, removed the flesh from his skeleton and kept the bones as a source of *mana* or spiritual power, a rite usually reserved for chiefs and elders.

In those years the Royal Navy was one of the only means of upward social mobility in Britain, as shown by Cook, the son of a farm labourer who rose to eminence on merit. But advancement through the ranks still depended in large part on elite connections and patronage. Bligh's talents had brought him so far, but with Cook's death he had lost his mentor, and he lacked other supporters on the *Resolution*. A vain and irascible man with a tendency to find fault with the men around him, Bligh failed to endear himself to his new superiors, and his colleagues seem to have shut him out. He was furious after the voyage when an official account gave his assistant the credit and royalties for charts he claimed were his own. He was also conspicuously passed over in the round of promotions after Cook's death, one of the only officers to miss out, even though he claimed the *Resolution*'s new commander, falling ill, had given him 'the power solely of conducting the ships'.* He was not promoted to lieutenant as he expected, but two of his subordinates were.

The young master returned to England vaguely humiliated, but he still carried the prestige of his association with the late James Cook. On the Isle of Man, the island off the north-west coast of England in the Irish Sea, he found distraction in the drawing rooms of the well-to-do, who were fascinated to hear firsthand about Cook's final voyage. Bligh had a whirlwind romance with Elizabeth Betham, the cultured and well-educated daughter of the local collector of customs. The pair married a few months after his return. Betsy's parents were pleased with their promising son-in-law, while Bligh was rapt with his new bride. Not only would Betsy prove his most

---

*   Preston, *Paradise in Chains*, ch. 3.

dogged supporter, but through their marriage he obtained the connections to elevated society that would dictate the rest of his career.

Betsy's uncle, Duncan Campbell, was a wealthy merchant whose ships transported convicts from England to the North American colonies and returned with tobacco. He also had ships plying the West Indian sugar and rum trade, and he owned a slave plantation in Jamaica. When the American Revolution broke out in 1775, England was barred from sending convicts to the colonies, and British prisons began overflowing. Campbell escaped financial ruin by winning a new contract to house the convicts in hulks, or de-masted ships, on the Thames River. The inmates sentenced to exile were held in the dark and disease-ridden holds of Campbell's hulks.

In the humiliating aftermath of the *Resolution* voyage, Bligh's uncle-in-law interceded on his behalf, urging the Admiralty that his charts had been miscredited and securing him a share of the royalties from the published account. Campbell also pulled strings to get Bligh appointed to the warship *Belle Poule* as master, only ten days after his marriage to Betsy. In 1781, Bligh saw action at sea in an explosive encounter with the Dutch known as the Battle of Dogger Bank, and finally won his commission as a lieutenant. In 1782, he sailed in the fleet that relieved the British fortress at Gibraltar from French and Spanish forces during the American War of Independence. Peace came in 1783, and

Bligh was dismissed on half pay, tough circumstances for a man with a young daughter and another on the way. But Campbell came to his rescue and gave him command of one of his merchant ships.

Bligh's appointment to the *Bounty* was another example of his uncle-in-law's influence. Campbell was an ardent supporter of the breadfruit mission and recommended his employee and nephew-in-law to Joseph Banks, who would not have required much persuasion. Bligh was well qualified for the position. He had South Seas experience from Cook's ill-fated voyage, and he was familiar with the waters of the West Indies, the destination of the breadfruit plants. His relatively low rank meant he was not above undertaking such a quirky command in return for promotion.

In August 1787, Bligh returned to England from Jamaica to find Campbell waiting for him with the news of his job offer. He accepted immediately and penned a grateful letter to Banks: 'I have heard the flattering news of your great goodness to me … I can only assure you I shall endeavour, and I hope succeed, in deserving such a trust.'[*] Thus Bligh's four-year stint in the merchant service came to an end and he resumed his naval career at huge financial cost, his salary dropping from five hundred to fifty pounds per year. He was now thirty-three years old, a father to three, soon to be four, daughters.

---

[*]   Alexander, *The Bounty*, ch. 2.

* * *

At Deptford dockyard on the Thames River, the *Bounty* was undergoing an overhaul. As per instructions from Joseph Banks, the navy had purchased a coastal trader to be refitted for the expedition. The botanist was convinced a small ship and crew was needed, to allow maximum room for the breadfruit plants. The *Bounty* was indeed small, a vessel of just 215 tons burden. But she was three-masted and full-rigged for ocean-going, and almost brand new.

The ship's great cabin was extended and converted into a greenhouse with skylights, a pipe system for runoff, and a stove to keep the plants warm. Her hull was sheathed in copper as protection from the wood-boring worms that turned hulls to honeycomb in tropical waters. As she began to assume her finished form, provisions for a year and a half at sea came aboard, including beads, looking glasses and iron adzes for trade with the Tahitians. Four cannon and ten swivel guns were hauled onto her decks, along with casks of liquor and salted meat. The Admiralty also supplied the expedition with the K2 chronometer, a newer and simpler version of the timekeeper used by Cook. The polished brass circle would fit in the palm of Bligh's hand as he made his longitude calculations. It was the most expensive item entrusted to him after the ship itself.

As he watched the labourers at work on the *Bounty*'s hull and rigging, Bligh's excitement at the prospect of his first naval command turned to disillusionment. Britain was bracing for war with the Netherlands, and it was obvious the Admiralty viewed Banks's mercantile project with indifference, if not exasperation. Most of the earlier government expeditions to the South Seas had been focused on discovery, whereas the *Bounty*'s voyage was a commercial venture, with elements of exploration tacked on. The Pacific was still mostly uncharted, and Bligh was expected to make valuable charts for future seafarers. The project had its admirers; Bligh's own father-in-law compared its significance to the bringing of the potato from America to Britain. But compared with the achievements of his mentor and idol, Captain Cook, the mission was unglamorous, a mere stepping stone to greatness.

Bligh's irritation was not unjustified. The ninety-foot-long *Bounty* was an underwhelming sight to any talented and ambitious commander. Although the Admiralty had spent triple what it intended in the ship's refit, there was no accounting for her small size. She was rated as a cutter, the smallest category of warship. That meant she was commanded by a lieutenant rather than a captain, and Bligh would yet again miss out on the promotion he was angling for; he also lacked the usual detachment of Royal Marines to act as his security force. On top of that, Banks's design specifications had made the already restricted living space on the vessel even more cramped. The great cabin, a spacious room with large windows at the stern, was usually the exclusive area where a captain kept his books, spread out his charts and entertained his officers. Bligh had lost that area entirely to the breadfruit plants, while his private cabin was a seven by eight foot cubby, and his dining area wasn't much larger.

Before the *Bounty* left England, there were already murmurings that the ship was ill-suited for a long voyage to the South Seas. The Scottish earl Lord Selkirk, a family friend of the Bethams, visited the ship at Deptford and wrote to Banks with his concerns: 'It is highly improper for so long a voyage; only twenty-four able seamen, and twenty-one of all others, without a lieutenant, or any marines, with only a surgeon without a surgeon's mate, but if Bligh's surgeon meets with any accident they must want all medical assistance God knows how long.'[*]

Selkirk also pressed Banks about Bligh's lack of promotion, writing that, given his lack of preferential treatment after his voyage with Cook, it would be 'no unreasonable thing' to make him a captain before the voyage. Soon after, when it was clear Selkirk's concerns would not be addressed, Betsy's father wrote to Bligh in a farewell letter: 'Government, I think, have gone too frugally to work; both the ship and the complement of men are too small.'[†]

Bligh complained bitterly about his superiors, but he was eager to prove them wrong. His ill feelings were expressed in a defiant resolve for him and his 'little ship' to succeed against the odds. In fact he planned to make the perfect voyage,

---

[*] Salmond, *Bligh: William Bligh in the South Seas*, ch. 5.
[†] Salmond, *Bligh: William Bligh in the South Seas*, ch. 5.

without a single case of scurvy or physical punishment. Such a clean record would allow him to showcase his ideas for managing a ship in the face of the stifling limitations imposed on him by the Admiralty.

CHAPTER THREE

The Voyage Out

For much of the voyage, Bligh's acting lieutenant, effectively his second-in-command, was one Fletcher Christian, twenty-three years old. Born in the Cumbria town of Cockermouth, north-west England, Christian was the seventh of ten children, four of whom died before reaching adulthood. He grew up within the stone walls of Moorland Close, a fortified homestead laid out like a small castle, its defences originally built to keep out Scottish border raiders. It was the sort of place where boyhood fantasies run rampant. When Christian rode to school in town, he would have passed through the square watchtower that guarded the complex's only entrance. The battlements must have looked epic to young eyes, perched on a lush and foggy hill on the outskirts of Cumberland.

His lawyer father, Charles Christian, died when Fletcher was still a toddler, leaving his mother, Ann Christian, to raise six children in genteel poverty. When Fletcher was a teenager, his mother was forced to sell the family home and move to a relative's estate on the Isle of Man, where the Christian family had a history dating back to the Middle Ages. How Ann fell into financial trouble is unclear, but it seems her eldest sons had borrowed heavily against her estates to fund their careers. Christian did not follow his elder brothers into higher education and a profession, perhaps because the family's fortunes had collapsed. Instead he went to sea aged eighteen and moved quickly through the ranks.

He served as a cabin boy on the HMS *Cambridge*, which took part in the relief expedition to Gibraltar. Coincidentally, William Bligh was on the same ship as a sixth lieutenant, but it's unlikely the pair had much contact. Christian's stint as a cabin boy, and his relatively old age for the position, suggest that, like Bligh, he had to earn his place among the socially superior midshipmen. His early career was not fast-tracked by a family member or friend. Evidently he proved himself, because after the voyage on the *Cambridge* he joined the naval ship *Eurydice* as a midshipman and sailed for India, where he was promoted to acting lieutenant after only one year, at a time when a lieutenant's commission required at least six years of service.[*]

---

[*]   Preston, *Paradise in Chains*, ch. 12.

On his return to England, the young man again crossed paths with Bligh, who was now the captain of the merchant vessel *Britannia*, owned by his uncle-in-law. Bligh probably met Christian through the Bethams, who were friendly with the Christians on the Isle of Man. Christian sailed with Bligh on two West Indian trading runs: on the first, he entered as a seaman and messed with the officers; on the second, Bligh made him second mate. Bligh most likely helped Christian to hone his navigational skills, taking a leaf from his mentor–pupil relationship with Cook. The *Bounty* expedition would be their third voyage together.

By now, Christian was aware that Bligh was a very passionate man, but he seemed to pride himself in knowing how to humour him. The young man had, however, very different ideas about leadership at sea. His older brother, Edward Christian, quoted him as saying: 'It was very easy to make one's self beloved and respected aboard a ship; one had only to be always ready to obey one's superior officers, and to be kind to the common men, unless there was occasion for severity, and if you are, when there is a just occasion, they will not like you the worse for it.'*

Christian was athletic, industrious, and well liked among his shipmates. He liked to lead by example, and boasted to his brother that he knew how to perform the labours of common seamen. Bligh, too, thought highly of Christian, and had wanted him to serve as the *Bounty*'s master, but the Admiralty

---

* Preston, *Paradise in Chains*, ch. 12.

turned down his request due to the young man's inexperience. Christian was retained as master's mate, the petty officer who assists the master. But halfway through the outward voyage, Bligh promoted Christian to acting lieutenant, a higher rank than master.

Unlike Bligh, there is no preserved portrait of Christian. The most detailed physical description we have of him comes from his *Bounty* commander, and was written after their relationship had devolved into mutual, boiling enmity. In his journal, describing Christian's appearance as an aid to the authorities who would be sent to hunt him, Bligh said Christian was 'strong made', with 'blackish, or very dark complexion', dark brown hair and a star tattooed on his left breast. He added that his acting lieutenant 'may be called rather bow legged', and was 'subject to violent perspirations, and particularly in his hands, so that he soils anything he handles'.*

Bligh was the only commissioned officer on the *Bounty*. Beneath him was a cohort of warrant and petty officers, including several men who had sailed with him and Cook on the *Resolution*. Before Bligh promoted Christian, the warrant officer directly beneath him in the chain of command was the 35-year-old sailing master John Fryer. A northerner from Norfolk, Fryer was considered a sober and competent man. Bligh, two years his junior, seems to have been pleased with his performance in the early days of the voyage; he wrote the

---

* Salmond, *Bligh: William Bligh in the South Seas*, ch. 12.

master was a 'very good man, and gives me every satisfaction'.* However, his feelings towards Fryer soon changed.

Next came the midshipmen or 'young gentlemen', an assortment of youths from privileged backgrounds who were pursuing naval careers. Bligh had taken on several more midshipmen than the two allowed, mustering most of them as seamen on paper, though they would all mess together in the ship's gunroom and enjoy officer privileges. Their sheer number was the result of family obligations on Bligh's part; three came recommended from Betsy or her father. But Bligh was no stranger to the mutual benefits of patronage, and he must have liked the idea of having so many beholden young men to enforce his command, at least before he grew to despise all of them.

The young gentlemen included the teenager Peter Heywood. Aged just fifteen when he joined the *Bounty*, Heywood had cut his education short to follow a family tradition of naval service, and the breadfruit expedition would be his first time going to sea. He joined the crew on the recommendation of Bligh's father-in-law, who knew his family on the Isle of Man. To see him safely to his ship, Heywood's father accompanied him on a boat to the mainland and sent him off in a carriage with two family friends, each armed with a pair of pistols to guard against highwaymen on the country roads outside London. The boy carried with him a Bible and prayer book

---

* Wahlroos, *Mutiny and Romance in the South Seas*, p. 279.

from his mother, which would prove a crucial means of recording his adventures. In London, Heywood stayed in Bligh's own lodgings before the ship sailed. Fletcher Christian would become Heywood's friend and mentor, teaching him Latin and Greek during the voyage. The pair had much in common. Both had grown up in Cumbria and could trace their ancestry to established families on the Isle of Man.

In the *Bounty*'s gunroom, simply a narrow space strung with hammocks and set aside for the midshipmen to sleep and mess, the young gentlemen quickly separated into cliques. On one side were Christian and Heywood, along with Edward Young, George Stewart, William Elphinstone and Robert Tinkler. Then there were the fifteen-year-old John Hallett and nineteen-year-old Thomas Hayward. The latter pair were kindred spirits, both appointed at Betsy's recommendation, and the arrogant Hayward seems to have been a bad influence on his junior. Both men were lacklustre in their duties and disliked by their colleagues.

James Morrison, a 28-year-old Scot with long black locks, had seen action against the French and passed his master gunner's examination, learning the science of naval artillery. But on the *Bounty* he was appointed boatswain's mate, a role that came with the responsibility of the cat o' nine tails in a red baize bag. The well-educated Morrison seems to have accepted a lesser position on the *Bounty* out of a simple desire to sail the South Seas. His diary would prove an important record of the voyage.

Finally, there were thirteen able seamen to carry out the actual work of sailing the *Bounty*. These were men from humble beginnings across Great Britain, their regional accents as variable as the scars they bore from brawls and accidents. Bligh would take the trouble of cataloguing their physical features in his notebook: 22-year-old Alexander Smith was pitted with smallpox; 23-year-old William McKoy had a scar from a knife wound in his belly; 28-year-old Charles Churchill had a crooked left forefinger, and 37-year-old Matthew Thompson was missing his right big toe.

In all it was a youthful crew, mostly aged under thirty, and, unusually for the time, the sailors were all volunteers. Two of the original crew were 'pressed men', rounded up by the press gangs that patrolled coastal towns, but they deserted and had to be replaced.

Poking around the *Bounty* for the first time, the new sailors were confronted with the cramped conditions that had troubled Bligh and his family for months. As the ship lacked any superstructures, much of shipboard life would take place belowdecks, reached via two separate hatchways. The aft hatchway led down to a lobby on the lower deck where the arms chest was kept. In this space were entrances to the great cabin at the stern, Bligh's cabin to starboard, Fryer's cabin to port, and the gunroom to fore. The room that served as Bligh's pantry, dining area and day room adjoined his cabin and the gunroom.

A canvas bulkhead separated the gunroom from the forecastle, the space reached by the fore hatchway where thirty-three men slept and spent their leisure time. Thus the seamen and their social superiors were separated by a flimsy barrier that could absorb neither sound nor smell. Bordering the forecastle was the galley, a cooking and dining area with an iron stove near the bow, and the pens holding sheep, goats and pigs. The seamen had six feet three inches of headroom and were allocated fourteen inches broad for their hammocks.

Sandwiched between the lower deck and the hold was a mezzanine deck, a warren of private cabins and storerooms where the surgeon, clerk, botanist, gunner, carpenter and bosun slept. Even the men who enjoyed the privacy of their own cabins lived in small, unventilated spaces, and in virtual darkness, since the ship had no portholes. When the *Bounty*'s crew members surfaced for air, they would have found her main deck no less crowded, taken up with the large boats Bligh had requested for the expedition: a 23-foot launch, a twenty-foot cutter and a sixteen-foot jolly-boat. As for toileting, the sailors would perch on small wooden chutes on either side of the bowsprit, while Bligh had his own privy at the stern.

If there had been any question about the Admiralty's attitude to the *Bounty*, it was made frustratingly clear in the days before her departure. Bligh was anxious to get underway, but the final paperwork for the voyage took weeks to arrive. By the time he received his sailing orders, favourable conditions had turned and the *Bounty* spent further weeks pinned in England by contrary winds. Bligh aired his irritation in a letter to Campbell: 'If there is any punishment that ought to be inflicted on a set of men for neglect, I am sure it ought on the Admiralty for my three weeks' detention at this place during a fine fair wind which carried all outward bound ships clear of the channel but me, who wanted it most.'*

He continued: 'This has made my task a very arduous task indeed for to get round Cape Horn at the time I shall be there. I know not how to promise myself any success and yet I must do it if the ship will stand it at all or I suppose my character will be at stake. Had Lord Howe sweetened this difficult task by giving me promotion I would have been satisfied.'

* * *

Cape Horn was a malevolent prospect in the mind of any sailor. The prevailing western winds in latitudes below forty degrees south could reach horrendous speeds because there was no land to interrupt them, giving rise to terms like the roaring forties, furious fifties and screaming sixties. Rounding the tip of Chile meant dipping to fifty-six degrees south latitude, well into the zone with the fiercest winds. The passage between South America and Antarctica was an effective funnel. By the time gales reached the Horn, they had screamed down the Andes mountains or up the Antarctic peninsula. The winds built up rogue waves that rolled

---

* Salmond, *Bligh: William Bligh in the South Seas*, ch. 5.

unimpeded through the Southern Ocean, reaching heights of a hundred feet tall, and shortening into near-vertical walls of water when they hit the shallow waters around the Horn.

The land itself was mountainous and bare, a Gothic landscape cut up with deep channels into peninsulas and islands. The aloof headland that sailors saw as they made the passage was the southernmost extremity of the Tierra del Fuego, a windswept archipelago and home to a people called the Yaghan, hunter–gatherers who coated their bodies with animal grease to keep warm.

In that eerie limbo, the sun never entirely left the sky, and sleet-filled headwinds could stop a ship's progress for weeks. A sailor who had rounded the Horn won the right to wear a gold hoop earring and dine with one foot on the table.

Tales of ships that met with disaster in the passage were legend. On his outward voyage, Magellan barely suppressed an outrage among his captains after he sentenced a boatswain to death for sodomising a cabin boy. On the coast of Patagonia he put down another uprising: two of his captains were drawn and quartered, and another was left marooned on a small island. In 1577 Britain sent a fleet under Francis Drake to raid Spanish colonies on the Pacific coast of the Americas. At San Julian, the grim point of no return before the Strait of Magellan, Drake was greeted by the bleached skeletons of Magellan's mutineers, still hung on gibbets more than half a century later. Drake sacrificed one of his own malcontents. He was convinced his gentleman crew member Thomas

Doughty was a witch and a conjurer of storms. Doughty was tried, convicted of mutiny and beheaded. Drake held up his severed head before the men on that barren coast, uttering the customary words, 'Behold the head of a traitor.'

The coast became a graveyard for mutineers and maroons. By the time early European expeditions reached South America across the Atlantic their crews were simmering with fear, paranoia and dissent.

In 1741, the Royal Navy ship *Wager* lost the rest of her squadron and ran aground on the Patagonian coast after weeks of foul weather. In those years, officers lost formal authority over crew members if their ship was lost. Some of the men promptly broke into the spirit room and got drunk. The shore camp of the survivors became a debauch, and most of the surviving crew mutinied against their captain, David Cheap, after he shot an officer in the face at point-blank range. The mutineers left the captain and his loyalists marooned on an island and sailed for England in an open boat, offloading men against their will along the frozen coast of Chile. Less than forty of the one hundred and forty shipwreck survivors returned home, including Captain Cheap and the ring-leaders of the mutiny, who were acquitted of any wrongdoing. The ordeal led to a law change extending naval discipline to wrecked, lost or captured ships, closing the legal loophole the mutineers had used in their defence.

* * *

The *Bounty* got underway on 23 December 1787. The ship's half-blind Irish fiddler, Michael Byrne, struck up shanty tunes on his violin as the men walked the capstan bars around, hauling up the dripping anchors. On Christmas Day, the crew dined on beef and plum pudding with an extra issue of rum. The mood among the sailors was a heady mixture of excitement and dread. Several of the older crew members had been to Tahiti before with Cook, and stories about its sultry shores and free-loving women would have spread rapidly through the ship. But a dangerous passage lay between the crew and their destination. The Admiralty's tardiness meant the *Bounty*, like the ill-fated *Wager*, would be attempting Cape Horn late in the sailing season, when the weather was at its fiercest.

Just days after her departure, and long before she reached the southern latitudes, the ship was already battling a storm. On Boxing Day, gale-driven seas collapsed the stern windows and flooded the great cabin. Seven full hogsheads of beer on deck were swept overboard, and casks of rum in the hold split open, their contents lost in the bilge. For the superstitious on board, these were grim omens about the voyage ahead.

* * *

The island of Tenerife, off the coast of north-western Africa, rose out of a thick haze to greet the *Bounty* in early January. Bligh brought his ship to anchor at Santa Cruz, an old

Spanish port and a common resupply point before a run to the Horn. He sent Christian ashore to greet the governor and tell him the *Bounty* had arrived for repairs and provisions. Christian also carried the message that Bligh would salute the governor with guns, providing a salute was returned with an equal number of guns. The Spanish dignitary refused on the basis he only returned the same number of guns to men of equal rank to himself, a snub that Bligh called 'extraordinary' in his journal.

The lieutenant had been to Tenerife before with Cook, and this time he was struck by the high price of food in the settlement, although he managed to buy several casks of the region's famous Madeira wine for Banks.

A week later the *Bounty* sailed from Santa Cruz and ran south-west across the Atlantic. In April, Bligh sighted Tierra del Fuego, the object of so much foreboding among his men, just as the ship came to a stalemate in westerly headwinds. The lieutenant tried for almost a month to get around the Cape, but it was hopeless. A shifting onslaught of drenching rains, snow and sleet lashed the ship, while the sailors swung like pendulums in the rigging. The *Bounty* surfed on towering peaks and dropped into dark and windless troughs. Her sails became heavy with snow and ice, and her sick list increased to eight as exhausted men nursed their bleeding hands. Swells tossed the ship so violently that the men could not stand on the deck without the assistance of a rope. The storms often reduced the ship to bare poles and battened hatches, a condition where all the sails were taken in and the hatches were sealed shut with metal battens, blocking out the little light and fresh air that could reach the quarters below. The man-made cave where the seamen rested was dank, smoky and dark save for the orange glow of the galley stove. The smell was a medley of bilge, vinegar, manure, and the tobacco that most of the men chewed or smoked. Sopping jackets and trousers hung about the ship.

'We had to encounter the most violent storms that I suppose were ever experienced,' wrote the midshipman Peter Heywood. The teenager had an especially good view of the rough seas because, for an unnamed infraction, Bligh had him 'mastheaded', or forced to stay up in the masthead during a storm.[*]

'I suppose there never were seas, in any part of the known world, to compare with those we met for height, and length of swell; the oldest seamen on board never saw anything equal to them, yet Mr. Peckover (our gunner) was three times sailing with Captain Cook.'[†]

On the evening of 22 April, Bligh admitted defeat. He summoned the crew, thanked them for their efforts, and announced that he would change course and take the longer route to the Pacific, around the Cape of Good Hope, the southern tip of Africa. The men received the news with three cheers. That evening the wind turned northward, causing

---

[*]   Salmond, *Bligh: William Bligh in the South Seas*, ch. 6.
[†]   Dening, *Mr Bligh's Bad Language: Passion, Power and Theatre on the Bounty*, p. 68.

Bligh to heave to and try again, but soon the wind was blowing west with redoubled fury, and he aborted his attempt for the final time. He must have been fuming at his superiors over the wasted effort; he believed he could have made the passage if he had arrived at the cape just a fortnight sooner.

But the ordeal had also been thrilling. As he boasted in a letter to Banks, perhaps no similar voyage had been undertaken with so few accidents, and there were no symptoms of scurvy, flux or fever among his men. 'I always thrive best when I have the most to do,' he wrote, 'and I was never better in my life.'* The letter was a continuation of the optimism Bligh expressed in Tenerife, where he said his crew were cheerful and content, he had no cause to inflict punishment on anyone, and 'everything turns out to my most sanguine expectations'.†

Contrary to Bligh's hopes, the voyage out was far from perfect. As Lord Selkirk had hinted, one of his immediate problems proved to be his surgeon, Thomas Huggan. Bligh had noticed Huggan's constant drunkenness before the *Bounty* sailed from Spithead and had tried in vain to have him replaced. Sensing the trouble to come, he took on a surgeon's mate. Huggan would die of 'intemperance and indolence' soon after the ship's arrival in Tahiti, but not before he caused the death of another crew member. The 28-year-old seaman James Valentine made the mistake of consulting him

*   Salmond, *Bligh: William Bligh in the South Seas*, ch. 6.
†   Salmond, *Bligh: William Bligh in the South Seas*, ch. 6.

over some 'slight indisposition', for which the surgeon bled him out of his arm, a common medical practice at the time. But Huggan's carelessness led to Valentine's arm becoming infected, and he wasted away belowdecks. The surgeon didn't tell Bligh about Valentine's condition until he was at the point of death. He died a few weeks out from Tahiti.

Adding insult to injury, Huggan formally reported the cause of Valentine's death as scurvy, perhaps in a deliberate attempt to tarnish Bligh's record. The lieutenant was incredulous. He viewed scurvy as a disgrace to a ship, and had been dutifully feeding his men antiscorbutic potions like malt essence and sweet wort, lining them up and making sure they swallowed every drop.

The ship was frequently washed down with vinegar, and aired out with fires, and once a week the crew assembled for an inspection of their clothing and even their fingernails. Bligh had also divided the *Bounty* crew into three watches (each led by either Peckover, Fryer or Christian, who was promoted to acting lieutenant). The system meant crew members could all enjoy eight hours of continuous rest, rather than the usual four hours on, four hours off system known as 'watch-and-watch'.

These were Cook's new and enlightened policies for keeping a crew healthy, and Bligh was fanatical in their enforcement, flying into temper tantrums about the ship's cleanliness and calling his entire company scoundrels, rascals and hounds. He wrote to Banks during the outward voyage that sailors could not be trusted to look after themselves and 'must be watched like children'.[*] Even the crew's leisure time was strictly regimented. He set aside three hours each evening for dancing sessions that saw the sailors shuffling to fiddle music like half-hearted marionettes. Two crew members who complained of aching joints and refused to dance had their grog cut off, a punishment second only to flogging in severity. Huggan diagnosed them with scurvy, too.

Other crew members showed signs of rebellion. Indeed, Bligh had fallen out with most of his officers before his ship reached Tahiti. The trouble seems to have started at Adventure Bay in Tasmania (then called Van Diemen's Land), where the *Bounty* stopped for two weeks to take on wood and water before her final run across the Pacific.

In the island's vaulting forest, the *Bounty* crew members planted pears and bananas and carved their ship's name into the trees. After some searching, Bligh encountered about twenty Indigenous Tasmanians who made a 'prodigious clattering in their speech' as they emerged on a rocky shoreline in the bay.[†] Bligh approached in a small boat and threw parcels of beads and nails, describing the group backhandedly in his journal as the 'most wretched and stupid people existing, yet the most inoffensive'.[‡] Morrison observed that the ochre-wearing Tasmanians showed little interest in

---

[*] Salmond, *Bligh: William Bligh in the South Seas*, ch. 6.
[†] Bligh, *A Voyage to the South Sea*, ch. 4.
[‡] Salmond, *Bligh: William Bligh in the South Seas*, ch. 6.

Bligh's presents. He was no less harsh in his summary, calling them 'the most miserable creatures on the face of the earth'.[*] Both men were copying almost verbatim the explorer William Dampier's racist description of Indigenous Australians as the 'miserablest people in the world'.[†]

For the most part, the *Bounty* crew were alone in the rolling wilds of a land seldom visited by Western ships, and their prescribed roles became a matter of contention. Bligh ordered the carpenter William Purcell to join a wooding party ashore. In the Royal Navy, a carpenter was charged with making daily reports about a ship's condition and undertaking repairs. Purcell was not required to do the work of common seamen, so it was with some reluctance that he obeyed Bligh's humiliating order.[‡] Soon Bligh was criticising the quality of the carpenter's woodcutting, and he shot back, accusing the lieutenant of coming ashore to find fault. As Purcell stormed back to the ship, Bligh shouted after him: 'I'll put a rope around your neck.'[§] When the lieutenant later tried to assert his authority again, ordering Purcell to help with loading water casks into the ship's hold, the carpenter simply refused. James Morrison wrote that, in Tasmania, not only were seeds of eternal discord sown between Bligh and the carpenter, but 'with all the officers in general'.[¶]

---

[*]   Morrison, *Journal on HMS Bounty and at Tahiti.*

[†]   Hughes, *The Fatal Shore*, ch. 3.

[‡]   Frost, *Mutiny, Mayhem, Mythology*, ch. 1.

[§]   Preston, *Paradise in Chains*, ch. 13.

[¶]   Morrison, *Journal on HMS Bounty and at Tahiti.*

Weeks out from Tahiti, Bligh proceeded to fall out with the master John Fryer, and the pair had a public stand-off that perturbed the crew. The master had refused to give the ship's expense books their bimonthly signature unless Bligh signed a certificate stating that he had done 'nothing amiss' during the voyage thus far.* In response, Bligh assembled all hands, read out the Articles of War, the rules governing naval discipline, and ordered Fryer to 'sign them books'.† Fryer grudgingly obeyed, but said within earshot of the assembled crew that his signature 'may be cancelled hereafter'.‡ It seems the master was trying to protect his career from any charges Bligh might lay against him as their relationship soured. But he might also have taken issue with Bligh's accounts of the ship's provisions, believing them false.

---

*   Frost, *Mutiny, Mayhem, Mythology*, ch. 1.
†   Morrison, *Journal on HMS Bounty and at Tahiti*.
‡   Morrison, *Journal on HMS Bounty and at Tahiti*.

CHAPTER FOUR

Landfall

James Cook, setting his eyes on Tahiti for the first time in 1769, was astonished at the apparent ease and luxury of island life. The Tahitians lived in shady groves of breadfruit and coconut, interlaced with sandy paths between houses. The climate was so warm that houses were almost unnecessary; their homes consisted of thatched roofs on posts. Cook marvelled at a 44-foot stone pyramid, the beginnings of a monumental architecture that, with a larger labour force, might have grown in the same direction as the pyramids of Mesoamerica. He saw double-hulled canoes up to seventy feet long, all built without iron tools. The Pacific Islands are mostly volcanic, with no usable metals; the Tahitians had had to make do with wood and rock. They lacked the navigation instruments of the Europeans, yet they were able to make long-distance voyages by reading the stars, winds, birds and currents. Tupaia, a Tahitian priest, was able to draw a chart showing all one hundred and thirty islands within a two thousand–mile radius of Tahiti. He joined the *Endeavour* as a navigator and interpreter for the rest of the voyage until he died of a tropical disease in the Dutch East Indies.

The Tahitians lived in a nuanced world of gods, spirits, omens and taboos that the Europeans struggled to comprehend. As white sailors discovered, the simple, absent-minded action of pulling a branch off a certain tree could render an entire property *tapu*, or spiritually restricted, forcing its inhabitants to pack up and move away. The sailors also marvelled at what they saw as the child-like caprice of Tahitian emotions. The islanders often wept, as Cook observed, yet their tears seemed forgotten as soon as they were shed. A funerary crowd might be found wailing with grief in one moment, then laughing hysterically at the sight of a British onlooker in the next. In bouts of grief or mourning, the islanders struck their heads with shark's teeth until blood streamed down their faces. Sex was a fertility rite, and the men were happy to share their wives with friends. Lovemaking also featured in bewildering public ceremonies: Cook witnessed one involving a girl as young as ten. And like numerous cultures throughout history, the islanders engaged in human sacrifice to appease their gods, felling a low-status villager with a stone for the occasion and collecting the skulls of past victims.

But the thing that most insulted the Christian morals of the white men in Tahiti, because it plagued them constantly, was theft. The Europeans came to view the pickpocketing skills of the Tahitians with begrudging admiration. In Europe itself, 'one cannot see more expert filchers',* observed one captain. In Tahiti, a European ship's tools, clothes and valuables were constantly going missing. Cook himself had his stockings stolen from under his head one night. The local chiefs seemed to have limited powers to prevent stealing (much to the captains' chagrin), and were often the victims or perpetrators of thefts themselves. The Tahitian attitude towards theft was ambivalent. Their code of vigilante justice allowed for thieves to be put to death, but a swift and undetected robbery was also something to be admired. Hiro, the patron divinity of thieves, had his devout followers, who sacrificed a portion of their spoils to him.

The Tahitians found their European visitors equally baffling. Their economy was based on a system of reciprocal gift-giving rather than bartering or trading, and they thought of the Europeans, so anxious to receive one item in exchange for another, as *piripiri*, or stingy. The all-male crews of European ships implied they had come from a sexually homogeneous if not a homoerotic land; Polynesian voyages of discovery always included women, so that the islands they reached could be colonised. (The Tahitians must have been

---

* Bougainville, *A Voyage Round the World*, p. 226.

even more intrigued when they exposed a sailor from a French ship as a woman in disguise, to the surprise of her own crew.) The average British sailor of the time was short, hairy and smelly, with a face pitted with smallpox scars and a mouth full of rotten teeth. The Tahitians were their physical opposites: tall and athletic with straight and white teeth, their bodies assiduously washed, scented and plucked of excess hair.

Cook noted the Tahitians seemed exempt from the Biblical curse that men must live 'by the sweat of their brow',[*] so abundant were Tahiti's fruit-bearing plants. Every meal made use of a seemingly endless supply of coconuts, breadfruits and bananas. He observed islanders eating up to fifteen bananas in a single meal. Their diet was mostly vegetarian, supplemented with pork, fish, and the occasional dog. Like the Aztecs, Polynesians bred dogs for eating; fattening them up with starchy vegetables and cooking them in earth ovens. Cook described the taste of dog as similar to English lamb. Dog meat was treated as a delicacy, and the leftover bones, teeth and fur were made into tools and ornaments.

The Tahitians spent their days in a 'round of various enjoyments',[†] wrote the German naturalist Georg Forster, who travelled with Cook on his second expedition to the Pacific. The landscape was pleasing, the temperature of the air was always warm and refreshed by sea breezes, and the sky was almost constantly serene. The routine of the

---

[*]   Cook, *Captain Cook's Journal During the First Voyage Round the World*, ch. 3.
[†]   Forster, *A Voyage Round the World* (Vol. 2), p. 110.

islanders began at sunrise when they washed their bodies in rivers. In the heat of the day they reposed under trees, anointing their hair with fragrant oils and playing the flute. At noon they ate dinner and then resumed their 'domestic amusements, during which the flame of mutual affection spreads in every heart'.[*] They jested, told stories and danced. The day concluded with another visit to the river. 'Thus contented with their simple way of life, and placed in a delightful country, they are free from cares, and happy in their ignorance,' Forster observed. 'No wonder then that a sailor, perhaps less guided by reason than the rest of his comrades, should hurry on headlong after the pleasures of the present moment.'

'I thought I was transported into the garden of Eden,'[†] wrote the French explorer Louis Antoine de Bougainville, who visited Tahiti a year before Cook. Bougainville claimed Tahiti for France and named it Nouvelle Cythere, after the island of the Greek goddess of love and fertility, Aphrodite. (He was unaware that Wallis had already claimed the island for Britain.) During his ten days in Tahiti, the French captain wrote rhapsodies about an earthly paradise populated by a race of tall and beautiful people, tilling a soil that he declared the 'most fertile in the universe'.[‡] He wrote about his men being offered young girls, a curious crowd of men and women

---

[*] Forster, *A Voyage Round the World* (Vol. 2), p. 111.
[†] Bougainville, *A Voyage Round the World*, p. 228.
[‡] Bougainville, *A Voyage Round the World*, p. 229.

gathering in a circle around the 'young victim of hospitality'.
He described a walk in the island's interior:

> We crossed a turf, covered with fruit-trees, and interlaced with
> little rivulets, which keep up a pleasant coolness in the air,
> without any of those inconveniences which humidity occasions. A
> numerous people there enjoy the blessings which nature showers
> liberally upon them. We found companies of men and women
> sitting under the shade of their fruit-trees: they all greeted us with
> signs of friendship; those who met us on the road stood aside to
> let us pass by; everywhere we found hospitality, ease, innocent
> joy, and every appearance of happiness among them.*

This was the Age of Enlightenment, and the European world
of ideas, long dominated by religion and superstition, was
quickly reorienting in favour of reason and evidence of the
senses. The rising bourgeoisie was awake from the long sleep
of serfdom, and suspicious of the divine rights of kings. In
London's coffee houses, men of all classes talked, argued and
heard the news in an atmosphere that was serious and civil, so
different from the torpor of alehouses and taverns. The earth
was no longer considered a flat square at the centre of the
universe, and disease was no longer thought to originate from
witches, evil spirits or divine retribution. Explorers set out to
probe, measure and categorise the world, and returned with

---

* Bougainville, *A Voyage Round the World,* p. 228.

tales of strange cultures that informed new ideas about how societies should be governed, and by whom. Almost a century before Europeans discovered Tahiti, John Locke drew on travellers' accounts of Native Americans in developing his thoughts about the 'state of nature'. Locke argued that all humans were born equal with natural rights to life, liberty and property, and the role of governments should be to protect those rights under a 'social contract' with the governed. His ideas would figure prominently in the American and French revolutions. Jean-Jacques Rousseau, another Enlightenment thinker who drew inspiration from Native Americans, went further than Locke, arguing man was inherently free, peaceful and good, and civil society made him evil.

If the Tahitians made sense of European ships as the vehicles of the gods, the whites saw Tahiti through an overlay of their own preconceived concepts and ideas. Grasping for references to describe the new world they saw, they resorted to classical imagery. Tahitian girls were 'Grecian',* and Tahiti itself the 'truest picture of Arcadia'.† Forster likened the Tahitian physique to Athenian sculpture. Bougainville could not seem to stop comparing Tahitian women to Venus. The reports of these men consisted of ethnographic notes infused with a heady mix of poetry, philosophy and myth. In Tahiti the whites had found paradise, and in the unaffected smiles of the Tahitians they traced the visages of true innocence.

---

* Preston, *Paradise in Chains*, ch. 2.

† Preston, *Paradise in Chains*, ch. 2.

Here was the theory of natural man writ large. Bougainville's surgeon, Philibert Commerson, claimed to have witnessed 'the state of natural man, born essentially good',* while Bougainville called it 'the true Utopia'.†

Joseph Banks travelled with Cook during his first visit to Tahiti in the *Endeavour*, along with a personal retinue of artists, servants and greyhounds. In those years the future instigator of the *Bounty*'s breadfruit mission was a young man about town, heir to a huge fortune, and he joined the *Endeavour* voyage at his own expense. He wrote at length about Tahiti and its people, penning the first European description of surfing when he observed Tahitians riding waves on a piece of an old canoe. Though engaged to be married at the time, he was thought to have slept with one of Queen Purea's attendants, who he described in his journal as 'my flame'.‡ On his return to England he was immediately famous, and Britain's well-to-do devoured his suggestive writing about the island, where 'love is the chief occupation ... both the bodies and souls of the women are moulded in the utmost perfection for that soft science'.§ Not everybody could stomach his prose, and he was also lampooned as a 'Botanic Macaroni'. Banks gave his critics ample fodder by sharing an account of himself going to sleep in a canoe with Queen Purea and waking up to find all of his clothes stolen. Officials in the Royal Navy, meanwhile,

---

* Dunmore, *French Explorers in the Pacific* (Vol. 1), p. 110.

† Preston, *Paradise in Chains*, ch. 1.

‡ Preston, *Paradise in Chains*, ch. 2.

§ Preston, *Paradise in Chains*, ch. 2.

found him a meddling dilettante. He had planned to join Cook's second voyage to the Pacific in addition to the first, and ordered extra cabins built on the *Resolution* to house his entourage of scientists, artists and French horn players. When the Admiralty found the cabins made the ship top-heavy and removed them, he withdrew from the voyage in anger.

Banks's writings were not the only reports from Tahiti that fascinated audiences in Europe. The English and the French read avidly the descriptions of free sex that ran so contrary to their own concepts of shame and decency. Stories of human sacrifice amazed and appalled them, even though hanging was a popular mass spectacle at home. In poems and satires they made fun of the tattooed backside of Wallis's Tahitian 'queen'. Some intellectuals seized on Tahiti as a foil for soul-searching European societies. Others scoffed at the growing romance of the South Seas, preferring Thomas Hobbes's claim that, without civilisation, the lives of men were 'poor, nasty, brutish and short'.*

Contrary to the rapt reports of certain Europeans, the Tahitians did not live in perpetual harmony and leisure. They were farmers, and like farmers everywhere, they lived at the whims of the harvest. Each year, the disappearance of the Pleiades constellation from the night sky marked the beginning of *Matari'i i raro*, or the season of scarcity, six months of relatively cool and dry weather when food was

---

* Hobbes, *Leviathan*, ch. 13.

limited. Far from an egalitarian free-for-all, Tahitian society was divided into three main castes: the *ari'i*, a hereditary noble class believed to be descended from the gods; the *ra'atira*, landed farmers, warriors, artists and craftspeople; and the *manahune*, or commoners. The island was also carved up into various chiefdoms that were often at war, each based around an open-air temple, or *marae*.

Despite the realities of Tahitian society, a seaman visiting the island might find his situation much improved compared to the one he had left behind in eighteenth-century London. Back home, the powdered wigs and mahogany furniture of Georgian England were the trappings of a small elite. As the Industrial Revolution lurched into life and London swelled to capacity, many residents were poor, illiterate and addicted to gin, living brief and desperate lives in decaying tenements. The crowded shanties of the East End reeked of urine and horse dung, and houses had cesspools beneath them, emptied by 'nightmen' who carted the sewage away through the streets. Graveyards were full, and some of the dead were tossed into partially covered 'poor's holes', left to decompose in the open air. To avoid getting muck on their clothes, members of the wealthier class rode around in sedan chairs carried by porters. Enlightenment thinking had yet to be reconciled with the hangings that drew rapt mobs of tens of thousands, or the use of orphaned children as slave labour in the city's factories. But in Tahiti, amid the clamour of welcoming canoes off the island, the seaman would quickly be made the *taio*, bond-friend, of a Tahitian nobleman, which meant free and lifelong access to the man's wife, house and possessions, and an unconditional welcome into his family. Suddenly he had become a landed gentleman in a warm and abundant paradise.

The Europeans didn't know it then, but the 'happy ignorance' of Tahiti, the 'simple way of life' that gave the seamen such respite from their wanderings in the Pacific, was under threat as soon as they arrived. Early visitors like Cook disturbed the Tahitian equilibrium of wars, hereditary rulers, harvests and gods. Up until first contact, Tahitian society had lacked central political organisation, and no chieftain had ever achieved supremacy over the entire island. Dozens of chiefs and nobles might come aboard Cook's ship in a single day, with varying degrees of authority over different districts. But it was expedient for the Europeans to treat the Tahitians as a single political unit, and it made sense to choose the chief of the particular district where they anchored as the sovereign of the entire island.

Wallis began this policy, christening the female chieftain Purea the 'queen of Tahiti'. But the *Dolphin*'s defeat of the Tahitians in 1767 with guns and cannon lowered Purea's prestige in the eyes of her people, and her authority rapidly diminished. Meanwhile, Wallis's visit inadvertently enriched other chiefs, such as Purea's brother-in-law, Tutaha, who was the chief of the district encompassing Matavai Bay, where the *Dolphin* anchored. Bougainville anchored in the same bay a year later, bestowing further status and gifts on Tutaha, while Purea fell further out of favour.

A year and a half after Wallis's visit, a number of chiefs, including Tutaha, allied against Purea and attacked her people. They destroyed houses and crops and massacred men, women and children, keeping their skulls as war trophies and leaving their bones to bleach white in the sand. Purea fled into exile in the mountains. When Cook arrived two years later in 1769, he regarded Tutaha as the 'chief man of the island',* observing that Purea had little authority over the islanders. In a subsequent visit he described Purea as a poor woman of little consequence.

The island had yet another sovereign in Tutaha, but his reign was similarly short-lived. By the time of Cook's second visit in 1773, Tutaha had been killed in battle. His mother seized Cook by the hands and burst into tears with the news; Cook was almost moved to tears himself. Tutaha's great-nephew Tu (whose name might be rendered in English as 'Standing Straight Up') was now the chief of a northern portion of Tahiti that included Matavai Bay (where, like the *Dolphin* had been, the *Endeavour* was now anchored), so Cook duly gave him the label of king, paying him official courtesies and showering him with gifts. But in so doing, the captain was conferring an authority on a young chief that was far beyond his resources and prestige. The Europeans

---

* Cook, *Captain Cook's Journal During the First Voyage Round the World*, ch. 3.

took years to realise that, in choosing sovereigns, they were placing the Tahitians in question and their families in grave danger. Cook acknowledged in his journal that his choice of Tu as king was arbitrary: 'In truth, we know not how far his power extended as king, nor how far he could command the assistance of the other chiefs, or was controllable by them.'*

The other Tahitian chiefs didn't just resent Tu, they openly cursed him. It seemed that Tu had refused to join them in a war against the people of Mo'orea, a small island off Tahiti's north-western coast. Cook had witnessed one of the expeditions sent to Mo'orea, a huge flotilla of war canoes that carried thousands of warriors. The battle was not as decisive as the chiefs hoped, and ended with an unsatisfactory truce. As Tu had refused to contribute to the battle, the chiefs blamed him for the outcome. Cook heard that his presence in Tahiti was the only thing stopping the other Tahitian chiefs from attacking Tu, and that they planned to do so when he departed. He waded even deeper into the island's politics and issued a threat: that if anybody attacked the king in his absence, he would retaliate on his return.†

For several years, the chiefs on Tahiti and Mo'orea heeded Cook's warning, biding their time. Naturally, it started to look as though Cook would not return, and indeed he never did. Five years after Cook's departure, Tu's enemies descended on his district of Pare, west of Matavai Bay, killing

---

* Cook, *A Voyage Towards the South Pole and Round the World* (Vol. 1), ch. 13.
† Oliver, *Ancient Tahitian Society*, p. 1249.

many warriors and looting and destroying the village, while the king fled to the mountains.

More than a decade passed before the Tahitians had their next British visitors. The Tahitians must have wondered at the sudden break in contact, their horizons empty of the pale sails that heralded iron tools, disease, and tectonic changes in local politics. The *Bounty*, a British naval ship with a peculiar mission, would attempt to pick up where the other expeditions left off, casting a beguiling influence over island life and reinforcing Tu's kingship. But the *Bounty* was not like her predecessors. On arrival in Tahiti, she was already a troubled ship, with cracks showing in the veneer of order and discipline that the Tahitians had come to expect from European sailors. Neither the ship, nor many of her crew, would ever return to England.

* * *

In October 1788, the crew members of the *Bounty* sighted Tahiti after ten months at sea. The first sign of the island was Point Venus, the peninsula forming the north end of Matavai Bay where Wallis, Bougainville and Cook had anchored. Huge numbers of Tahitians rolled towards the *Bounty* on a leafy carpet of canoes while the sailors watched, distracted and disbelieving, from the gunwales. The islanders climbed aboard, carrying pigs, fruit and rolls of bark cloth that unwound into long streamers. The riot of noise and colour that ensued, psychedelic in its novelty to the virgin sailors, almost insane in its hilarity and cheer, threw Bligh into temporary confusion; in a matter of minutes the deck was so crowded that he was struggling to locate his own crew. The ship had scarcely dropped anchor before every *Bounty* sailor made his *taio*, his amiable guide to the luxuries waiting ashore.

Bligh had nailed to the mizzenmast a list of rules for expected conduct on the island, a way of smoothing the crew into a uniform diplomatic unit. The first rule decreed that no sailor was to tell the Tahitians about James Cook's death in Hawaii. The late Cook had cult status in Tahiti; his portrait, regarded as an incarnation of the man himself, was kept wrapped in *tapa* cloth and brought out for ceremonial occasions. The Tahitians remembered Bligh from his visit with Cook on the *Resolution*, and he was anxious to leverage his association with the captain. When the Tahitians asked after 'Tute' (the name they had given Cook), Bligh told them his former commander was alive and well in England, and may yet return to Tahiti. The *Bounty*'s gardener, David Nelson, even told the Tahitians that Bligh was Cook's son, a lie that the lieutenant wasn't about to correct.

The second rule on the mizzenmast forbade the crew from revealing they had come to Tahiti with the sole objective of gathering breadfruit plants. Bligh guessed that the value of the plants would be greatly inflated if the Tahitians knew the truth of his mission, and instead, he planned to ask for them as casually as possible, giving only the usual trinkets in return. To lay the groundwork, he needed to re-establish relations with the 'king', Tu, so he sent Christian in a small boat to bring the chief on board. Tu arrived with his wife and attendants, and joined noses with Bligh in the customary Polynesian greeting. He was thirty-five years old and a large man, no less than six feet four inches tall, with a shy demeanour and a mop of curly hair. His wife, 'Itia, was the stronger personality of the pair, an eminent warrior, surfer and wrestler. She was about ten years Tu's junior, also very tall and with a 'very animated and intelligent countenance',* as Bligh observed. The lieutenant was surprised to learn that Tu was now going by the name Teina and acting as regent for a boy king, a common arrangement in Tahiti. The name of Tu, and the title of king of the island, had passed to his eldest son, who Bligh reckoned was about six years old. (A Tahitian chief could have several different names during the course of his lifetime. Tu later took the name Pōmare, Night Cougher, after his daughter died from tuberculosis in 1792.)

Bligh and Teina became *taio*, with the king adopting the Tahitian version of Bligh's name, Parai, and offering his wife to the lieutenant, although he seems to have remained chaste. For his part, Bligh gave Teina a present of hatchets, small adzes, gimlets, saws, looking glasses, shirts and red feathers (red and yellow feathers were associated with 'Oro and highly valued). To 'Itia he gave earrings, necklaces and beads, but

---

* Bligh, *A Voyage to the South Sea*, ch. 6

she asked for iron, so he ended up giving her much the same gifts as her husband. Teina wanted his gifts kept on the ship to prevent them being stolen and Bligh obliged him, storing the items in a locker in his own cabin. He spent the next several days touring the district and courting Teina with gifts and dinners. He had found the chief in a much weakened state than what Cook had left him in, a man only nominally possessed of power, with enemies on all sides. The large houses of Pare, once a rich and prosperous district, had been razed during the attack against Teina, replaced with small sheds that could be lifted up and carried away.

Bligh continued the British policy of 'king-making', even though he showed insight into its destructive effects, observing that Teina and his family's association with the British had 'brought him numberless enemies'.* He was confident that yet another joint attack would be made on Teina as soon as he left Tahiti: 'Their eligible situation for our ships has brought us intimately connected with them, and by this perhaps we have not only sown the seeds of discord but of revolution.'†

He confessed that he would have taken revenge on Teina's enemies if he had not thought it would jeopardise his mission. Instead, he tried to assist Teina in 'making friends', by showering the king's enemies with saws, shirts and other presents. Bligh seems to have interfered on the king's behalf despite feelings of personal distaste towards him. He was furious at Teina's

---

* Salmond, *Bligh: William Bligh in the South Seas*, ch. 10
† Oliver, *Ancient Tahitian Society*, p. 1253.

indifference about the fate of cattle left on the island by Cook (the people of Mo'orea had stolen them). He did not hesitate to point out Teina's enormous appetite whenever they dined together, and generally thought the regent lazy and cowardly. 'If Teina had spirit in proportion to his size and strength he would probably be the greatest warrior in Tahiti,' he wrote, 'but courage is not the most conspicuous of his virtues.'*

Active as Bligh was in trying to fix Teina's political troubles, the *Bounty*'s mission was one of deception, and after five days of wringing his hands like an overeager suitor, he cleverly raised the subject of the breadfruit plants. In reference to all the presents he was lavishing on the king, Bligh asked: 'And will not you, Teina, send something to King George in return?'† Teina replied that he would send anything in his power, and began listing all the possibilities, among which he happened to mention the breadfruit.

'This was the exact point to which I wished to bring the conversation,' Bligh raved, 'and, seizing the opportunity which had every appearance of being undesigned and accidental, I told him the breadfruit trees were what King George would like; upon which he promised me a great many should be put on board, and seemed much delighted to find it so easily in his power to send anything that would be well received by King George.'‡

---

* Bligh, *A Voyage to the South Sea*, ch. 10.
† Bligh, *A Voyage to the South Sea*, ch. 6.
‡ Bligh, *A Voyage to the South Sea*, ch. 6.

Once Bligh had Teina's blessing, it only took his sailors a matter of days to collect almost eight hundred breadfruit shoots in earthenware pots, but there was no rush to get them aboard. The Admiralty's delay in sending Bligh his orders meant he had reached the island on the verge of the western monsoon season. As he waited for the period of heightened rains and winds to pass, the *Bounty* would remain at anchor in Tahiti for five and a half months, much longer than any previous European ship.

CHAPTER FIVE

Yams and Coconuts

The *Bounty* was at least the ninth European ship to visit Tahiti, and detritus from the Old World was already scattered far and wide across the island: iron axes and nails, linen shirts, domestic cats and patches of wild-growing tobacco. The first islanders who climbed aboard the ship in Matavai Bay were selling capsicums, pumpkins and goats, all of which had been introduced to the island by Captain Cook. In the years since Cook's final departure in 1777, many islanders had died of venereal infections, or of a kind of consumption they called the 'British disease'. Despite this, for the crew members of the *Bounty*, Tahiti was an unspoiled paradise, and provided confirmation of the incredible stories they'd heard in England.

Bligh made Christian the leader of a shore party of nine men, including Peter Heywood, four armed seamen and the two gardeners. The party pitched their tents on Point Venus, the black sand peninsula where Cook had once set up an observatory, and lived ashore for the duration of their stay. Ahead of their tents were the hazy, fragrant groves of the Matavai settlement, and the jagged peaks of Tahiti's mountains. At their backs was the *Bounty*, a little nest of ropes and spars in the bay, and beyond her, the dull thunder of Pacific rollers.

At night, the islanders put on *heiva*, or concerts, and the women, fully bedecked in flowers, leis and perfumed oil, spun their hips to fast-beating drums. The women shed their clothes as they danced, in a display that was meant to excite the gods. It was all the same to British sailors, whose only reference was the allurements of London prostitutes. *Heiva* were not just dances, but a kind of variety show put on by the *arioi*, a travelling company of actors, dancers and comedians whose ranks comprised the most talented and charismatic men and women on the island. The whites were treated to pantomime dramas, some dry and religious but others farcical. In one play, a secret romance led to a female character giving birth on stage, and the newborn proceeded to run around with his umbilical cord trailing behind him and a midwife in pursuit, to peals of laughter from the audience.* Another *heiva* showcased a ring of *arioi* men who could perform ritualistic feats with their genitals. A

---

* Oliver, *Ancient Tahitian Society*, p. 342.

man wrapped his penis and testicles in twine and stretched them until they were a foot long; another performer pulled downward on the skin of his scrotum until it reached his knees. A horrified Bligh pleaded for the display to end, only adding to the hilarity of the crowd.

Christian's shore camp was by turns a plant nursery and trading post, off limits to the Tahitians except by permission. The ship's gunner, William Peckover, was in charge of trade with the islanders for official provisions. Peckover had been on all three of Cook's voyages; he spoke some Tahitian and knew the local customs. Meanwhile, the *Bounty*'s quiet and diligent gardener, David Nelson, reared the breadfruit seedlings in pots with the help of his assistant, William Brown. Nelson also spoke Tahitian. He was a student of Joseph Banks, and had sailed with Peckover and Bligh on Cook's third voyage, busily collecting botanical specimens.

While Peckover traded and Nelson gardened, the other members of the shore camp enjoyed relative freedom from Bligh's scrutiny, and began to bear the marks of life in a demarcation zone between the two cultures. They spoke a Tahitian–English pidgin, and motifs of *tatau*, or tattoo, spread across their chests, hips and buttocks, the ink printed into their skin with the searing rhythm of a shark-tooth comb.

Also a fixture at the shore camp was Moana, an elderly chief whose presence was supposed to discourage theft. The Tahitians were now highly aware of the wrath they could invoke from the whites through stealing. But pilfering still ensued around the *Bounty*, infuriating Bligh. A week after the ship's arrival, somebody stole the rudder gudgeon on a small boat, evading the crew member acting as sentry. Bligh decided to make an example of the sentry, John Adams, and gave him twelve lashes while many Tahitians were on board, Teina pleading in vain for the punishment to stop.

A flogging victim was tied prone and spread-eagled to a vertical grating like an inverted messiah, the lash administered to his naked back with the cat o' nine tails, or simply the 'cat', after the parallel wounds left from the tassel of nine knotted cords at the end of the whip. The boatswain's mate kept the cat in a little bag, hence the expression 'to let the cat out of the bag'. Nowadays, flogging is considered a form of torture; in the Royal Navy it was a staple of shipboard discipline, and not altogether outlawed until the late nineteenth century. The victim's skin was usually torn open by the fourth lash. After two dozen lashes, a common enough punishment, his back was a tattered mess said to resemble roasted meat. The pain, according to one contemporary source, was akin to being stabbed with a knife: 'I felt my flesh quiver in every nerve, from the scalp of my head to my toenails. I put my tongue between my teeth, held it there, and bit it almost in two pieces. What with the blood from my tongue, and my lips, which I had also bitten, and the blood from my lungs, or some other internal part, ruptured by the writhing agony, I was almost choked, and became black in the face.'* Then came a bucket of salt water over the wounds.

During the journey out, Bligh had already flogged Matthew Quintal after Fryer reported him for mutinous behaviour, scuppering the lieutenant's hopes for a punishment-free voyage. In Tahiti, he continued to order floggings, although he managed to flog his sailors less than most other Pacific navigators, including Cook. The *Bounty*'s butcher, Robert Lamb, got twelve lashes for 'suffering his cleaver to be stolen';† Isaac Martin received nineteen lashes for striking a Tahitian in an attempt to retrieve a stolen iron hoop. Bligh also wasn't above flogging the Tahitians: one received a hundred lashes for stealing. The thief had crept into the shore camp on a rainy night and made off with a compass and some bedding from Peckover's cot. Bligh rebuked Christian and his fellow officers for neglect of duty, but they responded that the night was so dark, and the rain so heavy, that they had not been able to see or hear each other, let alone the thief. After the Tahitian man was rounded up and flogged, he was put in irons, but he promptly escaped, further angering Bligh. It seemed he used a marlin spike to break his irons, then sprang out of the fore hatchway and jumped overboard in the night. A sentry heard him plunge into the sea. Hiro, god of thieves, must have been pleased.

One night in January 1789, three crew members deserted the ship. Charles Churchill, John Millward and William

---

* Wahlroos, *Mutiny and Romance in the South Seas*, p. 273.
† Wahlroos, *Mutiny and Romance in the South Seas*, p. 303.

Muspratt took eight muskets and ammunition and slipped away in the ship's cutter. Nine days earlier, Muspratt had been flogged for an unspecified 'neglect of duty'. Reaching the shore in the cutter, the deserters transferred into a Tahitian man's canoe and sailed to Tetiaroa, an atoll north of the main island that served as a kind of resort for local chiefs. The Matavai chiefs promptly told Bligh where his men had gone, and were relieved when the lieutenant did not take them hostage. Stormy seas prevented Bligh from reaching Tetiaroa for several days. When he arrived on the atoll, he stormed up the beach with his Tahitian guides, brandishing his cutlass, to the little shelter where his men were said to be hiding. They came out and surrendered, their figures harried and miserable. Their gunpowder was spoilt by the wet, and they claimed they had already resolved to turn themselves in. Bligh noted they probably did plan to return to the *Bounty* after being 'so much harassed by the natives'.*

He put the deserters in irons for a month and flogged them in two instalments, the second occurring just as the skin on their disfigured backs was beginning to heal. In Churchill's sea chest, he found a list including Churchill's own name and the names of three of the shore party. In those years, it was common for conspirators in a crime to put their names to paper. Bligh went ashore, called Christian and his men together and challenged them that they were in cahoots with

---

* Bligh, *A Voyage to the South Sea*, ch. 9.

Churchill and intending to desert. But the men denied it so firmly that Bligh was inclined to believe them.* Who among the nine men in the shore party had their names on the list is a mystery, but as the party's leader, Christian would have been held responsible. Morrison records Bligh's discovery of the list in his journal, but Bligh did not mention it in his own journal or log.

Two days after the second flogging, somebody slashed the ship's shore cable, leaving the *Bounty* tethered by a single thread. This act of sabotage could have proved disastrous for Bligh, running the ship aground and stranding him on Tahiti indefinitely. The lieutenant initially suspected the Tahitians, but concluded in his diary it was probably one of his own crew. Vaetua, Teina's younger brother, later revealed he had cut the cable because he was angered at Bligh's ill-treatment of his *taio*, Thomas Hayward.† Hayward, one of the young gentlemen, had been asleep on his watch when the deserters quit the ship. Bligh stripped him of his midshipman rank and put him in irons. Vaetua feared Bligh would have his friend flogged, so when the deserters' punishment took place, he stationed himself behind Bligh with a war club, preparing to bash his head in as soon as any blow landed on Hayward. But Hayward escaped the lash, instead receiving a severe rebuke. Bligh had no idea he came close to assassination, and Vaetua would later vow to kill the lieutenant if he ever returned to Tahiti.

---

* Morrison, *Journal on HMS Bounty and at Tahiti.*
† Morrison, *Journal on HMS Bounty and at Tahiti.*

After the floggings, Bligh, sweating in his full naval uniform, tramped around the district with Teina. The Tahitians swaddled him in bark cloth, flattering him with ceremonial honours while he scribbled ethnographic notes. Elsewhere on the island, his sailors enjoyed long days of beachcombing. When Bligh returned in the evenings to dine with Teina and 'Itia on the *Bounty* and naturally found something amiss, he exploded and damned his officers. At night, through the thin bulkheads of his stuffy cabin, he must have heard the revelries of his men and the Tahitian women who were allowed to sleep on board. Meanwhile, the silhouette of the *Bounty* haunted the convivial living arrangements at the shore camp. There's little record of what life was like for the shore party members, but they must have been the envy of the crew.

For all his careful diplomacy and gift-giving, Bligh was not popular among the Tahitians. Unlike Cook, he did not possess the physical height that the islanders associated with their hereditary nobles and leaders; Teina had to bend at the waist to press noses with him. Fletcher Christian, however, was tall and athletic, known to impress his shipmates by jumping from one barrel into another or balancing a musket on his outstretched hand.* The Tahitians came to look at him as a leader. 'Mr. Christian was beloved by the whole of them,' James Morrison later wrote of the Tahitians. 'On the contrary, none liked Mr. Bligh though they flattered him for

---

* Salmond, *Bligh: William Bligh in the South Seas*, ch. 6.

his riches, which is the case among polished nations, those in power always being courted."* Bligh tried to correct the Tahitians' view of Christian's status by telling the chiefs that Christian was his *teuteu*, or servant.

Bligh also embodied the anxious parsimony that so perplexed the Tahitians about the Europeans. The sailors were entitled to keep their own private stores of food, but the lieutenant began confiscating all the pigs they received from their *taio*, although he had more than forty of his own pigs in the ship's pens. When Fryer protested at having some of his pigs seized, Bligh said everything was his as soon as it came on board; that he would take nine-tenths of any man's property; and let him see who dared to say anything to the contrary.† The islanders started bringing hogs to the ship whenever the commander was on shore.

* * *

In early 1789, the *Bounty*'s crew made preparations to sail. Tahitians thronged the ship with broken iron tools, hoping to make the most of the ship's forge before her departure. The cabins were washed out with boiling water to kill the cockroaches that were so numerous the cables seemed alive with them, and cats were set free belowdecks to deal with the rats and mice.

---

*   Morrison, *Journal on HMS Bounty and at Tahiti.*
†   Morrison, *Journal on HMS Bounty and at Tahiti.*

Teina helped to stock the ship with wood, coconuts, bananas and pigs for the onward voyage. He brought two elaborate mourning costumes on board as gifts for King George, and couldn't help crying as he handed them over. He expected to be attacked after the ship sailed, so Bligh gave him 'two muskets, a pair of pistols and a good stock of ammunition'.* Bligh did not have high hopes for Teina's ability to defend himself, but he noted queen 'Itia had learnt to load and fire a musket with 'great dexterity'.† (Later, she would awe the crew of the *Mercury* by hitting the ship's buoy on her first shot.)

Bligh's breadfruit plants had rooted in their pots, and they were transferred from the shore camp onto the ship. When she weighed anchor and left Tahiti, the *Bounty* looked like a floating farm, bursting to the gunnels with plants, produce and livestock. The departure must have weighed heavily on the crew, many of whom had formed close relationships with Tahitian men and women in five months. According to Morrison, all hands received a double allowance of grog as the ship bore away in the evening, and 'everybody seemed in high spirits and began already to talk of home … One would readily have imagined that we had just left Jamaica instead of Tahiti, so far onward did their flattering fancies waft them.'‡

Bligh's excitement at being underway did not seem to quell his temper. Instead he got worse, and his petty fault-

---

* Bligh, *A Voyage to the South Sea*, ch. 11.

† Bligh, *A Voyage to the South Sea*, ch. 10.

‡ Morrison, *Journal on HMS Bounty and at Tahiti*.

finding and humiliating tongue were often directed at his acting lieutenant. 'Whatever fault was found,' one crew member recalled, 'Mr. Christian was sure to bear the brunt of the captain's anger.'* Bligh's penchant for public humiliation would soon send Christian over the edge, but it seems there was another issue with Bligh's command that caused other men to follow Christian: Bligh's stinginess with the ship's food stores. Although they lived in crowded squalor with few rights, navy sailors could at least expect precisely measured allowances of food and drink. Among their daily entitlements were a gallon of beer, and two pints of grog, or watered-down rum. If one food item was served in lieu of another, there was a fixed table of equivalents (for example, a gallon of beer was equal to a pint of wine). If their rations were reduced, the sailors could expect monetary compensation on their return to England, and they could also build up 'credit' if they decided to forgo any of their rations.

Usually a ship had a purser, an official responsible for dispensing the food stores and supervised by the captain, but on the *Bounty* that role fell to Bligh. It was in his interest to be close-fisted, so that he could supplement his salary through selling back the surplus provisions on his return. Indeed, the Admiralty had lowered Bligh's salary precisely because he could make an extra income as purser. The tension between his dual roles had been clear from the outset of

---

* Christian, *Appendix to Minutes of the Proceedings of the Court-Martial.*

the voyage, with Bligh's strange reaction to an instance of missing cheeses. He had ordered the ship's store of cheese to be aired out on deck. Noticing that two cheeses were missing, he declared somebody must have stolen them. But the cooper, Henry Hillbrant, reminded him in his German brogue that the cheeses had been sent to Bligh's own house in England before the ship sailed, on the orders of Bligh's clerk. Fuming, the lieutenant ordered the crew's allowance of cheese to be stopped and vowed the cooper would get a 'damned good flogging' if he said any more about it.* The crew were punished for a theft that never occurred.

As the ship entered the tropics and the sailors refused a ration of spoilt pumpkin in lieu of bread as an insufficient equivalent, Bligh was apoplectic, calling them 'damned infernal scoundrels'.† Soon after, the men complained to Fryer that it appeared the meat casks were not weighted correctly. Bligh again called all hands aft and informed them he was in charge of the provisions; no complaint would get any redress; he was the judge of what was right and wrong; and the next man to complain about food would get a severe flogging. Meanwhile, the quantity of boiled wheat and barley served up for breakfast was so small that brawls frequently broke out in the galley. In one such fight, the cook broke two ribs, and in another, the master-at-arms got his hand scalded in boiling water. Eighteenth-century seamen were a conservative

---

*   Morrison, *Journal on HMS Bounty and at Tahiti.*
†   Morrison, *Journal on HMS Bounty and at Tahiti.*

and hawk-eyed bunch, highly alert to breaches in shipboard customs. Whenever it seemed Bligh was stinting on them, they kept careful score. They were ordinarily entitled to complain to the captain if they suspected the purser of foul play, but in this case, they had no such recourse. Cook had been his own purser too, but his ships were so large that he was able to delegate the role to a secretary. On the *Bounty*, there was dangerously little distance between Bligh's role as commander and profit-seeking 'pusser'.

The latter was a demanding role, as he revealed in an unusually candid letter to uncle-in-law Campbell from Tenerife during the outward voyage: 'As my pursing depends on much circumspection and being ignorant in it with a worthless clerk, I have some embarrassment, but as I trust nothing to anyone and keep my accounts clear, if I fail in rules of office I do not doubt of getting the better of it.'* The tone, characteristic of many of Bligh's letters, implies a lonely and self-pitying commander surrounded by lesser men. By 'embarrassment', was he referring to general difficulties, or a specific incident, perhaps the missing cheeses? His clerk, John Samuel, does not seem to have been 'worthless', in fact Bligh would later praise Samuel in his journal. Was the letter intended as insurance against accusations of impropriety when he returned to England?

By the time they were three weeks out from Tahiti and anchored at the island of Nomuka in Tonga, the *Bounty* crew

---

* Salmond, *Bligh: William Bligh in the South Seas*, ch. 6.

members had long been wise to Bligh's tricks. Conscious that this was their final opportunity to spend their iron currency, they engaged in a frantic trade with the Tongans for clubs, spears, mats, and private loads of yams and coconuts, which they hid around the ship. The yam-hoarding must have galled Bligh, who was in a particularly foul mood of late. The visit to Nomuka had been a fiasco. Relations between the commander and his men were in freefall, and the Tongans threatened and stole from their demoralised visitors at every opportunity.

On 25 April, Bligh sent a party led by Christian to gather wood and water. He allowed the party to take muskets, but insisted the arms stay in the small boat and not be carried ashore. Tonga's name in those years, the Friendly Islands, was something of a misnomer; it was not the relatively benign paradise of Tahiti, and its people could be unpredictable. The men, women and children who crowded around the crew were covered in sores and marks of mourning: shorn hair, bloodied temples and amputated digits. Bligh noticed that even young boys were missing their pinky fingers. The islanders were eager to trade, but looked on Europeans with understandable pique. Captain Cook had not made things easy for future visitors to Tonga. When he anchored off Nomuka in 1777, he flogged Tongans for stealing, including a chief; and they conspired to kill him and his men, though the plot was never executed. The appearance of the *Bounty* inspired thoughts of mischief and revenge.

As Christian's men walked inland to the watering place, the Tongans made sport of them, and managed to make off with an axe and an adze. The sailors aimed their muskets, but the islanders only responded with derision, mirroring the action with their clubs and spears. Christian was at a loss, and circled back to the ship without filling all the water casks. He reported to Bligh, who called him a 'cowardly rascal' in front of the sailors, and asked if he was afraid of 'naked savages' when he had weapons in his hand. Christian replied that 'the arms are of no effect sir, when your orders prohibit their use'.[*]

Bligh knew from experience that the mere appearance of guns was not always a deterrent. In Hawaii, shortly after Cook's murder, he had been left to guard the *Resolution*'s mast under explicit orders not to fire on the rioting Hawaiians. He opened fire anyway, killing several stone-throwing warriors and enraging his superior, Lieutenant King.[†] In any case, Bligh had no sympathy for Christian. In fact he handed him the worst possible insult between gentlemen, at a time when the concept of honour took precedence over life itself. In civilian life, a charge of cowardice was cause for a duel.

Next day, it was Fryer who was in trouble. Bligh sent the master ashore in the cutter to supervise the watering party. After leaving two sailors in charge of the cutter and threading through a crowd of Tongans on the beach, Fryer went with Quintal along one of the paths that led through

---

[*]   Morrison, *Journal on HMS Bounty and at Tahiti.*
[†]   Dening, *Mr Bligh's Bad Language*, p. 159.

the plantations to the watering pool. The master had stopped to give out some nails when Quintal blurted, 'Mr. Fryer, there is a man going to knock you down with his club,'* and Fryer wheeled around to see a young chief holding a club above his head, and then running away in fright. The pair hurried to the pool, where they found Christian filling the water casks as quickly as possible while a group of islanders pelted him with stones and a chief threatened him with a long spear. Fryer told Christian to get the casks down to the boat empty or full, and started giving out nails in an attempt to cool the situation. When he returned to the beach, he found an enterprising islander had dived underwater and stole the cutter's grapnel.

Fryer jostled through the tumult at the ship (there were often about a hundred canoes surrounding her to trade). He informed Bligh about the theft, reassuring him that, as there were several grapnels on board, 'our loss was not very great', but the lieutenant was furious: 'By God! Sir, if it is not great to you it is great to me!'† He took some of the local chiefs hostage, threatening to sail away if the grapnel wasn't returned; a measure he had never resorted to in Tahiti. His threat didn't appear to inspire the Tongans into action, so he made good on it, taking the chiefs below and setting them the task of peeling coconuts for his dinner while the *Bounty* sailed for open water.

---

*   Alexander, *The Bounty*, ch. 5.

†   Salmond, *Bligh: William Bligh in the South Seas*, ch. 11.

When he returned on deck, he called his officers and men a 'parcel of lubberly rascals' and aimed his pistol at seaman William McKoy, threatening to shoot him for not paying attention.* The distressed Tongans followed astern in canoes, weeping and cutting their faces and shoulders. Bligh detained the chiefs 'till sunset, when their uneasiness and impatience increased to such a degree that they began to beat themselves about the face and eyes and some of them cried bitterly'.† It was more trouble than the grapnel was worth. Bligh gave the chiefs some presents and let them go into the sole canoe that was still following the ship. Their treatment would come back to haunt him.

On 27 April, Bligh came on deck in the afternoon and stopped to examine his store of coconuts, piled between the ship's guns on the quarterdeck. Some of the fruit was missing, he announced, and must have been stolen. He ordered the master's mate to bring every coconut in the ship aft, called the officers, and began interrogating each in turn about the number of coconuts he had bought in Nomuka. When he reached Christian, the acting lieutenant responded: 'I do not know, sir, but I hope you don't think me so mean as to be guilty of stealing yours.'‡

'Yes, you damned hound, I do,' replied Bligh. 'You must have stolen them from me or you could give a better account

---

* Morrison, *Journal on HMS Bounty and at Tahiti.*

† Bligh, *A Voyage to the South Sea*, ch. 12.

‡ Morrison, *Journal on HMS Bounty and at Tahiti.*

of them – God damn you, you scoundrels, you are all thieves alike, and combine with the men to rob them.'*

Bligh ordered his clerk to stop the crew's grog and cut the yam ration from a pound and a half to three quarters of a pound per day. He stormed below, leaving the officers in a dejected huddle on the quarterdeck. The seamen, meanwhile, were convinced Bligh would confiscate their yams next; he knew they had purchased large quantities and hidden as many as they could around the ship.

Christian, regarded as 'no milksop',† was seen in tears after the incident. 'I would rather die ten thousand deaths than receive this treatment,'‡ he was overheard saying. 'I always do my duty as an officer and a man ought to do, yet I receive this scandalous usage.'

The carpenter, Purcell, tried to console him, asking what was the matter.

'Can you ask me, and hear the treatment I receive?' replied Christian.

'Do not I receive as bad as you do?' replied Purcell.

'You have something to protect you, and can speak again; but if I should speak to him as you do, he would probably break me, turn me before the mast, and perhaps flog me.' (Christian feared Bligh would 'break' or disrate him to seaman, enabling him to be flogged.)

---

*   Morrison, *Journal on HMS Bounty and at Tahiti.*
†   Christian, *Appendix to Minutes of the Proceedings of the Court-Martial.*
‡   Christian, *Appendix to Minutes of the Proceedings of the Court-Martial.*

'Never mind it,' Purcell advised. 'It is but for a short time longer.'

Bligh had now branded Christian both a coward and a thief in front of the entire ship's company. Like the incident with the 'stolen' cheeses, he had once again reduced his crew's rations as punishment for a seemingly made-up infraction; an action which, as purser, he stood to profit from at the end of the voyage. In the hours afterward, witnesses noticed Christian acting strangely. He was seen tearing up his letters and papers and throwing them overboard. He asked for nails from the carpenter, who said he could take as many from the locker as he pleased.*

Bligh's mission was two-thirds complete, and he was about to reach an important lag of the journey, the part that, for him, was supposed to make it most worthwhile. On his journey to Jamaica with the breadfruit plants, he was under orders to map the Endeavour Strait (now known as the Torres Strait), a shallow, reef-strewn passage between northern Australia and New Guinea. It was Bligh's chance to bring an unknown and dangerous piece of water to heel. Only two previous European navigators had left the Pacific via the strait, including Cook in 1770. In mapping the strait, Bligh would be following in his mentor's footsteps, a much more exciting prospect than shipping breadfruit plants between hemispheres. But rather than lift his spirits, the upcoming task seemed to fill him with

---

*   Christian, *Appendix to Minutes of the Proceedings of the Court-Martial.*

anxious rage, and the Endeavour Strait became an object of terror among his crew. Bligh threatened that when the *Bounty* reached the strait, he would kill half his men. He would make the officers jump overboard and eat grass like cows.* Christian had confided to Purcell: 'In going through Endeavour Straits, I am sure the ship will be a hell.'†

Bligh didn't mention any of his rages or frayed relationships in his published accounts of the voyage. On the contrary, he wrote in an entry dated the day before the mutiny that, thus far, the voyage had 'advanced in a course of uninterrupted prosperity, and had been attended with many circumstances equally pleasing and satisfactory'.‡

After his tongue-lashings, screaming and shaking his fist in Christian's face, Bligh would seem oblivious and calmly invite the officers to dine with him in the small pantry adjoining his sleeping area. The officers, fed up with their commander's mood swings, had made a collective agreement to refuse his invitations. Christian was invited to dine with Bligh that very evening, after the coconut incident, but excused himself, claiming he was unwell. In fact, the acting lieutenant was preparing to desert the ship and take his chances on the islands.

---

* Christian, *Appendix to Minutes of the Proceedings of the Court-Martial.*
† Christian, *Appendix to Minutes of the Proceedings of the Court-Martial.*
‡ Bligh, *A Voyage to the South Sea*, ch. 12.

CHAPTER SIX

Mutiny

A quarter moon sent a pillar of light shivering across the water under a gentle breeze. The night of 27 April was calm, and in the east, the crew could see the volcanic island of Tofua, arrayed with flickering columns of steam and ash. The conditions were pleasing to Lieutenant Bligh, who came on deck between ten and eleven o'clock, giving his last orders for the night. The officer in charge of the watch was Fryer, who had been engaged in a personal feud with the lieutenant for months. Fryer had been the first officer to refuse to dine with Bligh, and in Tahiti, Bligh fumed in his log that, if it were possible, he would do away with the sailing master altogether. The pair no longer spoke except on duty.

'Sir, we have got a fine breeze and a moon coming on, which will be fortunate for us when we come to the coast of New Holland [Australia],'* Fryer said.

'Yes, Mr. Fryer, so it will,' said Bligh, before retiring to his cabin.

In the shadows on the moonlit deck, Christian got his things ready. He had a meagre bag packed with a bit of roast pork and some nails and beads, useful items for trading with islanders. He lashed together a raft out of planks, and got ready to launch it over the side, aiming for Tofua, thirty-five miles distant.

The men had some idea that their acting lieutenant was about to desert the ship. Through the night, Christian and the midshipman George Stewart were seen climbing up and down the fore hatchway to the cockpit where the boatswain's and carpenter's cabins were, an area of the ship they had no good reason for visiting. Morrison observed the boatswain and the carpenter conferring about something, and the boatswain concluding: 'It won't do tonight.'†

Fryer had the first watch, overseeing the ship until midnight. Then Peckover's group took over. Christian had to depart before four o'clock in the morning, when his own watch would start. But he couldn't find an opportunity to launch his raft. More men than usual were strolling around on deck, getting a look at the volcano. One witness saw Christian

---

* Linder, Transcript of the Court-Martial of the *Bounty* Mutineers, John Fryer's testimony.

† Morrison, *Journal on HMS Bounty and at Tahiti.*

drinking at midnight with the carpenter, who seemed to have become his confidant and helped him to gather supplies. Finally giving up, Christian lay down to rest at about half past three in the morning, and fell into an uneasy sleep.

* * *

Lieutenant Bligh was on the quarterdeck of the *Bounty* in his nightshirt, naked from the waist down, his hands tied behind his back. Christian, armed with a bayonet, held the cord that bound Bligh. The sun glowed red behind the volcano of Tofua, and the *Bounty* was noisy with laughter, curses and hasty orders.

Christian had slept fitfully for about half an hour while he waited for an opportunity to quit the ship. Then he was woken by an officer, Stewart, to take over the watch at four o'clock in the morning. He must have felt dazed and out of order as the wooden world of the ship rushed back to him. Stewart was aware that Christian was planning to leave, and had perhaps helped him get ready; he now tried to persuade his shipmate not to launch his raft. 'When you go, Christian, we are ripe for anything,'* the midshipman whispered, before going to bed.

Christian took over the watch. He looked east to the volcano. It had been a hopeless if not a suicidal plan. Desertions were common in the Society Islands, Christian knew, but captains were always able to compel the islanders to

---

* Christian, *Appendix to Minutes of the Proceedings of the Court-Martial.*

hunt down the deserters, offering a reward or simply holding the local chiefs to ransom. Had he succeeded in reaching Tofua, it would not have been possible for him to conceal himself for long. It would have been the talk of the islands.

Whatever his intentions, he had missed the opportunity to head for Tofua now. The distance between the ship and the volcano had steadily increased all night, and members of his watch were now emerging sleepy-eyed from the hatchways for their morning duties. The fuel and tinder had long been set for what was to follow, the necessary elements drawing together over many months: the Admiralty's careless approach to the mission, Bligh's stinting and abusive command, demoralised officers and men, and five decadent months in Tahiti. Now Christian supplied the flame.

The exact calculus in Christian's mind, if there was any, is not known. Perhaps the atmosphere of the time had some role: he lived on the verge of a revolutionary era in which mutiny became more conceivable and common among British sailors than ever before. Perhaps he drew dim inspiration from his great-great-grandfather, Illiam Dhone, who had led a mutiny against English rule over the Isle of Man only to be executed in 1663, his deeds immortalised in an island ballad. Or perhaps the impetus could be found even closer to home. Weeks before the *Bounty*'s departure, Fletcher's older brother, ship's surgeon Charles Christian, had been party to a 'mutinous conspiracy' aboard the East Indiaman ship *Middlesex*. Two officers were locked in their cabins after trying to intervene on behalf of a seaman they felt the captain mistreated. Charles Christian, moved by 'human sympathy' for the sailor and disgust at the 'capricious orders of tyranny',* was among the officers suspended from the service for his part in the episode. His sympathies must have been valid, because years later a civil court found in favour of the 'mutineers' as plaintiffs in a lawsuit against the captain, awarding them huge damages of three thousand pounds. Charles had returned to England a broken man, and it's likely he shared the tale with his younger brother before Fletcher Christian set sail on the *Bounty*.

What was meant by Stewart's whispered words at the conclusion of his watch? A strict and conscientious officer, it's unclear whether he was suggesting a rebellion against Bligh, or simply trying to persuade the ship's most popular officer to remain with the *Bounty* amid low morale. Could it nonetheless have been that ambiguous turn of phrase that sent Christian over the top?

Whatever the case, in the early morning hours of 28 April, the acting lieutenant made up his mind. The morning had presented a fleeting opportunity. In the grey pre-dawn, the sky clear and the water glassy as it had been the night before, the fellow officers of Christian's watch had not taken their posts. Thomas Hayward had emerged from his quarters, but proceeded to fall asleep on deck, while Hallett was still dozing in his hammock. Free of scrutiny, Christian quietly

---

* Preston, *Paradise in Chains*, ch. 12.

spoke to two of the seamen on his watch, Quintal and Martin, recruiting them to his cause. According to John Adams, Quintal required some persuasion, thinking the plan dangerous, while Martin slapped his thigh and declared, 'He was for it; it was the very thing'.[*] The seamen went below, moving quietly from hammock to hammock in the darkness and summoning other men they thought they could depend on: Churchill, Thompson, John Williams, McKoy and Adams.

In the meantime, Christian kept up the appearance of a regular morning, ordering the other seamen to clear the decks in preparation for washing. Charles Norman, coiling ropes up, looked over the side and saw a huge shark cruising alongside the ship, an uncanny presage to the dissent brewing on board. He shouted, 'There's a shark on the larboard quarter,'[†] rousing Thomas Hayward from sleep. Hayward told Norman not to make a sound and went off to get a shark hook. He returned with the hook and a sleepy Hallett, but the shark was gone. Hallett, scanning the water, realised he was in charge of organising dinner for the midshipmen that week, and ordered the seaman Burkett to 'draw those three fowls for me which are hanging to the mainstay'.[‡] Christian appeared again and ordered Norman to ready the gangway for drawing water, still giving the impression he wanted the

---

[*]   Beechey, *Narrative of a Voyage to the Pacific and Beering's Strait*, p. 73.

[†]   Linder, Transcript of the Court-Martial of the *Bounty* Mutineers, Charles Norman defence statement.

[‡]   Linder, Transcript of the Court-Martial of the *Bounty* Mutineers, Thomas Burkett defence statement.

sailors to wash the decks. Then he disappeared down the fore hatchway and woke the armourer, Joseph Coleman, asking for the keys to the arms chest and saying he wanted a musket to shoot a shark.

When Churchill emerged from the hatchway, Hayward was suspicious at his appearance so early in the morning. 'What are you about, are you going to exercise already?'[*] Churchill replied that Bligh had given orders for the men to exercise at daybreak. Hayward, not satisfied, began drifting towards the aft hatchway and Bligh's cabin. 'Hayward is going to tell the captain,' Churchill hissed. Now several men, Christian among them, were emerging with muskets and bayonets, priming and loading the guns as they went, ramming the ball and paper home with their ramrods. The group overtook Hayward, cutting off his route to the aft hatchway. When he protested Christian waved his cutlass and said, 'Damn your blood, Hayward, *mamu* [a Tahitian word for silence].'[†] Hayward froze and didn't interfere. Christian's men split up, securing both hatchways. Some went below to guard the officers, while Thompson stood sentry over the arms chest.

At five o'clock in the morning, Christian and three other men burst into Bligh's cabin. 'Bligh, you are my prisoner,'[‡]

---

[*] Linder, Transcript of the Court-Martial of the *Bounty* Mutineers, Thomas Burkett defence statement.

[†] Linder, Transcript of the Court-Martial of the *Bounty* Mutineers, Thomas Burkett defence statement.

[‡] Linder, Transcript of the Court-Martial of the *Bounty* Mutineers, Thomas Burkett defence statement.

were the words the lieutenant heard from his protégé as he awoke. The sounds of a muffled struggle came from the cabin. A glass broke. Fryer stirred next door and was ordered to stay in his room. Bligh ignored commands to stay quiet, calling out: 'What's the matter, what's the matter, murder!'* The mutineers tied his hands and marched him out on deck. Quintal and another seaman, John Sumner, secured Fryer in the cabin opposite Bligh's. Fryer saw Christian marching Bligh past in his nightshirt and nightcap. He asked what they were going to do with the captain.

'Damn his eyes,' Sumner said. 'Put him into the boat, and let the bugger see if he can live upon three fourths of a pound of yams a day.'†

'Into the boat?' replied Fryer. 'For God's sake, what for?'

'Hold your tongue,' said Quintal. 'Mr. Christian is captain of the ship and recollect that Mr. Bligh has brought this all upon himself.'

Other crew members woke from their hammocks at the noise and began to throng the deck. Christian first decided to leave Bligh on Tofua with three other men – Hayward, Hallett and Bligh's clerk, Samuel – who together comprised the most disliked men on board. The mutineers would put the men in one of the ship's boats, Christian reasoned, and tow them to the shores of the volcano. But when Norman

---

* Linder, Transcript of the Court-Martial of the *Bounty* Mutineers, Charles Norman defence statement.

† Linder, Transcript of the Court-Martial of the *Bounty* Mutineers, John Fryer testimony.

climbed into the smallest boat, the jolly-boat, he announced the bottom was so badly worm-eaten that it was sinking. And by the time the second boat, the cutter, was going into the water, many more men were asking to leave the ship. Purcell appealed for the launch, a 23-foot boat with a capacity of about ten people, saying anything smaller would 'make a sacrifice of us'.* Christian agreed, not for Bligh's sake but for 'the safety of those that were going with him'.† Soon the vessel was badly overloaded with eighteen men.

Christian's hair was loose, his shirt collar open. His bayonet, which he held by the socket at its base, was a seventeen-inch sliver of steel. He ordered Bligh's servant to bring up the lieutenant's clothes, and then to serve a dram of rum to the men under arms. For three noisy hours, Bligh tried to turn the tide of the mutiny while the launch was loaded up with boxes and trunks, his voice joining the din in Christian's ears. Hallett and Hayward, ordered into the launch, begged tearfully to stay aboard. William Cole, the boatswain, insisted on a compass for the launch. Quintal thought Bligh's men were being given too much equipment (and others agreed, warning that if Purcell were allowed to take his tool chest he would build 'another vessel in a month').‡

---

*   Linder, Transcript of the Court-Martial of the *Bounty* Mutineers, William Purcell testimony.

†   Linder, Transcript of the Court-Martial of the *Bounty* Mutineers, John Fryer testimony.

‡   Linder, Transcript of the Court-Martial of the *Bounty* Mutineers, William Purcell testimony.

When Bligh tried to reason, Christian shut him down: 'Mamu, sir, not a word, or death's your portion.'* Persisting, the lieutenant kept up his monologue, which sometimes devolved into furious instructions to the men nearby to 'knock Christian down'. Then he returned to bargaining: 'For God's sake, drop it and there shall be no more come of it.'

'Tis too late,' replied Christian.

'No, Mr. Christian, it is not too late yet. I'll forfeit my honour if ever I speak of it; I'll give you my bond that there shall never be any more come of it.'†

William Cole also begged Christian to desist, receiving in reply: 'You know, Mr. Cole, how I have been used.'‡

'I know it very well, Mr. Christian,' said Cole. 'We all know it, but drop it, for God's sake.'§

Bligh fell silent, gravely meeting eyes with the men who might help him retake the ship. He was aware that emotions might cool during the anticlimactic business of readying the launch. Suddenly he chimed in again, approaching the mutiny like an everyday problem: 'Can there be no other method taken?'

'No,' said Churchill. 'This is the best and only method.'¶

---

*   Morrison, *Journal on HMS Bounty and at Tahiti.*

†   Linder, Transcript of the Court-Martial of the *Bounty* Mutineers, Thomas Burkett defence statement.

‡   Linder, Transcript of the Court-Martial of the *Bounty* Mutineers, Thomas Burkett defence statement.

§   Linder, Transcript of the Court-Martial of the *Bounty* Mutineers, Thomas Burkett defence statement.

¶   Linder, Transcript of the Court-Martial of the *Bounty* Mutineers, Thomas Burkett defence statement.

The rough, bald-headed seaman had assumed the role of Christian's second-in-command throughout the morning, answering when his leader was engrossed in thought.

'This is a serious affair, Mr. Young,' said Bligh to Edward Young, a midshipman who was brandishing a musket.

'Yes, it is a serious affair to be starved,' replied Young. 'I hope this day to get a bellyful.'*

Amid the quarrelling and noise, the fiddler Michael Byrne had groped his way down into the leaky cutter, where he sat weeping in confusion. Stewart was clapping and dancing in the Tahitian manner, saying this was the 'happiest day of his life'.† Thomas Ellison, a sixteen-year-old seaman, had begun the morning at the ship's helm, and even obeyed a reflexive order from Bligh to steer the ship away from the volcano in the distance.‡ But he had since found himself caught up in the excitement, taking a musket and exclaiming of his commander, 'Damn him, I will be sentry over him.'§ Christian disapproved, ordering the musket off him: 'You little monkey, what business have you with that?'¶

The crew members who sided with Bligh did not try to overpower the mutineers. They only whispered and dithered. None of the lieutenant's men were prepared to risk their lives

---

* Christian, *Appendix to Minutes of the Proceedings of the Court-Martial.*
† Christian, *Appendix to Minutes of the Proceedings of the Court-Martial.*
‡ Linder, Transcript of the Court-Martial of the *Bounty* Mutineers, Thomas Ellison defence statement.
§ Linder, Transcript of the Court-Martial of the *Bounty* Mutineers, Thomas Hayward testimony.
¶ Christian, *Appendix to Minutes of the Proceedings of the Court-Martial.*

for him; the only officer who tried in earnest to stop the revolt was John Fryer, the master Bligh so despised. Held under guard in his cabin, Fryer persuaded Quintal and Sumner to call up to Christian, asking his permission to come on deck. After some hesitation, Christian allowed Fryer to come up, and he emerged blinking on the quarterdeck to see the stand-off for himself. 'Mr. Christian, consider what you are about,'* he blurted.

'Hold your tongue sir,' said Christian. 'I have been in hell for weeks past – Captain Bligh has brought all this on himself.'

The master calmly offered to mediate the dispute between Christian and Bligh: 'Mr. Christian, you and I have been on friendly terms during the voyage, therefore give me leave to speak; let Mr. Bligh go down to his cabin and I make no doubt that we shall all be friends again in a very short time.'† He even suggested that if Christian did not approve of Bligh's conduct, he should simply put him under arrest and proceed with the voyage.‡ But Christian was resolute: 'Hold your tongue sir; it is too late.'§

In the meantime, Fryer quietly told Bligh to keep his spirits up, whispering that if he stayed on board he might be

---

*   Linder, Transcript of the Court-Martial of the *Bounty* Mutineers, John Fryer testimony.

†   Linder, Transcript of the Court-Martial of the *Bounty* Mutineers, John Fryer testimony.

‡   Linder, Transcript of the Court-Martial of the *Bounty* Mutineers, William Cole testimony.

§   Linder, Transcript of the Court-Martial of the *Bounty* Mutineers, John Fryer testimony.

able to retake the ship. 'By all means stay, Mr. Fryer,' said Bligh audibly, betraying the plan. As ever, Bligh was smarting at Fryer; he thought the master had a pair of loaded pistols in his cabin and a 'firm resolution might have made good use of them'.* But Churchill had already confiscated the pistols and, in any case, according to Fryer they were not loaded.

Fryer had become a nuisance, appealing generally to the mutineers to lay down their arms, and Christian ordered him back to his cabin. On his way to the hatchway, he crossed paths with James Morrison and questioned him: 'I hope you have no hand in this business?'†

'No, sir,' Morrison replied, 'I do not know a word about it.'‡

Fryer lowered his voice. 'If that's the case, be on your guard; there may be an opportunity of recovering ourselves.'§

But the boatswain's mate dismissed the idea. 'Go down to your cabin, sir, it is too late.'¶

Fryer climbed down to the cockpit, the dark and fetid warren of cubbies beneath the lower deck, where he found Nelson the gardener and Peckover the gunner, the old South Sea hands, whispering about what to do. On waking up to

---

*   Preston, *Paradise in Chains*, ch. 11.

†   Linder, Transcript of the Court-Martial of the *Bounty* Mutineers, John Fryer testimony.

‡   Linder, Transcript of the Court-Martial of the *Bounty* Mutineers, John Fryer testimony.

§   Linder, Transcript of the Court-Martial of the *Bounty* Mutineers, John Fryer testimony.

¶   Linder, Transcript of the Court-Martial of the *Bounty* Mutineers, John Fryer testimony.

confused noises overhead, Peckover had assumed Tongans were attacking the ship. But Nelson appeared at his door and explained the ship was seized 'by our own people, Christian at their head, but we know whose fault it is'.* In the darkness, Fryer tried to convince Nelson and Peckover to remain in the ship, believing they could turn the tide of the mutiny in a short time. But the other two men disagreed, arguing if they stayed they would all be deemed pirates.

Returning on deck as the last of Bligh's supporters were hurried into the launch, Fryer asked to remain on the *Bounty*, but Christian directed him over the side with his bayonet. Martin was seen giving Bligh a conspiratorial look while feeding him some shaddock (Bligh had complained of his lips being parched), and he, too, was ordered into the launch. But once Martin sat down shoulder to shoulder with the other castaways, the carpenter Purcell said he would get him hanged when they reached England, and Quintal and Churchill ordered Martin back out at gunpoint. Martin wasn't the only crew member to swing between sides. The butcher, Robert Lamb, was initially with the mutineers, but on seeing so many men climbing into the launch he put down his gun and joined them.

The ship now stood in full daylight, and Christian ordered Bligh himself to go into the launch. A couple of sympathetic sailors were hurrying up and down the hatchways with

---

* Linder, Transcript of the Court-Martial of the *Bounty* Mutineers, William Peckover testimony.

bundles of clothes and other provisions to be tossed into the vessel. The lieutenant made his final pleas, swearing again on his honour 'never to think of this if you desist', and reminding Christian about his family: 'I have a wife and four children in England, and you have danced my children upon your knee.'[*]

Morrison heard Christian reply, 'If you had any honour, things would not have come to this; and if you had any regard for your wife and family, you should have thought on them before, and not behaved so much like a villain.'[†]

He now brought the lieutenant to the gangway and untied his hands. 'Never fear my lads,' Bligh said as he went over the side. 'I'll do you justice if ever I reach England.'[‡]

Once in the launch, Bligh stalled, asking to speak again to Christian, who did not appear. Worried the mutineers would begin firing into the launch amid calls of 'shoot the bugger',[§] Bligh's men pressed him to leave. Finally they cast off, while the two carpenter's mates, Norman and Thomas McIntosh, called out to the lieutenant from the gunwales of the *Bounty* to remember they were innocent. Bligh's launch had been too full to carry those men, and the mutineers also required their carpentry skills. Joseph Coleman, the armourer, in charge of repairing and maintaining the ship's guns, was kept on board,

---

[*]   Christian, *Appendix to Minutes of the Proceedings of the Court-Martial.*
[†]   Morrison, *Journal on HMS Bounty and at Tahiti.*
[‡]   Linder, Transcript of the Court-Martial of the *Bounty* Mutineers, Thomas Burkett defence statement.
[§]   Linder, Transcript of the Court-Martial of the *Bounty* Mutineers, John Fryer testimony.

too, and so was Byrne the fiddler, recovered from his refuge in the leaky cutter.

As the ship stood to the north-west, Bligh alone alleged he heard the mutineers calling out, 'Huzza for Tahiti'.* The men in the launch could see the young Thomas Ellison working his way up the rigging to loose the main topgallant sail. That was an added insult for the lieutenant, who had been entrusted with looking after the boy, a protégé of his uncle-in-law Duncan Campbell. At the beginning of the voyage Bligh had written to Campbell that Ellison was a 'very good boy and will do very well'.† So much for that assessment: Ellison was now an ardent mutineer, and had stood guard over his commander with a musket. Later Bligh remarked bitterly, 'even Tom Ellison took such a liking to Tahiti that he also turned pirate, so that I have been run down by my own dogs'.‡

The launch receded into the distance, Bligh's men rowing in the absence of wind. Back on the *Bounty*, the mutineers hoisted the cutter and stowed their weapons back in the arms chest. Far from triumphant, Christian was stunned at the present situation. The crew's passive obedience to his orders had surprised him, and he remarked that 'something more than fear' had stopped any resistance.§ He also regretted the fates of the men in the launch, saying he would readily sacrifice his own life if they could be safe in the ship again.

---

*   Preston, *Paradise in Chains*, ch. 11.
†   Alexander, *The Bounty*, ch. 3.
‡   Salmond, *Bligh: William Bligh in the South Seas*, ch. 12.
§   Morrison, *Journal on HMS Bounty and at Tahiti*.

But he hadn't necessarily handed Bligh a death sentence: it was assumed the lieutenant would sail to the Tongan island of Tongatapu, where he could wait for an English ship. As his adrenaline waned, it dawned on Christian with gradual, depressive force that, in the chaos of the morning, he had given up his status as an officer, a gentleman and an Englishman. He had veered off the tracks of Western civilisation entirely. He was now doomed to live as a fugitive around the edges of the known world; a prisoner, if not to the British authorities, then to the Pacific itself.

Indeed, death and suffering would haunt his project. More than half of the forty-four *Bounty* crew members would perish within the next four years, either drowned, hanged, murdered or succumbed to disease. More than eighty Polynesians would die violently, and thirty-one men sent to hunt the mutineers would be lost at sea.

'This is a hard case upon me, Mr. Christian, who have a wife and family in England,'* said Norman, kept aboard for his skills as a carpenter's mate.

'It is a hard case, Norman,' said Christian. 'But it never would have happened, if I could have left the ship alone.'†

Christian told the mutineers he had no right to the command, but they insisted he should be their captain.‡ After some persuasion from Christian, they accepted Stewart, an

---

* Christian, *Appendix to Minutes of the Proceedings of the Court-Martial.*
† Christian, *Appendix to Minutes of the Proceedings of the Court-Martial.*
‡ Christian, *Appendix to Minutes of the Proceedings of the Court-Martial.*

officer several years his senior in age and experience, as his second-in-command, the pair dividing two watches between them. The *Bounty*'s new commander had inherited the fragile hierarchy of her crew, whose ranks were divided along social class lines. The most active participants in the mutiny had been the seamen, not the fresh-faced young gentlemen (except the enigmatic Edward Young, who was the only midshipman to take up arms). Adding to that tension, four of the twenty-five men remaining on the *Bounty* were there under duress. Christian would keep a pistol in his pocket at all times in case of a further rebellion, while Churchill slept on the arms chest every night.

Meanwhile, Bligh was trying to get his bearings in the launch, which sagged in the water almost to the gunwales. The lieutenant had been given his private journal, a compass, some navigational books, a pocket watch, and Christian's personal sextant, a simple instrument used to estimate latitude and longitude. He was without his treasured K2 chronometer, which remained on the *Bounty*. The launch was also loaded with enough water and biscuit for a week. Bligh had asked the mutineers for guns, and at the last moment Burkett had thrown four cutlasses down into the launch. But the swords would not be much help in a contest with Polynesian warriors. Without muskets, a ship or a full crew, Bligh and his men would be seen as easy pickings.

CHAPTER SEVEN

The Debacle on Tofua

In the wake of the *Bounty*, William Bligh and his reluctant followers rowed about thirty-five miles north-east to the Tongan island of Tofua. The volcano was the nearest land within reach and, Bligh reasoned, a good place to bolster his provisions before moving on to Tongatapu, the main island in the archipelago. But the steep and rocky coast of Tofua was by no means a salvation. It was not as abundant as Tahiti, and the proud and warlike Tongans disliked Europeans.

Bligh wanted pigs and chickens, but had to be satisfied with small bunches of coconuts and breadfruit, and he was constantly on his guard. His open launch was a pathetic sight, so overladen that the freeboard remaining was less than a man's hand. The boat had been designed to cover short distances with ten passengers, not thousands of miles with nineteen men and a stack of supplies. Bligh wondered how to explain his circumstances to the Tongans, who could plainly see there were no ships anchored around the island. In the end he said his ship had sunk, which didn't inspire much sympathy.

Nageete, one of the chiefs Bligh had detained off Nomuka, happened to be visiting Tofua, forty miles distant, when the *Bounty* castaways arrived on the island.* Bligh wrote in his journal that Nageete seemed pleased to see him again. But there cannot have been much genuine warmth in the face of the high-born man who had been kidnapped and forced to prepare the lieutenant's dinner like a servant. Now the whites were under his power, and he must have been glad of an opportunity for revenge. Bligh kept up a line of patter, disappointed that the islanders did not have much food or water to offer him, but nonetheless giving out old shirts and knives as gifts. That night he and his men slept in a cave on a stony beach, keeping an uneasy watch over the entrance.

More days of frugal trading for island scraps, and the Tongans grew bolder. Hundreds gathered on the beach, clacking polished volcanic stones together in their hands, a sign of impending attack that Bligh remembered from Hawaii. The chiefs smiled and made platitudes. A group of islanders attempted to haul the launch ashore, cutting off any means of escape, and only desisted after Bligh angrily wielded

---

* Christian, *Appendix to Minutes of the Proceedings of the Court-Martial.*

his cutlass. During a lunch of coconut and breadfruit, the Tongans constantly asked the lieutenant to sit down, and he refused, believing they were looking for an opportunity to seize hold of him. 'Keeping therefore constantly on our guard,' he wrote, 'we were suffered to eat our uncomfortable meal in some quietness.'*

The Tongans were overstepping the usual boundaries, feeling out Bligh and his men for weakness. That night, rather than leave their visitors alone at the cave, they made fires along the beach, preparing to camp there for the night. It was almost sunset when the lieutenant, updating his diary in his cave, ordered his men to get the launch ready in the rough surf. A chief asked Bligh if he would stay on the beach all night. When Bligh replied that he would sleep in his boat and resume trade in the morning, the chief said, 'You will not sleep on shore? Then *mattie*,' which Bligh took to mean 'Then we will kill you.'† The chief stormed off. Bligh took Nageete by the hand and walked down the beach to the boat in a 'silent kind of horror'.‡

Nageete, discovering that Bligh was trying to leave, removed himself from the lieutenant's grip and left him. Bligh ordered William Peckover to run back to the cave and retrieve the ship's log. Peckover boldly pushed through the warriors, who sensed the book was of some value and tried to wrestle

---

* Bligh, *A Voyage to the South Sea*, ch. 14.
† Bligh, *A Voyage to the South Sea*, ch. 14.
‡ Bligh, *A Voyage to the South Sea*, ch. 14.

it from him. As soon as Bligh's men pulled him into the launch, hundreds of islanders attacked with volleys of stones, battering the sailors. John Norton, running up the beach to free the boat's stern line, fell in the attack, and the islanders were soon bashing his head in with rocks. Bligh would later confide to a relative that Norton's death was 'fortunate' in the greater scheme of the voyage, because he was the 'stoutest man in the ship, which circumstance would very materially have interfered with the boat's progress and the allowance of provisions'.[*]

The islanders now started pulling the launch ashore by the stern line, but Bligh severed it with a knife. His men bent at their oars, slowly rowing the launch through the surf amid a hail of stones, as canoes launched from the beach in pursuit. The crew tossed some clothes over the side as a distraction and, with daylight fading, the islanders gave up the chase.

Exhausted and bruised, the men took their bearings. The attack had shaken Bligh's faith in the hospitality of the Tongans, and he abandoned his plan to visit Tongatapu. Instead, he raised the masts, set the sails and aimed for the nearest outpost of Western civilisation, the Dutch settlement in the East Indies, thousands of miles to the north-west. He does not seem to have considered heading for the newly founded British penal colony at New South Wales on Australia's eastern coast; probably because it would have amounted to suicide, a

---

*   Preston, *Paradise in Chains*, ch. 12.

journey through unknown waters to a potentially abandoned settlement. He had considered calling at New South Wales during the *Bounty*'s outward voyage, but explained to Banks it would have left his mission in the 'power of chance'.* The East Indies, meanwhile, were dotted with busy Dutch-controlled cities, and Bligh knew at least vaguely where the city of Kupang was located on the island of Timor.

Other Polynesian canoes pursued Bligh's launch as he threaded through the uncharted Fiji islands, but he managed to keep ahead of them. In those years, the Fiji islands had a reputation for cannibalistic tribes and dangerous coral reefs, and Western sailors tended to avoid them. After the episode on Tofua, Bligh felt it was too risky to stop and find out the intentions of his Fijian pursuers, or to go ashore on any of the dozens of islands he passed, lush and inviting as they appeared. Much of the time he was bent over his quill pen, scribbling notes at the stern in his grim accounting of the boat journey.

During the mutiny, Bligh's servant, Samuel, had attempted, as he scrambled around the ship collecting his master's journal and warrant papers, to take the *Bounty*'s K2 chronometer and a box of charts. But the mutineers stopped him. Without the timekeeper, Bligh was using dead reckoning to make his way to Timor. In order to estimate longitude he needed to know the speed of the launch, so he fashioned a log line, a knotted

---

* Preston, *Paradise in Chains*, ch. 13.

piece of rope that his men threw into the water behind the boat. He determined speed by counting the number of knots that ran out of the boat over a set period of time.

When the lieutenant wasn't trying to outpace Polynesian canoes, he was struggling to maintain authority over his men, who teetered on another mutiny. Food had been a point of bitter contention on the *Bounty*, but it now became a matter of life and death, and Bligh retained his role as purser. The default ration, when they were not able to forage anything else, was one twenty-fifth of a pound of bread and a quarter of a pint of water, three times a day. That amounted to fifty-four grams of bread a day, about one slice. Bligh used a set of scales fashioned from coconut shells and musket balls to dole it out. An average man needs two and a half thousand calories per day to maintain his weight: the daily bread serving in the launch would have yielded about one hundred and forty calories. What the sailors knew as bread was ship's biscuit, a flour and water mixture baked into a hard rock to prevent spoilage during long voyages. It had to be rehydrated, and most of the men in the launch seasoned it with salt water. Bligh broke his share into small pieces and put them in his allowance of freshwater. He slowly ate the resulting porridge out of a coconut shell with a spoon, 'economically avoiding to take too large a piece at a time, so that I was as long at dinner as if it had been a much more plentiful meal'.*

---

* Bligh, *A Voyage to the South Sea*, ch. 15.

Soon Bligh's men were suffering from the dizzy spells, constipation and abdominal pains of starvation, and their bones and joints ached from their cramped sleeping positions in the bottom of the boat. Most would go two and a half weeks without evacuating their bowels. Water was not as great a problem as food, because the launch was frequently caught in thunderstorms and heavy rain. It meant the crew spent their nights saturated and cold, and they were constantly bailing water to prevent the launch from sinking, but if the weather had been drier they would almost certainly have died of thirst.

The men tried to supplement their meagre bread ration with whatever else they could find. A fishing line was always towing from the boat, but it produced almost nothing. On 25 May, somebody caught by hand a noddy, a seabird the size of a small pigeon, and it was divided into eighteen portions and devoured raw, bones, entrails and all. On 26 May, two boobies were caught, their fishy stomach contents saved to be divided and served the next day. On 29 May, Bligh found a break in the Great Barrier Reef off the eastern coast of Queensland, Australia. The crew grounded the launch on a small coastal island, staggering ashore like drunks. They feasted on a stew of foraged oysters, a full pint for each man. Bands of Indigenous Australians appeared across the water on the mainland and seemed friendly, gesturing for the crew to join them, but Bligh wouldn't take the risk.

His men were at their wits' end, and as they island-hopped along the scorched coast of Australia, discipline broke down. Somebody had started pilfering the provisions at night: on 30 May a portion of the pork was missing, and on 6 June some foraged clams disappeared. Robert Lamb, the butcher, became separated from his foraging party on an island and, in his solitude, ate nine raw seabirds to himself, an offence for which Bligh said he received a 'good beating'.[*] Purcell, the carpenter, clashed publicly with Bligh. He did not mention it yet, but he was convinced the lieutenant was secretly dropping pieces of bread while serving out the rations, and afterwards, when he thought no one was looking, plucking them up from the bottom of the boat and putting them in his mouth.[†] When the launch was beached on another desolate piece of land along the Great Barrier Reef, tensions between Bligh and the carpenter came to a head. Purcell refused to give up some clams he'd collected on the island; he thought it was 'every man for himself', while his commander insisted the clams should go in the communal pot. Purcell refused, and Bligh flew into one of his harangues.

'I have brought you here when, if I had not been with you, you would have all perished,'[‡] the lieutenant said, according to Fryer.

---

[*] Bligh, *A Voyage to the South Sea*, ch. 16.

[†] Wahlroos, *Mutiny and Romance in the South Seas*, p. 77.

[‡] Preston, *Paradise in Chains*, ch. 12.

'If it had not been for you, we should not have been here,' said Purcell.

'What's that you say, sir?'

'I say, sir, if it had not been for you we should not have been here.'

'You damned scoundrel, what do you mean?'

'I am not a scoundrel, sir, I am as good a man as you.'

Bligh took that last remark as mutinous and challenged the carpenter to a duel. He drew a cutlass and told Purcell to take another and defend himself. Purcell refused and called out for help, certain that Bligh was about to kill him. Fryer, at the sight of his commander swaggering with a cutlass over Purcell's head, burst into hopeless laughter and ordered the boatswain, William Cole, to put Bligh under arrest. The lieutenant responded that if Fryer interfered in his command he would put him to death, and as everybody stood around in suspense, the moment passed.

Bligh wrote in his journal that Purcell immediately made concessions and 'everything soon became quiet'.* But his authority hung by a thread, and like Christian with his pistol, he would keep his cutlass close at hand in case of further problems. Fryer later recalled the lieutenant was as tyrannical in the launch as in the *Bounty*, and his 'chief thought was his own comfort'.† That afternoon each man dined on a pint and

---

* Bligh, *A Voyage to the South Sea*, ch. 16.
† Wahlroos, *Mutiny and Romance in the South Seas*, p. 71.

a half of stewed oysters and clams, thickened with beans that Nelson the gardener had found.

William Bligh, parting with the northern tip of Australia and making his final, desperate run for Timor, watched as the faces of his men shrank into a uniform collection of sunken eyes and jutting cheekbones. A strange fact of starvation is its sufferers all begin to look alike. Bligh regarded their hollow faces and sleepy attitudes as 'melancholy presages of their approaching dissolution'.* When a seabird was caught, its blood was divided among the worst-affected crew members. Bligh took to giving his weakest men teaspoonfuls of wine, which seemed to help them. He confided in his journal that, despite their miserable situation, he did not believe he and his men could resort to 'destroying one another for food'.†

The famous *Essex* disaster was yet to occur, but survival cannibalism, usually through the drawing of lots, had long been an accepted last resort among castaways. Earlier that century, the British slave transport *Luxborough Galley* had caught fire and sank in the Atlantic. Twenty-two survivors were set adrift in the ship's yawl, without food, water or compass. Their number had been reduced to twelve before they were rescued by fishermen off the coast of Newfoundland two weeks later. They were not able to catch fish or birds, and resorted to eating the flesh and drinking the blood of their dead companions. Not until the late nineteenth century

---

*   Bligh, *A Voyage to the South Sea*, ch. 17.
†   Salmond, *Bligh: William Bligh in the South Seas*, ch. 12.

did the English criminal case *R vs Dudley and Stephens*, concerning two shipwrecked sailors who killed and ate their cabin boy, establish a precedent that necessity was not a murder defence.

Bligh accomplished his original task of passing through Endeavour Strait, albeit under very different circumstances than he and his superiors had imagined. Ever the cartographer, he drew careful charts along the way. He spotted the palm-lined coast of Timor at three o'clock in the morning on Friday, 12 June 1789. Friendly, betel-chewing locals directed him down the coast to Kupang, a small settlement centred around a Dutch fort. Bligh raised a pennant of distress and waited for permission to land, which must have struck his men as a pointless formality, given their dire situation. The voyage had spanned forty-six days and almost four thousand nautical miles.

'Our bodies were nothing but skin and bones, our limbs were full of sores, and we were clothed in rags,' wrote Bligh. 'In this condition, with the tears of joy and gratitude flowing down our cheeks, the people of Timor beheld us with a mixture of horror, surprise, and pity.'*

In Timor, Bligh's men swung between open defiance and abject apology while he reminded them he was still in control of their money, their passage to England and their freedom. Meanwhile, their wasted condition meant they

---

* Bligh, *A Voyage to the South Sea*, ch. 17.

were extremely vulnerable to disease in the island's tropical climate. It must have been obvious to the Dutch that these intrepid survivors could no longer stand each other; Bligh repeatedly called on Dutchmen to act as mediators in their disputes and as jailers for his men. He had ordered Fryer and his servant, John Smith, to stay behind and guard the launch once docked in Kupang, although the pair were near-death with hunger. Bligh and the rest of his men ate breakfast with a Dutch captain, who was shocked to hear his ragged guests had left two of their company behind in the launch. Meanwhile, a soldier took pity on Fryer and Smith and brought them some food. Feasting on tea and cakes, Fryer wept with gratitude.

Purcell confronted Bligh about the way he had conjured an extra piece of bread for himself during the voyage, and the quartermaster, Peter Linkletter, backed up the carpenter, saying he had also observed the bread trick.[*] Bligh retaliated by having both men imprisoned on the Dutch captain's ship. Fryer, meanwhile, secretly sent word to the Kupang governor that Bligh had overcharged the Admiralty for his expenses and given the *Bounty*'s crew short allowance throughout the voyage.[†] Bligh bought a schooner and prepared to carry his men to Surabaya on Java, fitting the vessel out with swivel guns as protection against pirates in the Java Sea. Nelson died of a fever before they set sail. Diligent and well liked, the

---

[*]   Wahlroos, *Mutiny and Romance in the South Seas*, p. 77.

[†]   Salmond, *Bligh: William Bligh in the South Seas*, ch. 12.

gardener had helped to identify edible plants as Bligh's men worked their way up the Australian coast.

At Surabaya, Bligh imprisoned Purcell and Fryer at the point of a bayonet. He discovered Purcell had spread a rumour that Bligh would be hanged or fired from a cannon when he reached England. The 'wretches' were confined in a separate canoe as the schooner made her way up the coast to Semarang, where Fryer was released after begging forgiveness. Purcell remained a prisoner all the way to Batavia, present-day Jakarta in Indonesia.

A hundred years after the Portuguese reached Asia, the Dutch and British had wrested control of trade with the east. While Britain developed a strong foothold in India, the Dutch controlled the East Indies, and Batavia was the centre of their trade network, a muggy city crowded with Chinese traders and Malay slaves. Here the European edge against fatal disease was reversed, and the malaria borne by the mosquitoes in the city's marshes and canals was known to kill white visitors in their droves. Bligh and several of his men fell sick.

The lieutenant quickly left the East Indies with his clerk and servant, filling the only three berths available on a voyage from Batavia to Cape Town, the Dutch way station to the east. As a passenger he was restive and irate, criticising the ship as unnecessarily slow, its captain as inept and 'dirty', and the Dutch crew in general as 'nasty beasts'.* On his way back

---

* Salmond, *Bligh: William Bligh in the South Seas*, ch. 12.

to England he dispatched letters with physical descriptions of the *Bounty* mutineers to New South Wales and India. Although all of his men save Norton had survived the open boat voyage to Timor, several died of tropical disease while awaiting their own transportation back to England in Dutch ships. Of the eighteen loyalists who had endured the open sea voyage in the launch, only eleven returned home.

CHAPTER EIGHT

Christian Holds a Vote

Christian moved into Bligh's cabin and leafed through his books, while the seamen cleared out the great cabin to be used as their commander's sanctum, throwing hundreds of breadfruit pots out of the stern windows and into the sea. In terms of spaciousness, the ship, with almost half its complement having departed in the open launch, had transformed into a rambling wooden manor. The mutineers cast lots to divide the hammocks, clothes and tools of the absent sailors among themselves, while Christian gave orders to steer the *Bounty* east, aiming for Tubuai, four hundred miles south of Tahiti. He kept up discipline on the ship, but he was often below deck with his head in his hands, and when the mutineers came down for orders, he seldom raised his head to answer more than 'Yes', or 'No'.

Tubuai is a small volcanic island that sits within a diamond-shaped membrane of coral reefs and sandy islets. Cook had charted it eleven years earlier, finding the sole opening in the reef and interacting briefly with the Tubuaians in their canoes, but never going ashore. Before the appearance of the *Bounty* in the island's blue-green lagoon, the islanders' contact with Europeans had been almost non-existent; they did not value iron and had no fear of guns. Christian faced the delicate task of making first contact, while one of his men, James Morrison, would play the role of an amateur ethnologist, recording the customs and culture of a people virtually unknown to the West. Morrison was critical of Bligh, but not an active mutineer; his writings imply he stayed on board with a plan to retake the ship that never eventuated. His narrative of the *Bounty* voyage, written as he awaited trial in England, provides a counterweight to Bligh's log and journal.

For example, Bligh wrote in his logbook on 23 March 1788, while he was trying to round Cape Horn: 'In the morning I killed a sheep and served it to the ship's company, which gave them a pleasant meal.'[*]

Morrison's corresponding entry reads: 'One of the sheep dying, this morning Lieut. Bligh ordered it to be issued in lieu of the day's allowance of pork and peas, declaring that it would make a delicious meal and that it weighed upwards

---

[*] Wahlroos, *Mutiny and Romance in the South Seas*, p. 327.

of fifty pounds; it was divided and most part of it thrown overboard, and some dried shark supplied its place for Sunday's dinner, for it was no other than skin and bone."[*]

Morrison, his longing for a South Seas adventure more than satisfied, was watching with typical attention to detail on the *Bounty* as his new commander prepared to make landfall at Tubuai. The island appeared as a green smudging on the horizon within half an hour of Christian's prediction. He ordered the mutineers to sew matching jackets out of studding sails, giving up his blue officer's uniform for edging. He reasoned that some semblance of a uniform might impress the Tubuaians. Donning their new garb, the sailors moved the *Bounty* through the opening in the reef that Cook had found, entering a shoal-strewn bay.

On the beaches ahead they could see the islanders stirred into activity with clubs and long spears, their red-dyed tunics stark against the white sand. Their heads were enlarged with conical helmets woven from coconut fibres. Conch shells droned and the crowds on the beach grew. Soon canoes were coming out and the *Bounty* went into a holding pattern, the sailors trying to invite the Tubuaians aboard in the Tahitian language when they came within earshot. Canoes full of women lined up on one side of the ship, and an armada of several hundred warriors on the other, echoing the display Wallis of the *Dolphin* had witnessed on his arrival in Tahiti.

---

[*] Wahlroos, *Mutiny and Romance in the South Seas*, p. 327.

An old man, perhaps a chief, climbed aboard and was astonished at everything he saw, but seemed carefully to be reckoning the numbers of the white men.

When the mutineers tried to land ashore in a small boat, the islanders threw hails of stones. The whites opened fire with muskets, killing eleven men and a woman.* The beach crowds fled inland and the mutineers turned and rowed back to the ship. Regrouping, the *Bounty* crew weighed their options. Christian was set on building a settlement on the island. It lacked an enticing anchorage and its nearness to Tahiti meant there was little reason for passing ships to call there. He reasoned the Tubuaians could be won over in time, notwithstanding their first violent encounter. But he could not depend on the prospect of their hospitality. He sailed back out through the reef and aimed north for Tahiti.

Some weeks later, the *Bounty* returned to Tubuai loaded with hundreds of livestock and a handful of Tahitian men and women who had willingly joined the mutineers. Their number included Christian's partner Mauatua, a high-born woman from the Pare district with whom he had only recently formed an attachment, and the female companions of several other Englishmen. In Tahiti, Christian had forbade the mutineers from deserting the ship or divulging their plan to settle Tubuai. He also refrained from telling the Tahitians about the mutiny. Instead, he said he had run into Captain

---

* Morrison, *Journal on HMS Bounty and at Tahiti*.

Cook at Aitutaki in the Cook Islands, and after transferring Bligh and the breadfruit plants to Cook's ship, he was sent back to Tahiti under orders to gather supplies for a new settlement in those islands. Whether or not they believed him, the Tahitians graciously brought out pigs, goats and cats to the ship. The *Bounty*'s new, biracial cohort were optimistic as they weighed anchor in Matavai Bay with all the ingredients for a colony.

Several stowaways emerged from the hatches when it was too late to put them ashore. Christian agreed to proceed to sea with them, but made clear they would never see Tahiti again, to which they were 'perfectly easy and satisfied',[*] according to Morrison. Among the stowaways was Hitihiti, a high-born adventurer from Bora Bora who had travelled widely across the Pacific with Captain Cook. When Cook met Hitihiti on Tahiti during his second voyage, the intrepid young man had recently arrived in a voyaging canoe from his native island. Cook took him on a seven-month odyssey to Tonga, the Marquesas, Easter Island and New Zealand, then dropped him back at Tahiti with a certificate of his service. Hearing the *Bounty* crew were off to see his old friend at Aitutaki, Hitihiti happily secreted himself on board.

Nine days after Bligh had reached Timor in the open launch, Christian was manoeuvring his ship through Tubuai's reef passage for a second time. He braced for another attack

---

[*] Morrison, *Journal on HMS Bounty and at Tahiti*.

from the Tubuaians, but as they came alongside in their canoes the mood was much changed: now they seemed to desire peace, offering young plantain trees to the mutineers. After the *Bounty*'s first visit, the Tubuaians had suffered a bout of illness, which they took as a punishment from the gods for going to war with a wrong cause.

Soon after dropping anchor, two of Christian's men went ashore without leave for a night, flouting the rules of the ship. On their return the next day, they explained that the 'ship is moored and we are now our own masters',[*] to which Christian put a pistol to one of their heads and raged, 'I'll let you know who is master',[†] ordering them in irons. Morrison thought the incident showed 'he was not to be played with'.[‡] Christian understood the *Bounty*'s crew could not dispense with naval discipline, and in fact it was the key to their survival, though rules were becoming increasingly difficult to enforce. The two misbehavers spent a day in irons and when it came time to release them, they begged for forgiveness. Christian relented a little, now allowing two men to sleep ashore each night, and as many as wanted to on Sundays.

The mutineers chose a tract of sandy, palm-studded land to settle, hoisting the Union Jack on a staff and drinking an extra allowance of grog. The plan was to build a quadrangular fort that could be defended against warships and Tubuaians alike,

---

[*]   Morrison, *Journal on HMS Bounty and at Tahiti*.
[†]   Morrison, *Journal on HMS Bounty and at Tahiti*.
[‡]   Morrison, *Journal on HMS Bounty and at Tahiti*.

complete with the *Bounty*'s guns and a drawbridge spanning a ditch. The men christened the project Fort George. Perhaps Christian took the name from the British Fort St George in the Indian coastal city of Madras (present-day Chennai). As a teenager, he would have seen that imposing stone building from the decks of the *Eurydice*. Neither he nor any of his men knew much about fort-building, but they got to work felling trees, digging ditches and building up the walls. Ambitious plans described a ditch eighteen feet wide and twenty feet deep from the top of the walls, and walls eighteen feet thick at the base. The drawbridge was planned for the fort's north side, facing the beach, with a four-pounder cannon on each corner. Christian joined in the labour himself, and everybody got an extra pint of porter per day for their efforts.

While the mutineers were working away on Fort George, a European ship passed within miles of them. At eight o'clock on the night of 9 August 1789, the brig *Mercury*, a Swedish vessel with an English crew, was sailing two miles off Tubuai on her way to Tahiti. In the darkness, her crew could see the dim glow of fires on the island. They fired two guns to get the islanders' attention, but it was too dark to see anybody, or to spot the *Bounty* anchored inside the island's reef. Indeed, it was so dark that the crew failed to see the reef itself, and came dangerously close to foundering on it, which would have left them stranded with the mutineers. The *Mercury* moved on and reached Matavai Bay, where her captain was mystified by all the talk of Titerano, the Tahitian name for Christian, who was said to have sailed just fifteen days earlier. If the mutineers heard the guns of the *Mercury* on the night she passed Tubuai, there is no record of it.

Tensions again flared between the mutineers and the islanders as Christian became mired in local politics. As usual, the presence of white sailors, with their superior firepower and coveted gifts, had warped the tribal dynamics of the island. Christian's choice of the location for Fort George, four miles to the east of the reef passage, had been welcomed by the chief of that district, Taaroatahoa. Christian purchased the land for a quantity of red feathers, which the Tubuaians valued above axes and metal. But the arrangement was taken as an insult by the other two chiefs on the island, whose districts were larger and better resourced. The chiefs boycotted trade with the Europeans, putting a strain on provisions, and a tit-for-tat rivalry emerged. A naked John Adams had to be rescued from a rival chief's house after he was kidnapped from his shore camp. Tensions were not helped by the more than three hundred pigs the mutineers had introduced to the island; the animals were roaming free and uprooting crops. Before that the only mammals the Tubuaians had known were rats.

Christian was also faced with dissent from his own men. The mutineers hated Tubuai, so different from free-loving Tahiti. They were struggling to lure local women to Fort George, and insisted they should abduct women from their villages in an armed raid; a wife for each man. They refused to do any more work in the meantime. 'As Mr. Christian's desire was to persuade rather than force [the women],' wrote Morrison, 'he positively refused to have anything to do with such an absurd demand.'[*]

The mutineers were also thirsting for more grog, but a double allowance didn't satisfy them and they took more by force, breaking the lock of the *Bounty*'s spirit room. They got drunk, fought and threatened to kill each other, while the men in command nervously primed their pistols. The momentum of their shared mission had slackened, replaced with an angry torpor. But Christian was forging ahead, and he had begun to talk of dismantling the ship. That frightened Morrison, Peter Heywood and George Stewart, who whispered about stealing the cutter and making for Tahiti, where they hoped to flag down an English ship. The cutter needed repairs, which Christian tactfully refused to allow until the work on the fort was finished, but the trio plotted to sail in her anyway. Morrison estimated the passage would take five or six days, but 'had we the chance to meet with bad weather our crazy boat would certainly have made us a coffin'.[†]

* * *

Christian's plans for Tubuai were a lost cause. After a couple of months, his fort stood half-finished and his men were running rampant. He called the company together and let

---

[*] Morrison, *Journal on HMS Bounty and at Tahiti*.
[†] Morrison, *Journal on HMS Bounty and at Tahiti*.

them vote on how to proceed. Sixteen men out of twenty-five voted to return to Tahiti, despite the high risk of capture. Christian relented and promised to land the men wherever they wanted on one condition: 'that you will grant me the ship, tie the foresail, and give me a few gallons of water, and leave me to run before the wind: and I shall land upon the first island the ship drives to'.* He explained he could not remain in Tahiti himself, and instead planned to continue searching the Pacific for an island to settle: 'I will never live where I may be carried home to be a disgrace to my family.'† Eight men pledged to remain with him, and then all hands began preparing to leave Tubuai in the *Bounty*.

But when they were trying to round up the hundreds of pigs they'd released on the island, they found one of the rival chiefs, Tinarou, unwilling to give them up. The mutineers assembled a war party, and as they marched along a thickly wooded trail in search of Tinarou's men, they came under ambush, a spear flying out of the bush and into Burkett's side. A hundreds-strong force of Tubuaians came out of the trees, bristling with spears and clubs. The mutineers responded with coordinated gunfire. Their flintlock muskets allowed about three shots per minute, accurate up to one hundred yards (91 metres). But muskets were prone to misfire, and after continual use, fouling in the barrel made it increasingly difficult to ram a charge home.

---

* Christian, *Appendix to Minutes of the Proceedings of the Court-Martial.*
† Christian, *Appendix to Minutes of the Proceedings of the Court-Martial.*

The *Bounty* crew made a fighting retreat to an open taro ground, where the Tubuaians lost heart, preferring to stick to the trees. While they greatly outnumbered the whites, the psychological edge of the muskets had kept them from making a substantial charge. The skirmish cost them sixty men and six women, who were supplying the men with spears and stones.* On the mutineers' side, Burkett and several of the Tahitians were wounded, but none fatally. One of the young Tahitians was 'much displeased' when the crew refused to let him collect the jawbones of their slain enemies and hang them around the ship as trophies.

---

* Morrison, *Journal on HMS Bounty and at Tahiti.*

CHAPTER NINE

A Hero's Welcome

William Bligh, arriving in England on 13 March 1790, was hailed a national hero. His open boat voyage to Timor was touted in the international press as a triumph over absurd odds. 'In navigating his little skiff through so dangerous a sea,' commented the *London Chronicle*, 'his seamanship appears as matchless, as the undertaking seems beyond the verge of probability.'* The Admiralty quickly dispatched a frigate to hunt the mutineers.

Bligh had spent the journey home from the Dutch East Indies preparing his account of the *Bounty* voyage. His time with Cook had taught him the importance of controlling a narrative, especially after catastrophe. On his arrival in

---

* Frost, *Mutiny, Mayhem, Mythology*, introduction.

London, he presented his effort to the king, and a few months later it was published with the Admiralty's stamp of approval as his *Narrative of the Mutiny on the Bounty*, while a London theatre presented a pantomime titled *The Pirates, or, The Calamities of Capt. Bligh*. The lieutenant's narrative was a bestseller, and he followed it with an expanded account in 1792, *A Voyage to the South Sea*. The books told of a more or less trouble-free voyage before the fateful incident in the Tongan Islands, and of a Bligh who, moments after being cast adrift, felt an 'inward satisfaction' at the thought of his own integrity.*

Later in 1790, Bligh was honourably acquitted of losing the *Bounty* at court martial and made a post-captain, the promotion he had hoped to receive before sailing for Tahiti. Basking in public accolades, he wasted no time in settling old scores, and brought charges for misconduct and insubordination against Purcell. The carpenter's court martial, held two weeks before Bligh's, found his charges proven in part and handed him a reprimand. As Diana Preston writes, it's possible the carpenter was given a mild punishment in return for not creating further trouble; when he was called to give evidence at William Bligh's own court martial, he voiced no complaints about Bligh's command.

Bligh also sent off fiery letters to the family of Peter Heywood, the young gentleman who had remained with the

---

* Bligh, *A Voyage to the South Sea*, ch. 13.

mutineers. Bligh was convinced Heywood had been one of the mutiny's chief instigators. When the lieutenant returned to England and Heywood's recently widowed mother wrote to him asking about the fate of her son, Bligh didn't disguise his hatred for the boy, which had fomented during his voyage to Timor. 'His baseness is beyond all description,' he wrote in reply to Mrs Heywood, 'but I hope you will prevent the loss of him, heavy as the misfortune is, from afflicting you too severely.'* Bligh really let his pen fly in a letter to Heywood's uncle, saying the young man's 'ingratitude to me is of the blackest dye ... I very much regret that so much baseness formed the character of a young man I had a real regard for, and it will give me much pleasure to hear his friends can bear the loss of him without much concern.'† He wrote that he imagined Heywood was in Tahiti with the other mutineers, a hypothesis that would turn out to be true.

In his *Voyage*, Bligh described the mutiny as a 'close-planned act of villainy' prepared with 'so much secrecy and circumspection' that there had not been the smallest hint he was about to lose his ship. Christian, in particular, he had been on the most friendly terms with, he wrote; so much so that he had invited the acting lieutenant to dine with him the night before the mutiny. He insisted the motive of the mutineers was a return to Tahiti, where the 'allurements of

---

*   Preston, *Paradise in Chains*, ch. 13.

†   Preston, *Paradise in Chains*, ch. 13.

dissipation are beyond anything that can be conceived'.[*] Bligh, whose writing about Tahitians had thus far comprised a relatively cool ethnography, was suddenly echoing the European romance about Tahitian women, described in the official account of Cook's first voyage as having 'dissolute sensuality wholly unknown to every other nation ... and which no imagination could possibly conceive'.[†]

He claimed the warmth and idleness of island life and the siren song of Tahitian women had led his men astray: 'I can only conjecture that the mutineers had flattered themselves with the hopes of a more happy life among the Tahitians than they could possibly enjoy in England, and this, joined to some female connections, most probably occasioned the whole transaction.'[‡]

The British public had no reason to question Bligh's explanation for what happened, at least in the beginning. It squared with familiar accounts of Tahiti as a utopia in the Pacific. The *General Evening Post* put its own spin on his account, reporting that the mutineers 'were so greatly fascinated by the Circean blandishments of the Tahitian women, they took this desperate method of returning to scenes of voluptuousness unknown, perhaps, in any other country'.[§]

Just one year after arriving back in England, Bligh was appointed to command a new breadfruit expedition. The

[*]   Bligh, *A Voyage to the South Sea*, ch. 13.
[†]   Preston, *Paradise in Chains*, ch. 2.
[‡]   Bligh, *A Voyage to the South Sea*, ch. 13.
[§]   Salmond, *Bligh: William Bligh in the South Seas*, introduction.

mission was unchanged, and Banks was still its overseer; but this time, the Admiralty spared no expense. Bligh was given command of a brand-new sloop, the *Providence*, with double the *Bounty*'s complement, including twenty marines, and a brig as the ship's tender. Two of the *Bounty* crew members sailed with him again, the sailmaker Lawrence Lebogue and his personal servant, John Smith. William Peckover, the Pacific veteran who had bravely retrieved the ship's log from the cave on Tofua, had his application to join the voyage turned down. Bligh wrote in a letter to Banks he should ignore any correspondence from that 'vicious and worthless fellow',[*] and he wanted nothing to do with him. His lasting hatred for the gunner was never explained.

---

[*]   Preston, *Paradise in Chains*, ch. 13.

CHAPTER TEN

The Island

When the *Bounty* returned to Tahiti after the disaster on Tubuai, the sixteen men who had chosen to disembark began to land their guns, pots, tools and wine (about three gallons per man). The group naturally included the four sailors who had been kept on the ship against their will, and the two officers who appeared to play no clear role in the mutiny, Stewart and Heywood. But there were also active mutineers among them, including Christian's enforcer Charles Churchill, who now had leadership aspirations of his own, and the young Thomas Ellison.

Meeting the usual welcoming party of islanders, they nervously trusted some of their supplies to Tahitian canoes, but made sure their ammunition only went ashore in a small boat, a suspenseful task in the high surf. Each man was given his own musket, pistol, cutlass and bayonet, except Byrne the fiddler, who had lost the trust of his shipmates. Despite the strangeness of their second reappearance, the crew were received happily among the Tahitians, and 'all were glad when we informed them we intended to stay with them',* recalled Morrison.

Christian had resolved to sail to an uninhabited island and burn the *Bounty*, living out his days 'without seeing the face of a European',† except those of his eight remaining followers. He told those who had disembarked that he intended to stay a day or two, and he hoped they would assist him in gathering freshwater. But this was a feint. That night, Morrison was surprised to see the ship sailing out of the bay already. He guessed the quick departure was to prevent Christian's hardcore supporters from changing their minds about the coming voyage. Perhaps Christian feared a plot by the Tahitians to capture the ship, an easy undertaking with only nine Europeans left to guard her; it was now obvious the *Bounty* was a rogue vessel without the weight of Britain behind her.

According to Heywood, before Christian left he passed on a message for his family in England, emphasising that he was solely responsible for the mutiny. He also revealed 'other circumstances' that Heywood said were not a defence of the crime, but somewhat excused it, and 'may not be laid before

---

* Morrison, *Journal on HMS Bounty and at Tahiti.*
† Morrison, *Journal on HMS Bounty and at Tahiti.*

the public' until after the deaths of Christian's relatives.* Those details remain a mystery. Heywood recalled Christian also told him and Stewart to give themselves up when a warship inevitably arrived at Tahiti.

About nineteen Tahitian women were belowdecks on the *Bounty* having supper when one of the Europeans quietly cut the anchor cable. Some of the guests noticed the ship was in motion, but Christian assured them he was only moving her to the neighbouring district of Pare. Coleman, who elected to stay in Tahiti but had come on board for dinner, sensed what was happening and jumped overboard. His skills as an armourer would have been useful in a future settlement.

Next morning, the women could feel from the movements of the ship that she was beyond Tahiti's outer reef. Some of them were distraught: one jumped overboard and swam a mile to shore, while several others, who were somewhat elderly, were allowed to go ashore at Mo'orea in canoes. That left twelve Polynesian women on board, one with a baby girl, and six Polynesian men, three of whom had been recruited specifically for the voyage, and another three who emerged as stowaways.

The mutineers seem to have left Tahiti with thoughts of investigating the Marquesas to the north-east, keeping a constant watch on the horizon for uncharted islands or the sails of other navy ships, which would have meant a swift end

---

* Barrow, *The Eventful History of the Mutiny and Piratical Seizure of HMS Bounty*, ch. 3.

to their plans. According to Adams, they searched in vain for islands discovered and incorrectly charted by the Spanish, probably the Solomon Islands. At some point Christian steered the *Bounty* west, and the trade winds carried her towards Tonga. Off a small island, likely in the Cook group, islanders came alongside in canoes offering pigs and breadfruit. A man ventured aboard and took a special interest in the pearl shell buttons on Christian's jacket. The commander happily gave him the jacket, and the man was standing proudly on the *Bounty*'s gunwale, showing off his present to his countrymen, when a mutineer blithely shot him dead and he fell into the sea. Christian was 'highly indignant' at this, but with his authority again in doubt, could do nothing more than 'reprimand the murderer severely'.*

The crew stopped at Tongatapu, the main island in Tonga, and stayed there for two days, trading with the Tongans and listening to stories of Tute, Captain Cook, who had left cattle on the island. The mutineers were now more or less back where they had started on the day of the mutiny, only a day's sail from the volcano of Tofua. They continued west from Tonga for a few days, stopping in Fiji's southern Lau Islands and investigating an atoll (maybe Vatoa or Ono-i-Lau), but pulling back when they saw islanders on the beach. After the failure on Tubuai, Christian didn't want to start another settlement in competition with locals; an almost futile aim,

---

* Teehuteatuaonoa (Jenny) interview, transcription from *United Service Journal*, 1829.

since Polynesians had colonised virtually every piece of land in the Pacific worth living on.

In the candlelight of Bligh's library, he came across Philip Carteret's description of Pitcairn Island, a great rock rising out of the sea that seemed to be uninhabited but was covered with trees, with a small stream of freshwater running down one side of it. Carteret would have stopped to investigate further if heavy surf hadn't rendered a landing impossible. The brief description, buried in Carteret's account of his voyage across the Pacific, must have seemed heaven-sent. As Dening points out, Pitcairn was probably the only uninhabited high island in the whole Pacific. Christian turned the *Bounty* around and sailed her east against the trade winds. He was not relying on navigational guesswork. The fine gears and springs of K2 kept time with London even as he sailed further into oblivion. He found nothing but open sea at the coordinates where the island was marked, but correctly guessed that Carteret's longitude was a mistake. He continued along the line of latitude, until he raised Pitcairn on a summer's evening in January 1790.

If a mixture of remarkable seamanship and a mysterious providence had seen Bligh safely to Timor, the same combination must have been at play in Christian's discovery of Pitcairn Island. As the location for a band of fugitives to start a surreptitious colony, the island was ideal. Not only was it well shaped to deter invaders, but it was still obscured in the fog of Carteret's dead reckoning. Warships searching for the mutineers would begin at Tahiti, and likely continue west from there; they would not sail east towards Pitcairn Island, against the prevailing trade winds. The island would also fall outside all shipping lanes for more than a century hence. (It was only in 1914, when the Panama Canal opened, that Pitcairn fell in the path of traffic to and from New Zealand.)

The settlers burnt the *Bounty*, stranding themselves on a tiny perch in a backwater of the South Pacific. After a few weeks, they explored the high land, and started to plant the crops taken from Tahiti to supplement the existing fruit trees. The sails of the *Bounty* became tents, and then clothing. The mutineers divided up the island into nine equal portions. The interior was hot, oppressively dense and eerily quiet, the ground uneven and pockmarked with pits for trapping pigs. When it rained, the ground around the settlement became a muddy quagmire. Nerves would be frayed when the liquor and tobacco ran out. Almost immediately, each settler began to jealously guard his share.

Meanwhile, the Polynesians were faced with the horrendous realisation that their adventure with the white men was at an end, the destination was reached, and, for them, it amounted to little more than an open-air prison. Of the six Polynesian men on the island, at least two came from nobility: Titahiti from Tubuai was a chief; Tararo from Raiatea was also high-born. But they were abruptly stripped of the status they had enjoyed in their respective societies. The whites did not deviate from the Zeitgeist of the eighteenth century that viewed Indigenous people as lesser beings. While the mutineers fenced and planted their new estates, the Polynesians remained landless servants. They were left to share three Tahitian women among themselves, while each Englishman had a wife of his own. In setting up their little society so unequally, the mutineers had set a course to conflict and murder.

* * *

A priest put a girdle of red feathers around the waist of the boy king. Then he turned to the corpses of three human sacrifice victims, arranging them with their heads facing the king like supine witnesses. His lips moved in prayer as he used a piece of split bamboo to pluck an eye out of each corpse. He gave a long speech as he held out the eyes, the most valuable part of the body, as a symbolic offering to the young sovereign. The boy sat with his mouth open throughout the ceremony, allowing the spirits of the sacrificed to enter his soul.[*]

It was February 1791. The mutineers who elected to stay behind at Tahiti, while Christian sailed on, had been living on the island for more than a year. In that time, they had thrown themselves into the island's tribal conflict, allying with Teina and fighting as mercenaries against his enemies. The mutineers had turned Tahitian warfare, hitherto based

---

[*]   Morrison, *Journal on HMS Bounty and at Tahiti*.

more on ceremony than strategy, into bloody carnage. Teina's soldiers wore uniforms, marched in formation and fired musketry. He had become the most powerful leader on the island. He had captured the *maro ura*, the length of fabric covered with red feathers that was a potent symbol of chiefly power. The garment was a record of Tahiti's social history, with feathers and patterns marking the ages. The red pennant from the *Dolphin* was sewn into it, as was a lock of hair from Richard Skinner, *Bounty* mutineer.

In the ceremony at the *marae*, Teina's son, now seven years old, was invested with the *maro ura*, and hailed as the supreme king of Tahiti. It was a grand affair, with chiefs from other parts of the island descending on Pare with human sacrifice victims and droves of pigs. The new king was taken on a triumphal march in a cloak of black feathers, always riding on men's shoulders, because any ground he trod on was rendered *tapu*. A Union Jack covered with red feathers served as the king's banner. Most of the other chiefs, intimidated by the military power of the mutineers, were in a state of begrudging submission.

After Christian's departure, the remaining mutineers had discovered they were not the only white maroons on the island. Another European ship, the *Mercury*, had recently called and left behind a man named John Brown who was said to be visiting the island's southern shores. Nervous, the mutineers dispatched Churchill and Millward to go and find out who he was. Meanwhile, they told the Tahitians the truth about the mutiny, and for their part, the islanders revealed they were angry at Bligh. The captain of the *Mercury* had told them in no uncertain terms that Cook was dead and Bligh was not Cook's son.

The mutineers realised it would be wise to pay their respects to Teina's son, the boy king. They gathered on the banks of a river opposite his sacred house, removing the *tapa* cloth draped around their shoulders as a customary show of respect. The boy appeared on the shoulders of an attendant, bundled in white cloth with a garland of feathers on his head like a bulbous plant. He welcomed each of the mutineers in turn, calling them by the names of their *taio*. A crowd of spectators gasped in wonder as Hitihiti, stripped naked, held up some carved god images from Tubuai and told a long story in Tahitian. The carvings were sent across the river to the king, along with gifts of red feathers and cloth; then the mutineers 'formed three divisions and discharged their arms, at which the young chief was so much pleased that he told us to follow our own country fashion in everything, and take no heed of the ceremonies, when we retired'.*

With the king's blessing, the Englishmen set about building new lives in Tahiti. Brown, the English rogue, arrived from the south and told the mutineers his story. He was left behind on the island at his own request, he said, after getting into an argument with one of his shipmates and

---

* Morrison, *Journal on HMS Bounty and at Tahiti*.

slashing the man's face with a knife. That was only the latest episode of trouble in his itinerant and criminal life, the broad strokes of which he didn't bother to conceal. The mutineers found a letter left by the *Mercury*'s captain that seemed to confirm Brown's story; it described him as 'an ingenious handyman when sober but when drunk a dangerous fellow'.* He seemed unpredictable, but the mutineers treated him kindly and gave him some English clothes.

Each mutineer took a different approach to his sojourn on Tahiti. Peter Heywood, the fair-haired teenager from the Isle of Man, embraced island culture; as he would later explain, he resolved to live by the maxim, 'when I was in Rome to do as Rome did'.† He lived in a cottage at the end of an avenue of shaddock trees near Matavai Bay. He learnt the Tahitian language and compiled a dictionary that would keep him occupied for years. He adopted the local dress and had his body heavily tattooed. The tattooing was done to fulfil the desires of his hosts, he later explained; in Tahiti a man without tattoos was an outcast. Heywood roamed the far corners of the island, dressed in a simple loincloth. Sometimes the islanders plotted to rob him, but as he had given away the last of his European possessions, there was nothing left to steal.‡ He later wrote to his mother about the experience: 'Whilst we remained there we were used by our friends (the

---

* Morrison, *Journal on HMS Bounty and at Tahiti*.
† Heywood, *Innocent on the Bounty*, p. 98.
‡ Morrison, *Journal on HMS Bounty and at Tahiti*.

natives) with a friendship, generosity and humanity almost unparalleled, being such as never was equalled by the people of any civilised nations, to the disgrace of all Christians.'* Notwithstanding his generous treatment by the Tahitians, Heywood was unhappy. In his island poetry he described himself as despondent and miserable, wandering around at night or sitting under a breadfruit tree to ruminate on his life in exile.

Some of his fellow shipmates were also restless, and set their sights on returning to Britain. Morrison led a secret effort to build a European-style boat from island materials, which he hoped to sail to Timor. He was not a boatbuilder, so he had to marshal the reluctant shipmates among him who had carpenter's and armourer's skills. He also had to wade into Tahitian politics to secure key materials, such as matting for the boat's sails, while he insisted the boat was only a pleasure craft to avoid sabotage. When the mutineers divided up the possessions of Bligh and his supporters, Thompson had taken Hayward's quadrant and navigational books; Morrison got them for a gallon of wine and a hatchet.

After seven months of hard labour, during which his charges repeatedly threw up their hands and walked away from the project, he had a thirty-foot, two-masted schooner, caulked with the gum of the breadfruit tree. Morrison christened his vessel the *Resolution*, after the flagship of

---

* Heywood, *Innocent on the Bounty*, p. 48.

Cook's final voyage. He spent his days salting hundreds of pounds of pork for the run to civilisation.

Churchill and Thompson, the roughest of the mutineers, were not satisfied with a peaceful existence and arced into chaos. Churchill had offered to lead his shipmates, and when they refused, he and Thompson moved to another part of the island. Here he managed to satisfy his aspirations and become a local chief, succeeding his Tahitian *taio* when the man died without heirs. Thompson ran rampant, and responded with violence when the local women refused his advances. One day, after attempting to rape a chief's daughter and being knocked down by the woman's brother, he stormed home, vowing to shoot the next Tahitian he saw. The usual crowd of curious onlookers was standing outside his hut, hoping to catch a glimpse of the local *popa'a*, the white man. Thompson fired a musket into the crowd, killing a man and his baby and breaking a woman's jaw.[*]

Thompson and Churchill's friendship devolved into a paranoid rivalry, and Brown was 'active in promoting their quarrel'.[†] Churchill was afraid of his former shipmate, and ordered one of his servants to steal Thompson's muskets from his hut. When Thompson found out about the plot, he shot and killed Churchill. The Tahitians then avenged Churchill's death by killing Thompson, bashing his head in with a rock.

---

[*]   Morrison, *Journal on HMS Bounty and at Tahiti*.
[†]   Morrison, *Journal on HMS Bounty and at Tahiti*.

Teina, consolidating his chiefly power, steeled himself for a final battle, hoping to secure a lasting reign over all of Tahiti. When his son was invested with the *maro ura* and proclaimed king, some of the island's chiefs were conspicuously absent. Those chiefs who refused to submit came from the Taiarapu peninsula, across the isthmus in the island's south-east. Teina and his allies forged a plan to force his rivals into submission. A grand feast would be held in Papara, the southern district, giving the king an excuse to amass his warriors near the isthmus. He could then cross onto the peninsula under the cover of night.

This was not one of Teina's usual defensive battles, but an all-out conquest, and four mutineers refused to be involved. But the rest pledged their assistance, with their new comrade John Brown the most eager promoter of war among them. They sailed down the coast in Morrison's schooner. On 24 March 1791, they arrived at Papara, but found themselves with little time to enjoy the festivities. A courier arrived with a message that a British warship named the *Pandora* had anchored in Matavai Bay the day after they left. Three of the men who stayed behind – Heywood, Stewart and Coleman – had all voluntarily boarded the ship and been put in irons. Now two launches from the *Pandora* were on their way to Papara to arrest them, led by none other than Thomas Hayward, the unpopular midshipman from the *Bounty*.

CHAPTER ELEVEN

Pandora's Box

Edward Edwards, forty-eight years old, was a dour and humourless man with a visceral hatred for mutineers. In 1782, when he was patrolling the eastern coast of revolutionary America as the newly appointed captain of the *Narcissus*, Edwards had been the object of a mutiny himself. Forty-six of his men signed up for the plot. When the code word 'wine' was uttered, they planned to put their captain and his officers into a longboat and sail to the American mainland, where they would sell the ship and join the revolutionaries in Philadelphia. Edwards caught wind of this from a nervous quartermaster and managed to apprehend the would-be mutineers. Six of the conspirators were hanged and more than a dozen flogged, one of them receiving five hundred lashes. The captain never forgot the experience; indeed, he used his obsessive fear of 'pirates' to justify his cruel methods of command. As far as his credentials, he seemed an excellent choice for a police mission to round up the *Bounty* mutineers. But his voyage to the Pacific was disastrous.

The frigate *Pandora* set sail in November 1790. Her crew of one hundred and sixty men was composed mostly of landlubbers rounded up by press gangs, because every trained seaman in the Royal Navy had gone to the fleet assembling at Portsmouth ahead of a potential war with Spain. A fever epidemic was raging in England at the time and it was introduced on board. The expedition was hopeful of finding the *Bounty* fully intact and sailable; the ship's sick bay, and even the officers' cabins, were crammed with provisions for the *Bounty*'s return voyage to England, leaving no accommodation for the sick. The fever-stricken men seem to have recovered by guzzling tea and sugar. After a smooth run around Cape Horn and into the Pacific, Edwards sighted Ducie Island, a barren atoll that lies less than three hundred miles east of Pitcairn Island. If Edwards had only kept a westward course, he would have found Christian and his pirate colony. Instead, he turned north, passed within a hundred miles of the mutineers over the next day, and continued on to Tahiti.

When Edwards anchored in Matavai Bay he found Teina, as always, mired in political troubles. George Hamilton, the *Pandora*'s surgeon, described a chief in the southern district of Papara as the 'proper king of Tahiti', and Teina's family as 'usurpers', the two parties being on the verge of war.* Teina was a tall, handsome-looking man, good natured and affable in his manners, according to Hamilton. His wife, 'Itia, who had learnt how to handle a musket from earlier visitors, was as interested as ever in European customs, and became very fond of tea during the *Pandora*'s stay. Teina's entourage now included a concubine, who Hamilton called Aeredy, a 'pretty young creature, about sixteen years of age: they all three sleep together, and live in the most perfect harmony'.†

After receiving word of the *Pandora*'s arrival, Coleman, Heywood and Stewart rowed out to the ship in canoes to surrender. They were clad in bark cloth, and so heavily tanned and tattooed that the crew initially mistook them for Tahitians. Morrison too, decided to walk to Matavai Bay from Papara and give himself up, along with Norman, the carpenter's mate who had exclaimed his innocence to Bligh from the gunwales of the *Bounty*. That left several fugitives outstanding, and Edwards required help from the local chiefs to find them. He sent Teina a bottle of rum and invited him on board. The king yielded to the captain's authority in the matter of the rogue Englishmen, and Edwards gradually cut off their resources and support, plying the other chiefs with gifts. Brown, the maroon from the *Mercury*, assisted in the round-up as a guide and interpreter. He does not seem to have thought twice about betraying the *Bounty* pirates,

---

*   Hamilton, *Voyage of HMS Pandora*, ch. 1.
†   Hamilton, *Voyage of HMS Pandora*, ch. 1.

insisting he had only associated with them for his own safety. Brown and Edwards somehow became friends, and Brown left Tahiti on board the *Pandora* as a valued member of her crew.

'He had lived upwards of twelve months amongst the natives,' wrote Hamilton about the maroon, 'adopted perfectly their manners and customs, even to the eating of raw fish, and dipping his roast pork into a coconut shell full of saltwater, according to their manner, as a substitute for salt.'* Hamilton described Brown as a 'keen, penetrating, active fellow, who rendered many eminent services, both in this expedition and the subsequent part of the voyage'.†

Mutineers like Heywood, who surrendered as soon as Edwards arrived, were shocked to find themselves being put in chains. Coleman, McIntosh and Norman, too, were indiscriminately clapped in irons, despite Bligh having already exonerated them. These men had been kept on the *Bounty* against their will.

Edwards was not interested in sorting the guilty from the innocent. All of the captured *Bounty* crew received the same treatment, kept naked and manacled in a stinking roundhouse on the decks of the ship known as 'Pandora's Box'. Sweat ran in streams from the box to the scuppers, and the tubs that the men used as toilets were squirming with maggots. Heywood noticed a familiar face among the crew of

---

* Hamilton, *Voyage of HMS Pandora*, ch. 1.
† Hamilton, *Voyage of HMS Pandora*, ch. 1.

the *Pandora*: the officer Thomas Hayward from the *Bounty*, who had survived Bligh's open boat voyage to Timor. This was the same Hayward who Bligh had demoted for being asleep on his watch on the *Bounty*. Evidently he was moving up in the world, but hopes that he would verify the innocence of his former shipmates were quickly dashed. He received the captured mutineers 'very coolly, and pretended ignorance of our affairs',* wrote Heywood.

Although the island's leaders were accommodating of the *Pandora* crew (and Hitihiti even acted as their guide despite his *taio* being among the fugitives), Teina and the other chiefs were worried about the ship's safety, and kept personal watch over her cable. The mutineers had formed bond-friendships with many of the Tahitians, and their imprisonment was a sorry spectacle with the potential to cause unrest. There were miserable scenes as the prisoners' wives visited the ship daily, bringing food and children in tow. Stewart had to request that his wife, who he called Peggy, and their small daughter not be allowed on board; whenever she saw Stewart in irons, Peggy cried bitterly and gashed her head in ritual mourning, allowing blood to stream down her face. Months later, Peggy would continue to appear before visiting crews with Stewart's little daughter, Charlotte, tearfully asking after the fate of her husband. A subsequent, perhaps over-sentimental report claimed she had died of a broken heart.

---

* Heywood, *Innocent on the Bounty*, p. 49.

Hamilton described the visits between the Tahitian women and their English husbands thus: 'To see the poor captives in irons, weeping over their tender offspring, was too moving a scene for any feeling heart.'[*]

The *Pandora* readied for sea, and Teina, 'Itia and Aeredy persistently asked Edwards to take them back to England; they now faced an inevitable tribal uprising in the absence of their white mercenaries. Eventually, Teina's dynasty would consolidate its rule over a unified Tahiti, which included surrounding islands, but for now he faced another exile in the mountains. Canoes hovered around the *Pandora*, the islanders mourning her departure, cutting their heads with shells and smearing their breasts and shoulders with blood. Teina, with tears streaming down his cheeks, asked to be remembered to King George.

Edwards sailed westward. His orders directed him to search in the Leeward, Cook and Tongan Islands, before heading home through the Endeavour Strait. Hitihiti, ever the adventurer, joined the expedition as a guide, but did not return aboard from a kava-drinking session with his friends on his native Bora Bora.

Six days out from Tahiti, Henry Hillbrant, the *Bounty*'s German cooper, asked to speak to the captain. Hillbrant told Edwards that on the evening before Christian left Tahiti for good, he privately revealed his destination: an uninhabited

---

[*]   Hamilton, *Voyage of HMS Pandora*, ch. 1.

atoll west of Danger Island (Pukapuka, in the Cook Islands). Edwards knew from his charts that Christian must have been referring to the Duke of York Islands (Atafu). He took Hillbrant at his word and steered for the alleged hideout, unaware the ruse by Christian was leading him further away from the mutineers. If Hillbrant had hoped to improve his situation by revealing Christian's stated plans, he must have been disappointed, because he remained shackled in Pandora's Box.

Edwards, ever alert to insurrection, was terrified the *Bounty* pirates might infect his crew with mutinous thoughts. He took great pains to prevent the two parties from speaking, but fretted that he had not been successful, and even suspected his men of corresponding with the pirates by letter.

On Palmerston Island, an atoll in the Cook Islands, Edwards found some worm-eaten spars marked *Bounty*. A party of armed men crept ashore to comb the island. The sound of an explosion sent them grasping for their muskets in terror, but the 'attack' they anticipated from the bushes was an imagined one; a coconut had burst on the embers of their campfire. The spars that teased Edwards's hopes of apprehending another batch of mutineers had drifted almost a thousand miles westward from the island of Tubuai. Next day, as the captain continued his vain search of the atoll, a jolly-boat containing five of his crew was blown away in a heavy squall and never seen again. Edwards searched for the boat for five days before giving up. When he reached Atafu,

Christian's supposed destination, he only found an abandoned Polynesian fishing camp and a wooden ship's buoy washed up on the beach.

In Tahiti, the captain had confiscated Morrison's schooner, the *Resolution*, and turned her into the ship's tender, renaming her the *Matavy*. He now sent the boat out from *Pandora* to conduct her own search for the mutineers. But in the Samoas, the tender and mothership lost each other in a rain shower.

Passing the Santa Cruz Islands in the Western Pacific, Edwards saw smoke signals coming from the island of Vanikoro, but ignored them, reasoning that the remaining mutineers he was hunting would not reveal their location so willingly. The smoke was probably a distress signal from the survivors of the La Pérouse expedition, a French voyage of discovery that wrecked on Vanikoro's reefs in 1789. It's thought that some of the survivors were killed by Polynesians, while others, including Captain Jean-Francois La Pérouse, remained on the island for many years.

In August 1791, after almost a year at sea, the *Pandora* was hovering near the Great Barrier Reef on her homeward voyage. In his rambling search of the Pacific, Edwards had lost fourteen men, and the scent of the mutineers had grown ever fainter. As he later declared in his report to the Admiralty, Christian's claimed intention to settle an uninhabited, harbourless island was 'too vague to be followed in an immense ocean strewn with an almost innumerable number of known and unknown islands'.* In short, Christian, with his twenty-month head start in an incalculable wilderness, could have been anywhere. Edwards was preparing to sail through the Endeavour Strait and return to England; surveying the strait as he went, to make the passage safer for future expeditions.

But first Edwards had dispatched a yawl to find a way through the jumble of surf, coral spires, turquoise shallows and sandy cays that span more than a thousand miles off the coast of north-eastern Australia. The Great Barrier Reef had horrified its first European discoverer, James Cook, and had almost been his undoing. Cook declared the reef system an 'insane labyrinth' after it suddenly materialised around him and he ran aground on a shoal. Edwards must have been anxious, having lost both the tender and the jolly-boat already, while his men probed the reef for a passage. By the time they signalled their success, night was falling and the sky was dark with storm clouds. The yawl regained the mothership by following musket flashes through the gloom.

At seven o'clock, the same moment the boat reached the ship, the *Pandora* was thrown onto the reef in a series of sickening lurches. In the pitch dark of Pandora's Box, the mutineers knew instantly the ship had suffered mortal damage.

There was a flurry of activity on deck. Coleman, Norman and McIntosh were removed from the box and ordered to the pumps, amid cries that nine feet of seawater had collected in

---

* Hamilton, *Voyage of HMS Pandora*, Captain Edwards' Reports.

the hold. Morrison and the other ten mutineers begged in vain to be able to join them. As the *Pandora*'s crew rushed to and fro, the imprisoned mutineers managed to break their shackles in preparation for abandoning ship, but they remained trapped in the box, with the hatch bolted from the outside. When Edwards was told they had broken their irons, he had them shackled again and stationed two armed men as sentinels over them, with orders to shoot if they made any further attempt to escape. The water in the hold rose to eleven feet. The mutineers lay down and prayed in the dark as they listened to the officers bundling their things into the small boats. 'I'll be damned if they shall go without us,'* a *Pandora* crew member was heard saying.

Efforts to save the *Pandora* devolved into confusion. The ship began to heel to one side, and some of the cannon the crew were attempting to throw overboard broke loose, crushing a sailor to death. A topmast fell down from the booms and struck another man, killing him. A small boat broke adrift with only two men aboard, and another boat had to be sent out to bring her back. By now the water was coming in faster at the gunports than the pumps could discharge, and the ship was listing heavily. At daybreak the mutineers could see the officers, armed with muskets, getting ready to climb into the small boats.

Edwards sent his crew member Joseph Hodges to retrieve Muspratt, Skinner and Byrne; Hodges climbed down into

---

* Morrison, *Journal on HMS Bounty and at Tahiti*.

Pandora's Box and began fussing with their irons. Skinner was so desperate to escape that he clambered out with his hands still manacled. Then somebody shut the scuttle again, leaving Hodges trapped inside while he freed Morrison and Stewart from their manacles.

Morrison begged one of the sentinels to let him out, but the guard was defiant: 'Never fear, my boys, we'll all go to hell together.'* The words were scarcely out of his mouth when the ship rolled to port amid cries of 'There she goes'.† The sentinels fell overboard and water surged up the decks as far as the mainmast, then began pouring into the box holding the mutineers.

The *Pandora*'s boatswain's mate, William Moulter, had scrambled on top of the structure, and heard the screams of the mutineers inside. He pulled off one of the heavily barred scuttles on the box and threw it overboard, and quickly followed it himself. Everybody in the box managed to scramble out except Hillbrant. The ship now heeled over completely, and the sea around her became a boil of bodies and debris. 'The cries of the men drowning in the water was at first awful in the extreme,' wrote Hamilton, 'but as they sunk, and became faint, it died away by degrees.'‡

The ship had taken eleven hours to sink. Thirty-five crew members drowned, along with four *Bounty* crew: Henry

---

* Morrison, *Journal on HMS Bounty and at Tahiti*.
† Morrison, *Journal on HMS Bounty and at Tahiti*.
‡ Hamilton, *Voyage of HMS Pandora*, ch. 3.

Hillbrant, locked in irons, went down in Pandora's Box; Richard Skinner drowned with his hands still manacled; George Stewart and John Sumner were killed when the ship's gangway collapsed on top of them. Among the ten surviving prisoners were Morrison and Heywood, paddling on planks of wood after the small boats that now lay in the distance. Clenched in Heywood's teeth was a prayer book that contained scribbles about key dates and events, the entries written in Tahitian rather than in English. Naked and exhausted, they landed with the other survivors on a desolate cay a couple of miles from the wreck.

The *Pandora* crew set up two tents on the cay, for the ship's officers and men respectively. The prisoners were left exposed to the withering sun on their own section of the cay, and Edwards refused their pleas to use a spare sail as shade. Meagre provisions and very little water had been saved from the ship. The master, sent to visit the wreck, returned with little more than an angry cat, which he found clinging to a broken masthead. The day's meal was a mouthful of bread and a glass of wine. That night, the mutineers shivered under rain showers in the open air. One of *Pandora*'s men spent the night collecting steam from a kettle of boiling saltwater until he had a teaspoonful. Another man went delirious drinking seawater.

The ship's crew sailed for Timor in four open boats. The voyage took two weeks, and some of the men suffered so horribly from thirst that they drank their own urine and died of dehydration regardless. For Thomas Hayward, this was the second time in as many years that he was sailing desperately for Timor in an open boat, and following much the same route as Bligh. The men of the *Pandora* were even using the same method to dole out rations, a makeshift scale of coconut shells and musket balls, and drinking the blood of the seabirds they caught. They proceeded up the barren coast of north-eastern Australia, cowering in their camps at the sound of howling dingoes, which they mistook for wolves. Morrison kept an indignant record of Edwards' conduct. On 9 September the captain ordered the mutineer to be pinioned and lashed to the boat's bottom, while Ellison, then asleep in the boat, received the same punishment:

> I attempted to reason and enquire what I had now done to be thus cruelly treated, urging the distressed situation of the whole, but received for answer, 'Silence, you murdering villain – are you not a prisoner? You piratical dog, what better treatment do you expect?' I then told him that it was a disgrace for a British man-o'-war captain to treat a prisoner in such an inhuman manner, upon which he started up in a violent rage, and snatching a pistol which lay in the stern sheets threatened to shoot me.*

After thirteen days at sea, the four boats reached Kupang, where the situation of the mutineers did not improve. Handed

---

* Morrison, *Journal on HMS Bounty and at Tahiti*.

over to the Dutch authorities, they were kept in a cell in the town fort. They spent a week in stocks, forced to relieve themselves where they lay before the fort's commander took pity on them and put them in irons. A surgeon sent to check on them refused to enter their cell until it had been washed by slaves. Also in the fort's jail were William and Mary Bryant, the notorious convicts from New South Wales.

It might have been the news of Bligh's open boat voyage that inspired William, a convicted smuggler, and Mary, a female highway robber, to flee the penal colony in the governor's cutter. They had reached Timor after a sixty-nine-day, 3250-mile journey up the Australian coast with a compass, quadrant and chart. The Bryants had made their voyage with two children, including a baby at the breast, and seven other convicts. Even Bligh was impressed, praising William Bryant as a 'determined and enterprising man'.[*] The group had been enjoying fine hospitality in Timor, claiming they were the survivors of a whaling shipwreck on the Great Barrier Reef. With the arrival of the *Pandora* crew the runaways were exposed and arrested. According to Hamilton, locals assumed Edwards was the Bryants' captain, but on being told the happy news of his arrival Mary exclaimed: 'What captain? Damn me, we have no captain.'[†]

In the jail at Kupang, the mutineers were still naked, and set about making hats out of leaves in the Tahitian style,

---

[*]   Preston, *Paradise in Chains*, ch. 20.
[†]   Preston, *Paradise in Chains*, ch. 18.

hoping to sell them and raise funds for clothing. But clothes proved too expensive, and they settled for tobacco instead.

From Kupang they proceeded to Java, and in Semarang along the island's northern coast, they had a surprising reunion with the crew of the *Pandora*'s tender *Matavy*, Morrison's homemade boat that had lost contact with the *Pandora* in a rain shower five weeks before. The tender's crew had been provisioned with little more than muskets and a bag of salt and had sailed westward, delirious and near-death with thirst. In the Fijian islands they established the first proper contact between Europeans and the 'savage and cannibal Feegees',* as Hamilton called them. In fact the Fijians they met were hospitable, providing them with desperately needed sweet potatoes and coconuts (although men from other islands did attack them). They then limped to the Great Barrier Reef, the Endeavour Strait and Surabaya in the Dutch East Indies.

The Dutch were growing highly accustomed to offering refuge to British castaways, but in this case the nine men in the schooner perfectly matched the description of the *Bounty* pirates, and on their arrival, they were put under guard. Despite their insistence they were in fact hunting the *Bounty* mutineers, the men of the *Matavy* had no commission or warrant to prove it, and their ragged appearance in a freshly built boat, made of Tahitian materials, was incredibly suspicious. Indeed, their boat had been built by the mutineers.

---

* Hamilton, *Voyage of HMS Pandora*, ch. 1.

Edwards only devoted a small passage in his journal to their death-defying voyage. Hamilton wrote that the joyful reunion of the surviving *Pandora* crew and the *Matavy* crew in Semarang brought everyone to tears.

On their arrival in Batavia, dead bodies floated out of the canals into the sea and struck the boat, an omen that had a 'very disagreeable effect' on the ship's crew, as Hamilton wrote.* During their seven weeks at the port, the prisoners were allowed on deck only twice.

* * *

Heywood, Morrison and the other surviving prisoners arrived in England on 19 June 1792, nine months after the sinking of the *Pandora*. They did not set foot on land, but were transferred directly to the moored warship *Hector*, where they waited a further three months for trial. For Heywood, fifteen years old when the *Bounty* sailed from Spithead and twenty by the time of his court martial, the *Pandora* voyage had been a spiritual odyssey of Tolstoyan proportions. As he wrote to his mother surreptitiously from Batavia, he was now 'young in years but old in what the world calls adversity', and had come to view the ordeal as the 'most beneficial incident that could have occurred to me at my years.

---

* Hamilton, *Voyage of HMS Pandora*, ch. 5.

'It has made me acquainted with three things which are little known: first, the villainy and censoriousness of mankind; second, the futility of all human hopes; and third, the enjoyment of being content in whatever station it pleases providence to place me in. In short it has made me more of a philosopher than many years of a life spent in ease and pleasure could have done.'*

---

* Heywood, *Innocent on the Bounty*, p. 50.

CHAPTER TWELVE

The Trial of the Mutineers

On the Isle of Man, Peter Heywood's family lived in the capital town, Douglas, on the parade, a tidy strip of houses overlooking a pebbled beach where herring boats were drawn up in winter. As with Fletcher Christian's family, financial troubles had figured prominently in the Heywood family story. When Peter was a year old, his father was forced to sell his estate on the island and move the family to Whitehaven on the coast of Cumbria, a town with close associations to Douglas due to its proximity across the Irish Sea. In 1779 the family moved back to Douglas, a year before Ann Christian arrived on the island with a teenage Fletcher Christian.

By 1790, the Heywood household, overseen by an old woman-servant called Birket, was crowded with seven brothers and sisters (not counting twelve-year-old Henry, who was on his first voyage to Jamaica, and seventeen-year-old Peter, who was in Tahiti). In February 1790, Mr Heywood died, and one month later, Peter's widowed mother received a report that there had been a mutiny on her teenage son's ship the *Bounty*. For the next two years, the family received a series of distressing updates about Heywood's situation. He was thought to be among the mutineers; a frigate had taken him prisoner in Tahiti; the ship was wrecked and he had made his way to the Dutch East Indies; and he was now bound for England on a Dutch ship. During this period there was never any word from Heywood himself. He managed to scribble a letter to his mother in Batavia in November 1791, but by the time she received it seven months later, he had already arrived in England for trial. Once he was moored in Portsmouth and allowed to correspond, his family spent still more time in anxious waiting. Douglas was a lively town, but its residents were always behind on news from the mainland, relying on a mail packet from Whitehaven that could be held up for days or even weeks in bad weather.

After hearing the news of the mutiny, Mrs Heywood wrote a frantic letter to Bligh, who made no secret of his expectation Heywood would be executed, prompting Mrs Heywood's family to intercept the letter and hide it from her. At a time when bad news was thought to pose a health risk to the recipient, Heywood's elder sister, Hester 'Nessy' Heywood, twenty-four years old, largely took over the quill pen from her mother. In the family's drawing room, Nessy spent hours writing letters, assiduously practising the organ, and contemplating a drawing, done by Peter, of the Iranian ruler Nader Shah that hung over the mantlepiece. She had begun a self-appointed mission to gather intelligence, shore up her brother's spirits and lobby family connections, especially her uncles James Modyford Heywood and Commodore Thomas Pasley, both men of consequence in the Royal Navy.

The first responses to Nessy's letters did not bode well for her brother. James Heywood, after meeting with Bligh, tried to brace her for the worst, writing from London on 14 April 1792: 'You must have the philosophy for the present to consider him as lost forever.'* On 8 June 1792, Commodore Pasley wrote from Sheerness: 'I cannot conceal from you, my dearest Nessy, neither is it proper I should – your brother appears by all accounts to be the greatest culprit of all, Christian alone excepted. Every exertion, you may rest assured, I shall use to save his life, but on trial I have no hope of his not being condemned.'†

On 3 June, Heywood was still en route to England in a Dutch ship, but Nessy wrote to her brother from the Isle of Man. She sent the letter to Mr Hayward of Hackney, Thomas Hayward's father, who promised to give Peter the letter when he reached Portsmouth. The *Pandora*'s people had been long

---

* Heywood, *Innocent on the Bounty*, p. 35.
† Heywood, *Innocent on the Bounty*, p. 41.

expected in England but had not yet arrived, and Nessy was 'in the most painful uncertainty' whether Peter was still alive.[*]

Nessy wrote:

Oh! My ever dearest boy, when I look back at that dreadful moment which brought us the fatal intelligence that you had remained in the *Bounty* after Mr. Bligh had quitted her and were looked upon as a mutineer! When I contrast that day of horror with my present hopes of again beholding you, such as my most sanguine wishes could expect, I know not which is the predominant sensation – pity, compassion and sorrow for your sufferings, or joy and satisfaction at the prospect of their being near a termination and of once more embracing the dearest object of our affections![†]

Nessy's letters bore the self-conscious and sentimental flourishes of the Romantic era, but the devotion she expressed to her brother was very real. She was busy trying to muster all possible support for him at his inevitable trial, and warned him that Bligh's representations to the Admiralty about the mutiny had been, 'I am told, very unfavourable, and hitherto the side of public opinion has been greatly in his favour.'[‡] She also informed Peter about the death of their father, who had not been alive to hear the news of the mutiny.

---

[*] Heywood, *Innocent on the Bounty*, p. 39.
[†] Heywood, *Innocent on the Bounty*, p. 38.
[‡] Heywood, *Innocent on the Bounty*, p. 40.

On 20 June, from the moored warship *Gorgon*, which had carried him from the Cape of Good Hope to England, Heywood wrote to Bligh's father-in-law Richard Betham, hoping to clear his name, and giving an account of the mutiny and his subsequent adventures similar to the one he had passed to his mother. He did not know it, but Betham was dead; his son forwarded the letter to Nessy. Later that month, after Heywood was transferred to the *Hector* in Portsmouth Harbour, Nessy informed him that Bligh had 'gone to the South Sea [in the *Providence*], but we must hope the best', She allowed space at the bottom of the letter for six of his brothers and sisters to scribble their own messages.

In July, Nessy wrote: 'Do you know I envy you exceedingly – to have borne with such heroism your misfortunes, to become the idol of all your relations and friends, and to be held up as an example of worth and suffering virtue – tell me, is not such a triumph worth the purchase?'[†]

Heywood's uncles, meanwhile, though initially glum about his prospects, had become invested in Nessy's mission. By July, James Heywood's daughter was visiting Heywood daily on the *Hector*, taking him fresh vegetables and books. Commodore Pasley engaged no less than three legal advisers, including his good friend Aaron Graham, and wrote to Nessy that Heywood's strongest points of defence were his extreme youth and his willing surrender to the *Pandora* in Tahiti. He

---

*   Heywood, *Innocent on the Bounty*, p. 64.
†   Heywood, *Innocent on the Bounty*, p. 82.

also met with Fryer and William Cole, describing them as 'both favourable evidences',* and made plans to track down several other *Bounty* crew members in London.

In August, at Nessy's request, Peter bought some pencils and paper and drew a portrait of himself, with the caveat that he hadn't seen himself in a mirror in at least a year. When it arrived in Douglas, Nessy was incredulous at the result: 'I must tell you that it cannot be like you, that's positive, except a little resemblance in the nose and the upper lip'.† Peter also sent Nessy a few locks of his hair, which Nessy divided among their siblings.

On 11 September, Peter wrote to his mother: 'The awful day of trial now draws nigh where I shall see another day – or – die!'‡

* * *

The court martial of the mutineers was held in September 1792 on board the warship *Duke*, moored in Portsmouth Harbour on England's southern coast. Heywood, Morrison and the other prisoners were rowed across the harbour in choppy weather. In the great cabin of the *Duke*, a jury of eleven post-captains in blue livery and powdered wigs were assembled to hear the evidence. The rest of the space was

---

* Heywood, *Innocent on the Bounty*, p. 66.
† Heywood, *Innocent on the Bounty*, p. 94.
‡ Heywood, *Innocent on the Bounty*, p. 106.

packed with high-ranking spectators. Heywood was wearing an officer's uniform with a strip of crepe around his arm as a mark of mourning for his father. His defence statement was read to the court by one of his lawyers, Francis Const.

His account went like this. On the morning of the mutiny, he woke in his hammock to see Thompson the seaman sitting on the arms chest in the aft hatchway with a drawn cutlass in his hand. He asked the seaman what was going on. Thompson replied that Fletcher Christian had confined the captain and was going to carry him home as a prisoner.

Heywood went on deck to see the mutiny for himself, and assisted in hoisting out the launch. One of the armed mutineers told him Bligh and his supporters were going to be left on Tofua. Heywood saw going into the open launch as tantamount to committing suicide. He told his fellow midshipman and messmate, Stewart, of his intention to remain aboard; but Stewart, the more senior officer, persuaded him such an action would brand him a mutineer.

The pair resolved to go into the launch, but first they jumped down the hatchway to gather a few belongings. Once below, Churchill called down to Thompson to keep guard over them, and when Stewart attempted to leave, Thompson pointed a pistol at his chest. By the time Churchill told Thompson to let the pair come up, Bligh's launch was a long way astern. Thus did Heywood remain on the *Bounty*. In Tahiti, while the mutineers gathered livestock for the settlement on Tubuai, he hoped to escape, but the mutineers kept watch over him, fearful that a deserter would reveal their plans to a passing ship.

There was no evidence that Heywood had played any active role in the mutiny, and other witnesses confirmed he had gone below deck partway through the event and never re-emerged. But some of the testimony from his fellow shipmates cast him as a neutral party. As Commodore Pasley had advised Nessy, according to martial law 'the man who stands neuter is equally guilty with him who lifts his arm against his captain in such cases'.*

The evidence began favourably for Heywood with the testimony of John Fryer. During the mutiny, Fryer had not seen Heywood on deck at all. The next witness, boatswain William Cole, remembered seeing him appear briefly. He told the court he believed the midshipman had wanted to come away in the launch, but was kept on the *Bounty* against his will.

Meanwhile, the fate of James Morrison also hung in the balance. As he reeled from Fryer's recollection that he had answered a proposal to retake the ship with 'it is too late', Morrison received some vindication from Cole. The boatswain said his mate kept obeying his orders during the mutiny and helped to hoist the launch out. The pair had parted with a handshake, with Morrison saying he planned to take his chances in the ship; though for what reason, it

---

* Heywood, *Innocent on the Bounty*, p. 76.

was not clear. By contrast, prisoners like the young Thomas Ellison were remembered as musket-wielding mutineers and made desperate attempts at cross-examination. 'Are you certain whether it was me or not,' Ellison asked Cole, 'as I was then a boy, and scarcely able to lift a musket at that time?'*

Next on the stand was the carpenter Purcell, who threw doubt over the positive testimony about Heywood thus far, saying he had seen the midshipman leaning on a cutlass during the mutiny. He said he called out to Heywood, 'In the name of God, Peter, what do you do with that?'† and the teenager instantly dropped the weapon. Purcell conceded, however, that Heywood looked like a 'person confused',‡ and did not seem to realise his hand had been resting on the sword. He also hastened to add Heywood had been well liked and respected during the voyage, his behaviour 'in every respect becoming the character of a gentleman'.§ Purcell recalled that Morrison, for his part, had asked him to take notice in front of the mutineers that he had been prevented from getting in the launch.

The most damning evidence against Heywood came from his fellow midshipman John Hallett. The young man had overslept when the mutiny broke out, a fact he never

---

* Linder, Transcript of the Court-Martial of the *Bounty* Mutineers, William Cole testimony.
† Linder, Transcript of the Court-Martial of the *Bounty* Mutineers, William Purcell testimony.
‡ Linder, Transcript of the Court-Martial of the *Bounty* Mutineers, William Purcell testimony.
§ Linder, Transcript of the Court-Martial of the *Bounty* Mutineers, William Purcell testimony.

answered for during the trial. Later he pleaded with Christian to remain on the *Bounty*, then got in the launch with the loyalists. Bligh had described the midshipman in a letter to Betsy from Timor as a 'worthless impudent scoundrel'.* But since his safe return to England, Hallett had become one of the lieutenant's most vocal supporters. He singularly claimed, for example, that Bligh never accused anyone of stealing his coconuts. At the court martial, Hallett was employed as a devastating witness for the prosecution. He told the court that during the commotion of the mutiny he saw Bligh speak to Heywood, who responded by laughing and walking away. He also claimed he saw Morrison armed with a musket as the launch pulled astern, jeering down at Bligh's party: 'If my friends enquire after me, tell them I am somewhere in the South Seas.'†

The court martial ran for a week. Across the Channel, an atmosphere of fevered paranoia had descended on France. Mobs fearing a counter-revolutionary plot had raided Parisian jails and massacred more than a thousand prisoners, many of them priests and aristocrats. The English received news of the revolution with growing horror. Britain had had her own revolution more than a century earlier, emerging as a constitutional monarchy with a new king and queen, an empowered parliament and a Bill of Rights. But as the

---

* Salmond, *Bligh: William Bligh in the South Seas*, ch. 12.
† Linder, Transcript of the Court-Martial of the Bounty Mutineers, John Hallett testimony.

French Revolution progressed, comparisons to the Glorious Revolution wore thin. This was an all-out uprising that had turned Europe's greatest and most populous country on its head. Law and order had collapsed; while the National Assembly calmly legislated for its new vision of France in Versailles, undisciplined crowds caused mayhem in Paris. Aristocrats were fleeing the country as peasants set fire to chateaux and manor houses. The monarchy was overthrown, and King Louis XVI was soon to be executed.

The court martial of the captured *Bounty* mutineers was a delicate affair for the British establishment. The jurors at the trial had to strike a careful balance. The mutiny had been presented to the public as a political act; it was widely regarded as a British equivalent of the fall of the Bastille.* Bligh's official story, that his officers had abandoned king and country to live in the paradise of Tahiti, stoked a public feeling that the mutiny was something bigger than itself. The most famous visual representation of the mutiny, printed a few months after Bligh's return to England by Robert Dodd with the lieutenant's approval, also alluded to the radicalism sweeping Europe. The painting shows the launch being pulled astern of the *Bounty*; Bligh stands in his shirtsleeves, pale and ghostly, his hand outstretched in a pathetic gesture of entreaty; about him is the distressed frieze of his eighteen supporters. Christian, standing on the flag box of the *Bounty*,

---

* Salmond, *Bligh: William Bligh in the South Seas*, introduction.

is shown wearing a hat, which was such a potent symbol of radical working-class politics in Britain that 'rioters, arsonists, rabble rousers, pamphleteers were made to wear hats in any representation of them',* Dening writes.

The mutineers received their sentences on 18 September; but from 17 to 24 September, contrary winds prevented the mail packet from reaching the Heywood family with the news. When they did hear of the result, it came not from a letter but a little boy, the son of a family friend, who ran into their house on a Monday evening and blurted that the trial was over and all the prisoners condemned to death, but Peter had been recommended for the king's mercy. The news had been brought to the island by a man in a fishing boat who had seen it in a newspaper in Liverpool; maddeningly, he had forgotten to bring the paper with him.

A week earlier, the court had agreed the charges were proved against six of the *Bounty* crew, who were sentenced to death by hanging, but Heywood and Morrison were recommended for the king's mercy, and the cook's assistant, William Muspratt, had launched an appeal. Four others were acquitted as expected: Norman, Coleman, McIntosh and Byrne; the men who were detained on the *Bounty* and who Bligh had already exonerated.

On 29 September, Nessy wrote to James Heywood: 'We are in agony of suspense, and I can scarcely support my

---

*   Dening, *Performances*, p. 171.

own misery, much less keep up my poor Mama's dejected spirits.'* But she added that everybody assured her there was 'not the smallest danger' of Peter's being executed.[†] A recommendation for mercy from a court martial was as good as an acquittal; the king had never refused one. As the eighteenth century went on, the number of people convicted of capital crimes had begun to outweigh the number who were actually hanged. Despite the fatal laws of the land, judges were good at finding reasons to commute sentences. When an appeal reached King George, he made liberal use of his royal prerogative of mercy.

Aaron Graham, too, was confident Peter's life was safe. The lawyer had been prompted to assist Peter through his many obligations to Commodore Pasley, but since then he had grown personally fond of Heywood and Nessy. His anxiety during the trial had taken a toll on his health and left his head aching 'most wretchedly'.[‡]

Peter assured Nessy he was in good spirits, and his writing, hitherto sprinkled with references to divine providence, reached a new level of religious fervour. 'There is a heavenly king and redeemer,' he wrote, 'ready to receive the righteous penitent, on whose gracious mercy alone I (as should we all) depend, with that pious resignation which is the duty of every Christian.'[§]

---

* Heywood, *Innocent on the Bounty*, p. 110.
† Heywood, *Innocent on the Bounty*, p. 110.
‡ Heywood, *Innocent on the Bounty*, p. 113.
§ Heywood, *Innocent on the Bounty*, p. 117.

At breakfast on 1 October, Nessy heard a fishing boat was leaving for Liverpool in half an hour; she quickly gathered some things and rushed aboard. She arrived at Liverpool after a rough and sleepless two-day passage, and began the overland journey to London, arriving at six o'clock on the morning of 5 October. Heywood's legal adviser, Aaron Graham, was waiting for her at his house on Great Russell Street in the fashionable suburb of Bloomsbury. He gave her personal assurances that she should not fear for Peter's life. For the next few weeks, she lived at Graham's house with his young daughter, and got letters to Peter through her younger brother, James, who visited him on board the *Hector* daily in Portsmouth. After talking with Graham in person, Nessy wrote home that the testimony given by Hallett, the 'vilest of wretches',* had led the jury to condemn Heywood.

On 27 October, Captain Montague of the *Hector* read Heywood the king's unconditional pardon, and Heywood declared: 'I receive with gratitude my sovereign's mercy – for which my future life will be devoted to his service.'† Graham retrieved Heywood from the *Hector* and brought him to London, where two days later, Heywood, Nessy and James reunited.

Morrison, who mounted his own defence, also received the king's pardon. William Muspratt, a thirty-year-old seaman with a black beard covering his scarred chin, appealed

---

* Heywood, *Innocent on the Bounty*, p. 129.
† Heywood, *Innocent on the Bounty*, p. 155.

his death sentence on the basis he had been denied the opportunity to call his desired witnesses. He was represented by the attorney Stephen Barney at the court martial; it's unclear how Muspratt alone among the seamen was able to afford legal representation. He was one of the three sailors, along with Churchill and Millward, who deserted the *Bounty* in Tahiti before her inward voyage. He had received a total of sixty lashes under Bligh. Later when the *Pandora* arrived in Tahiti, he was one of the fugitives who absconded to the mountains. The testimony of his shipmates during the court martial had depicted him as an active mutineer, but four months later, he won his appeal and walked into Portsmouth a free man.

Thomas Ellison, Thomas Burkett and John Millward were not so fortunate. Ellison, sixteen years old at the time of the mutiny, the 'little monkey' who had his musket taken off him by Christian, mounted his own defence at the court martial. It was very much his own work, complete with phonetic misspellings typical of his Cockney dialect:

I hope, honorable Gentlemen, yo'll be so Kind as to take my Case into Consideration as I was No more than between Sixteen and Seventeen Years of age when this of [sic] done. Honourable Gentlemen, I leave my self at the Clemency and Mercy of this Honourable Court.[*]

---

[*] Linder, Transcript of the Court-Martial of the *Bounty* Mutineers, Thomas Ellison defence statement.

The plea did not sway the court, and the convicted mutineers were transferred to the *Brunswick* in Portsmouth Harbour. They spent the night before their execution in a cell in the ship's gunroom. Millward, the most educated man among them, led the prayers. People came to look at them. Most of the visitors were solemn, even sorrowful, but some were unsympathetic; the hangman took their nightcaps as souvenirs and called twenty-year-old Ellison a 'hardened dog'.[*]

Next day was grey and rainy. At nine o'clock a cannon fired on the *Brunswick*, and a yellow flag appeared in her shrouds, compelling the other ships in the fleet to send delegations to witness the punishment. A ring of boats pressed in around the ship and the surrounding shores were crowded with thousands of spectators. At eleven o'clock the prisoners came on deck with four clergymen and Morrison, who wanted to give them moral support in their final moments. They either confessed to the mutiny in their speeches, or maintained their innocence to the end; witness accounts differ. Given the social unrest in France, the Admiralty might have thought it wise to represent the mutineers as penitent in their final moments.

Their hands and feet would have been bound. Perhaps a weight was tied to their feet to speed the process. Civilians, before they reached the gallows, were sometimes paraded through the streets like Caesars, stopping at taverns along the way; the three mutineers had no such luxury. This was

---

[*] Alexander, *The Bounty*, ch. 10.

a naval hanging, meaning they would be hoisted rather than dropped, the *Brunswick*'s company using ropes and pulleys to haul them to the yardarms, where their convulsions might not cease for a quarter of an hour. Waiting for the final signal, they stood on the catheads, the beams projecting from the ship's bow. Bags were placed over their heads, and nooses around their necks. At 11.26 another cannon sounded and the crews assigned to each rope pulled the mutineers skyward. Their bodies hung for two hours in the rain.

* * *

Nessy was not able to enjoy her brother's freedom for very long. Little over a year later, while visiting a family friend on the English mainland, she caught 'a violent cold, and not taking proper care of herself, it soon turned to inflammation of the lungs',* according to her mother. An uncle took Nessy to Hastings with hopes being near the sea would help, but she died, probably of pneumonia or tuberculosis, on 25 September 1793. She was twenty-six.

* * *

The court martial was a blow to the reputation of William Bligh. It was held while he was still at sea on his second

---

*   Heywood, *Innocent on the Bounty*, p. 126.

199

breadfruit mission, which should have made things harder for the defence because he couldn't be cross-examined. But the trial had aired damaging testimony about Bligh's command of the *Bounty*. The mutineers, when they took the ship, were muttering about short rations; Christian had been 'in hell' due to the 'frequent quarrels ... and the abuse which he had received from Mr. Bligh'; and the day before the mutiny, 'Mr. Bligh challenged all the young gentlemen and people with stealing his coconuts'.* Rumour spread through the Royal Navy that there was more to the *Bounty* mutiny than Bligh had revealed in his narrative. Drafts of Morrison's journal might have been circulating among navy personnel, a striking departure from Bligh's version of events. Caroline Alexander points out that Joseph Banks probably intervened to stop Morrison from publishing the journal; it did not surface until many years later.

For centuries, the printed pamphlet had been used as the mass medium for everything from political dialogue to erotic fiction, and it was in pamphlet form that the discrepancies in the *Bounty* story first reached the wider public. In 1794, Fletcher Christian's older brother, a law professor at Cambridge named Edward Christian, published minutes of the *Bounty* court martial taken by Muspratt's lawyer (the Admiralty had refused to give him the official minutes). To this document he attached an appendix that was essentially a defence of his

---

* Linder, Transcript of the Court-Martial of the Bounty Mutineers, John Fryer testimony.

brother's character and a critique of Bligh's narrative. The appendix drew on more than ten interviews with *Bounty* crew members and listed the names of prominent people as witnesses to the interviews. It was compelling, not solely because it presented evidence about Bligh's temper tantrums and abuse, evidence not heard during the court martial, but because it was an older brother's inquiry into the crime, disappearance and probable demise of his younger sibling. It had been Heywood who encouraged Edward Christian to begin the project. Free to speak his mind after his court martial, the young man wrote to Edward hoping to clear Christian's name, telling him that his younger brother was not the 'vile wretch' he had been portrayed as, 'but, on the contrary, a most worthy character, ruined only by having the misfortune (it can be so called) of being a young man of strict honour'.*

Edward applied his legal mind to the case, seeking out the *Bounty* crew members Coleman, Byrne and Lebogue in Greenwich Hospital, the cluster of colonnaded buildings on the southern banks of the Thames River that served as a permanent home for retired sailors. Among the bustling docks and tenements of Wapping, East London, he located Peckover, the Pacific veteran. He also spoke to Fryer, Hayward, Purcell, John Smith, Heywood and Muspratt, and corresponded with Morrison. Most of the interviews were held at the Crown and Sceptre public house or in his legal

---

* Heywood, *Innocent on the Bounty*, p. 212.

chambers. Edward brought 'respectable gentlemen' in tow, a committee of attorneys and reverends who sat in on the interviews as witnesses.

The result was antithetical to Bligh's account, which began to look like a whitewash. Edward contended that the mutineers were far more preoccupied with their food rations than with the allure of Tahitian women. The coconut incident, glancingly referred to by Fryer in the court martial, was now covered in detail; Bligh had shaken his first in Christian's face and called him a 'thief'.[*] He had cut the yam ration to three quarters of a pound, and the ship's company were 'greatly discontented at their short allowance of provisions, and their discontent was increased from the consideration that they had plenty of provisions on board, and that the captain was his own purser',[†] During the mutiny, the midshipman Edward Young spoke to Bligh of being 'starved'.[‡]

Edward's argument was supported by the talk among *Bounty* crew members during and after the mutiny. Fryer recalled the mutineer John Sumner telling him Bligh would be cast adrift to 'let the bugger see if he can live upon three fourths of a pound of yams a day'.[§] Heywood, when he asked the mutineer Matthew Thompson what was going on, received in reply that Bligh was now a prisoner and the men

---

[*] Christian, *Appendix to Minutes of the Proceedings of the Court-Martial.*
[†] Christian, *Appendix to Minutes of the Proceedings of the Court-Martial.*
[‡] Christian, *Appendix to Minutes of the Proceedings of the Court-Martial.*
[§] Linder, Transcript of the Court-Martial of the *Bounty* Mutineers, John Fryer testimony.

would have 'more provisions and better usage than before'.[*] In the Dutch East Indies, both Fryer and Purcell told the Dutch authorities that the mutineers took the *Bounty* because Bligh had cut their rations, specifically the yams.[†] John Adams also said decades later that the crew yielded so easily to Christian because 'the captain stinted them in their allowance'.[‡]

A very different voyage was emerging from the one of 'uninterrupted prosperity' in Bligh's narrative.[§] Edward's pamphlet told of a journey full of conflict, and a commander who had abused and humiliated his officers, and skimped on the rations of his seamen; demoralising his crew to the point that a spontaneous rebellion could occur with little resistance.

'The sufferings of Captain Bligh and his companions in the boat, however severe they may have been, are perhaps but a small portion of the torments occasioned by this dreadful event,' Edward concluded.

> And though public justice and the public safety can allow no vindication of any species of mutiny, yet reason and humanity will distinguish the sudden unpremeditated act of desperation and frenzy, from the foul deliberate contempt of every religious duty and honourable sentiment; and will deplore the uncertainty of human prospects, when they reflect that a young man is

---

[*] Heywood, *Innocent on the Bounty*, p. 120.

[†] Frost, *Mutiny, Mayhem, Mythology*, ch. 1.

[‡] Alexander, *The Bounty*, ch. 12.

[§] Bligh, *A Voyage to the South Sea*, ch. 12.

condemned to perpetual infamy, who, if he had served on board any other ship, or had perhaps been absent from the *Bounty* a single day, or one ill-fated hour, might still have been an honour to his country, and a glory and comfort to his friends.[*]

Caroline Alexander argues that Edward used his influence in a conspiracy to smear Bligh's name and vindicate his brother. She points out that Edward was well connected in eighteenth-century British society; he counted among his close friends the anti-slavery campaigner William Wilberforce, himself a friend of Prime Minister William Pitt. The committee of gentlemen who witnessed Edward's interviews included slave abolitionists and revolutionary sympathisers who might have looked unfavourably on Bligh and his mission to feed the human chattels in the West Indies. Alexander includes Peter Heywood's family in the plot, because Peter had several uncles with high-ranking positions in the Royal Navy. In all, the 'sea of intrigue in which Bligh found himself entangled remains unfathomable',[†] she maintains. In his pamphlet, Edward had elicited 'the perfect Romantic hero' and Bligh was faced with 'a force more formidable and unassailable than any enemy he would meet at sea – the power of a good story'.[‡]

In fact, the reverse is true; it was Bligh and his own elite connections who participated in an intrigue after the mutiny.

---

[*] Christian, *Appendix to Minutes of the Proceedings of the Court-Martial*.
[†] Alexander, *The Bounty*, ch. 11.
[‡] Alexander, *The Bounty*, ch. 11.

He and the editors of his *Voyage*, James Burney and Joseph Banks, worked together to turn the story into a work of propaganda through the omission of key details. For Bligh, Banks and the Admiralty, the failed expedition had to be portrayed with extreme care. Bligh stood to lose money and career prospects, while the failure of Banks's pet project threatened his courtly prestige. For the Admiralty, the mutiny was an untimely reminder of the fragility of naval discipline, and a disaster it might have avoided with greater attention to the *Bounty* mission. The best course of action, for all involved, was to paint Bligh as the commander of a trouble-free voyage, blindsided in a plot by his corrupt officers. As Banks expressly told Bligh about the narrative: 'We shall abridge considerably what you wrote in order as far as we are able to satisfy the public and place you in such a point of view as they shall approve.'* The notorious incident the day before the mutiny, where Bligh publicly accused Christian of stealing his coconuts and reduced the yam ration, is absent from his narrative, as is any mention of trouble with Christian, or of cutting food allowances to punish the crew. How could readers achieve a true understanding of the mutiny without the inclusion of those events?

Alexander overlooks the reality that Bligh was able to publicise his distorted account of the *Bounty* voyage to a huge and admiring audience, without challenge, for several

---

* Frost, *Mutiny, Mayhem, Mythology*, introduction.

years. It was not unusual or sinister that Edward and the Heywoods wanted to counterbalance Bligh's version of events in public. The fact that Edward was a man of influence does not discount the charges in his pamphlet, which Bligh never directly addressed. At any rate, Bligh was well connected himself; Joseph Banks had the king's ear, and as Alexander allows, his 'tentacles of influence stretched to the remotest corner of all parts of the globe'.*

The pamphlet was a collection of corroborated evidence from the most reliable witnesses it was possible to wrangle. Of the interviewees, half had chosen to go into the launch with Bligh, and only one, Muspratt, seems to have been an active mutineer, although he was acquitted in his court martial. Edward listed the names and addresses of all the crew members he spoke to, but didn't directly attribute their statements, because they had an understandable fear of retribution. The men weren't only speaking out against Bligh, but the establishment-ordained version of the *Bounty* voyage. It wasn't in their interest to defend Fletcher Christian, a wanted criminal and the man ostensibly responsible for their sufferings at sea. Yet far from blaming him, they told Edward he was a person 'adorned with every virtue and beloved by all, as good and generous a man as ever lived'.†

It's true that Bligh was wronged by history in one sense: twentieth-century films portrayed him as a sadistic tyrant who

---

* Alexander, *The Bounty*, ch. 1.
† Christian, *Appendix to Minutes of the Proceedings of the Court-Martial.*

relished physical punishment. It was a myth that arose from the hyperbolising power of Hollywood, not the Christian or Heywood families.

Bligh's response to Edward, a pamphlet of his own titled *An Answer to Certain Assertions*, was a small collection of documents that he hoped was sufficient to 'do away any evil impression'.* It included sworn affidavits from Lawrence Lebogue, John Smith and Joseph Coleman. The degree of coercion involved in procuring their statements is unclear, but Bligh did demand that one of his former sailors receive physical punishment when he declined to cooperate. The *Bounty*'s fiddler, Michael Byrne, refused to change his evidence. Bligh wrote to Francis Bond, who was serving on the same ship as Byrne: 'As to the blind scoundrel, I can only beg of you to make the best of him, and get him flogged nobly whenever he deserves it for he is certainly a very great villain.'†

The statements all sought to defend the key claim in Bligh's narrative: that the mutineers overthrew him so that they could return to Tahiti. All three affidavits claimed Christian had a permanent attachment with a Tahitian woman before the mutiny, and mentioned the mysterious cutting of the ship's cable at Tahiti. They said that the sailors were never on short food allowance (except bread, by their consent) and that Bligh never abused his officers (although they conceded

---

* Bligh, *An Answer to Certain Assertions*, p. 2.
† Salmond, *Bligh: William Bligh in the South Seas*, ch. 23.

he did 'damn the people').* Smith said he never told Edward 'anything about the coconuts' in his interview, but admitted 'the captain found fault at a heap of coconuts being taken away'.†

Each affidavit contained more or less the same points in the same order. And there were new accusations against Bligh's critics. Coleman claimed Morrison, the acquitted mutineer whose journal of the voyage was circulating, 'threatened to blow my brains out'.‡ Lebogue said on the day of the mutiny, he saw a musket at 'Purcell, the carpenter's door'.§

Bligh also fired scandalous interest in the case by including allegations about Christian's sexual exploits and drinking habits. He quoted a letter from Edward Lamb, who had sailed with Bligh and Christian on a West Indiaman years earlier: 'In the appendix it is said that Mr. Fletcher Christian had no attachment amongst the women of Tahiti; if that is the case he must have been much altered since he was with you [Bligh] on the *Britannia*; he was one of the most foolish young men I ever knew in regard to the sex.'¶ Smith said Christian had free access to Bligh's personal case of grog. Lebogue said the acting lieutenant was drinking with Purcell at midnight on the night before the mutiny, although he had to be up at four o'clock in the morning to keep his watch. In all, it was a

---

*   Bligh, *An Answer to Certain Assertions*, p. 21.
†   Bligh, *An Answer to Certain Assertions*, p. 21.
‡   Bligh, *An Answer to Certain Assertions*, p. 19.
§   Bligh, *An Answer to Certain Assertions*, p. 26.
¶   Bligh, *An Answer to Certain Assertions*, p. 30.

surprisingly lame rejoinder, not as damning as Edward's, who responded in yet another pamphlet.

The public spat did not cost Bligh the patronage of his rich benefactor, Joseph Banks, who was ecstatic when the *Providence* returned to England with a huge cargo of exotic plants. For his part, Banks kept track of the allegations arising from the court martial and Edward's interviews and asked Bligh to answer for them in private letters. Bligh, undergoing eighteen months in a kind of professional exile on half-pay, had little else to do but mount an epistolary defence of himself. But in his draft replies to Banks, he began to make concessions. He admitted, for example, that he had argued with Christian after the *Bounty* left Tahiti, and that he had words with his men about coconuts. He maintained that Christian had had a permanent female attachment in Tahiti and said the woman was still living on the island when he called there on the *Providence*: a self-defeating claim, since Christian's only known Tahitian partner was then living on Pitcairn Island.

For Banks, Bligh's answers must have been satisfying enough, or at least, the truth about the mutiny was now so muddied that he could give his protégé the benefit of the doubt (although he never defended Bligh in public). Their professional association would continue for years. Indeed, Banks was destined to handpick Bligh for another appointment, which would prove just as catastrophic for him as the *Bounty* mission and put an end to his active career.

CHAPTER THIRTEEN

Bligh's New Post

William Bligh's second attempt to procure breadfruit plants from Tahiti was a success. As captain of the *Providence* he transported a cargo of the plants from the Pacific to the Caribbean, unknowingly sailing within five hundred miles of Christian and his pirate colony on Pitcairn Island. During the voyage he suffered from terrible headaches, perhaps a symptom of the malaria infection he contracted in the Dutch East Indies. Decreeing that noises distracted him, he kept his ship in a state of profound silence. The seamen nicknamed him 'the Don', likening his arrogant and prideful manner to that of a Spanish grandee.

As on the *Bounty*, there was discontent among the crew of the *Providence*. In the run from Tahiti to the West Indies, Bligh was parsimonious with freshwater, ensuring most of it went to the breadfruit plants. The crew suffered so much from thirst that the midshipmen took to licking beads of water off the gardener's buckets.* In an act of protest, somebody poured seawater on the plants. An enraged Bligh 'longed to flog the whole company', but never found the culprit.† This was mutinous behaviour, but the possibility of a full-blown mutiny was now far more remote with twenty marines on board.

Bligh also continued to clash with his officers. His midshipman, a budding navigator named Matthew Flinders, was derated to seaman after an argument over the authorship of some charts.‡ Flinders would go on to complete the first circumnavigation of Australia and give that country its modern name; he would resent Bligh's treatment of him on the *Providence* for the rest of his career. The ship's armourer, Henry Smith, was stripped of his warrant and reduced to a seaman, and later jumped overboard in an apparent suicide. As happened on the *Bounty*, Bligh's deputy seems to have borne the brunt of his abuse. Bligh took his step-nephew Francis Bond on the *Providence* as his second-in-command. According to Bond, 'he has treated me (nay all on board) with the insolence and arrogance of a Jacobs: and notwithstanding his passion is partly to be attributed to a nervous fever, with which he has been attacked most of the voyage, the chief

---

*   Wahlroos, *Mutiny and Romance in the South Seas*, p. 270.
†   Scott, *The Life of Captain Matthew Flinders*, p. 33.
‡   Preston, *Paradise in Chains*, ch. 20.

part of his conduct must have arisen from the fury of an ungovernable temper'.*

In a draft letter to his brother, Bond reflected that he had hoped to receive instruction from Bligh as his student, until 'this imperious master … publicly exposed any deficiency on my part in the Nautical Act etc'.†

'The very high opinion he has of himself makes him hold everyone of our profession with contempt, perhaps envy: nay the navy is but a sphere for fops and lubbers to swarm in, without one gem to vie in brilliancy with himself,'‡ Bond wrote.

> Every officer who has nautical information, a knowledge of natural history, a taste for drawing, or anything to constitute him proper for circumnavigating, becomes odious; for great as he is in his own good opinion, he must have entertained fears some of the ship's company meant to submit a spurious narrative to the judgement and perusal of the public.§

Bond's letter, which he thought better of sending, might be dismissed as a subordinate's private venting if it didn't bear so many similarities to accounts of Bligh's conduct on the *Bounty*. The captain seems to have gone out of his way to make Bond miserable, stripping him of 'every dogma of power

---

* Christian, *Fragile Paradise*, p. 186.
† Christian, *Fragile Paradise*, p. 186.
‡ Christian, *Fragile Paradise*, p. 186.
§ Christian, *Fragile Paradise*, p. 186.

and consequence', accusing him of laziness, keeping him 'menially active' at all times and mocking him for keeping a private journal.*

It wasn't unusual for sailors on scientific expeditions to be barred from publishing their journals. During Cook's third voyage, the officers were ordered to hand over their diaries, charts and drawings, Bligh not excepted, and the seamen were searched for stray bits of paper. The order had come from the Admiralty to prevent the 'scramble for publication' known to follow such expeditions.† On the *Bounty*, Bligh was unconcerned about this, because he wasn't on a voyage of discovery (although during his open boat voyage, he had refused Fryer a pencil or paper to write down what was happening). On the *Providence*, his attitude changed. He was so concerned about subversive accounts of his voyage that to Bond, 'among many circumstances of envy and jealousy he used to deride my keeping a private journal and would often ironically say he supposed I meant to publish'.‡ Bond wrote that every officer was expected to hand over their private logs when the ship anchored at Saint Helena, an order he considered arbitrary and 'illegal' because the ship's mission was a mercantile one.§

Bligh was away at sea for more than two years, and in that time, his professional reputation began to suffer at home with the court martial of the captured mutineers. When Bligh

---

* Christian, *Fragile Paradise*, p. 186.
† Besant, *Captain Cook*, p. 172.
‡ Christian, *Fragile Paradise*, p. 186.
§ Christian, *Fragile Paradise*, p. 187.

returned to England from Jamaica in 1793, his superiors had lost all enthusiasm for him. The head of the Admiralty, Lord Chatham, simply refused to grant him an audience, and he was left waiting day after day in the department's corridors while other captains came and went. He complained to Banks that his lordship's evasiveness was 'certainly a slight'.* The Admiralty also would not support the publication of a book about the successful voyage of the *Providence* (even though it had rushed to publish Bligh's account of the mutiny on the *Bounty*). Bligh was left without an assignment on half-pay for a year and a half. Jamaican planters paid him a handsome reward for his efforts, but the plan to turn breadfruit into a Caribbean staple proved futile. The slaves refused to eat the fruit and fed it to their pigs instead.

In 1796, Bligh finally received an important naval command on board the *Director*. A year later, he was mutinied again, as part of a general strike action involving fifty thousand seamen in more than a hundred warships. The mutineers deposed their captains at the Nore, an anchorage in the Thames Estuary, sending their commanders ashore and setting up a 'Floating Republic'. The liberal sentiments rippling across Europe had led to a spike in the number of mutinies in the Royal Navy in the 1790s. At the Nore, sailors demanded pardons, higher pay and an end to war with revolutionary France. The mutiny was quelled, with

---

* Preston, *Paradise in Chains*, ch. 20.

dozens of rebels hanged and imprisoned, and Bligh regained control of his ship. But news of the uprising fuelled more unrest on lower decks around the globe. In the Caribbean, the crew of the *Marie Antoinette* murdered their commander and turned their ship over to the French, whereupon most of them disappeared. Sailors on the *Hermione,* drunk on stolen rum, hacked at their captain with cutlasses and threw him overboard. They went on to murder eight officers and two midshipmen. The mutineers handed the *Hermione* over to the Spanish in Venezuela, claiming they had set their captain adrift as the *Bounty* mutineers had done.

Bligh later commanded warships in the Battle of Camperdown against the Dutch, and in the Battle of Copenhagen against the Dano–Norwegian Navy. In 1805, while commanding the HMS *Warrior*, he was court-martialled over allegations of 'tyrannical and oppressive and un-officer-like behaviour'.* John Frazier, one of his lieutenants, stated that Bligh did 'publicly ... grossly insult and ill treat me in the execution of my office by calling me a rascal, scoundrel and shaking his fist in my face'.† The ship's surgeon had put Frazier on the sick list with a swollen leg. Bligh thought Frazier was malingering. He removed the lieutenant from the sick list and ordered him back to duty, though according to the other officers Frazier could barely walk. When Frazier refused to follow orders, he was arrested; his court martial later acquitted

---

* Preston, *Paradise in Chains*, ch. 21.
† Preston, *Paradise in Chains*, ch. 21.

him. Bligh's own trial found the charges against him partly proved and he received a reprimand, the court warning him 'to be in future more correct in his language'.*

Shortly after that ignominious episode, the captain's lifelong patron, Banks, was writing to him with the offer of another appointment: the governorship of New South Wales. It had been Banks who first proposed the eastern coast of Australia as the site for a British penal colony decades earlier. Transportation, or the forced exile of criminals to foreign lands, had been a lawful punishment in Britain for almost a hundred years. Tens of thousands of English convicts were siphoned off to the American colonies up until the Revolutionary War. Duncan Campbell's prison hulks in the Thames River, meant as a temporary measure, had become floating shanties where prisoners either died of disease or graduated as hardened criminals. Canada, the Falkland Islands and West Africa were considered as new destinations at one time or another. So, too, was a proposal to simply continue sending convicts to America without permission. (The *Mercury* tried in vain to impose her convicts on Georgia and unloaded them in Honduras instead.) Meantime, convicts kept marching into the hulks.

Giving evidence before a committee of the House of Commons on the problem of transportation, Banks had described New South Wales in glowing terms: the weather was

---

* Preston, *Paradise in Chains*, ch. 21.

mild and moderate, the grass long and luxuriant. His proposal bore similarities to his *Bounty* project; both were aimed at exploiting British discoveries in the Pacific. Indeed, Banks nearly combined them into a single mission before thinking better of it. The First Fleet of convict ships left England just six months before the *Bounty* sailed for Tahiti. The fleet's mission was to set up the most extravagant gulag in history, a penal colony without precedent both in terms of distance from the mother country (fifteen thousand miles) and the sheer foreignness of the land to its colonisers. Captain Cook had glimpsed the coast of New South Wales and claimed it for Britain almost two decades earlier; in the interim, no European expedition had landed there. It was as if the modern United States decided to send its felons to the moon.

When the captain of the fleet, Arthur Phillip, disembarked at Botany Bay he was disappointed. Contrary to Banks's description, the bay was an unsheltered sweep of arid ground and scrappy trees that rolled off into a dry immensity as impartial and unvarying as the ocean itself. Phillip moved the settlement north to modern-day Sydney, overcoming severe food shortages to establish an open-air jail with a growing population of free settlers. Meanwhile, the effect of the colony on Indigenous Australians was catastrophic. Notwithstanding the fact that they were driven from their ancestral lands and dispossessed of their diverse languages and cultures, the fallout from the diseases the colonists carried was akin to biological warfare. From 1788 to 1921, the total Indigenous population in Australia would decline by eighty per cent, from an estimated three hundred thousand to sixty thousand.

By 1806, Britain's grip on the colony at Sydney was slipping. Officers in the New South Wales Corps, charged with guarding the convicts, were undercutting the governor's authority as a military junta. The corps officers had taken over the courts and the supply of convict labour, building up their own profitable estates. They had a monopoly on rum, the colony's de facto currency, as well as the goods arriving on merchant ships, which they sold at inflated prices. The third governor of New South Wales, Philip Gidley King, was constantly at loggerheads with corps officers and failed to stop the rum trade. He grew despondent, his health suffered, and he asked to be recalled. Joseph Banks had lost the use of his legs to gout and had to be wheeled to his meetings in a wheelchair, but his mind was as sharp as ever and he remained an adviser to the British government on Australian affairs. He suggested William Bligh as King's replacement.

Bligh, now fifty years old, was reluctant to accept the offer. He pointed out that he would not be able to take Betsy on the voyage to New Holland because she was terrified of the sea. Banks was persuasive, promising him his salary would be double that of King's, and he could take his daughter Mary to function as his hostess, while her husband Lieutenant Putland served as his aide. Bligh could not resist a chance to improve his finances, and in 1805 he was made the fourth governor of

New South Wales. It was hoped his disciplinarian style would bring the military corps to heel and remind them that they were run by British fiat.

There were problems even before Bligh arrived in Sydney to occupy his new post. During the voyage out, he assumed his authority exceeded that of the captain of the convoy, Joseph Short, and the pair quarrelled bitterly. Bligh, in command of a transport ship, refused to obey Short's signals, and the captain had to resort to firing across the ship's bow. Once in Australia, Bligh forced Short back to England to face a court martial, and Short's wife and child died on the return journey. The court martial acquitted Short, found he had been unjustly treated, and recommended he be compensated for his losses. In the aftermath, an indignant Betsy wrote in defence of her husband to Banks, who in turn used his influence to prevent Bligh's recall.

In Sydney, now a busy port city with a population of about ten thousand, Bligh was just as irascible and politically inept as ever, and he quickly alienated the most powerful settlers in the colony. Chief among these was John Macarthur, a cunning and ambitious man who had originally come to Sydney as a lieutenant in the corps. Macarthur had been arrested under King's watch and sent to England for court martial after he wounded his commanding officer in a duel. But he managed to reverse his fortunes and return to New South Wales with a five thousand–acre grant of pastoral land and official permission to set up a merino wool industry.

Joseph Banks opposed the project, arguing it should be done on English soil. Nonetheless, Macarthur secured rare Spanish sheep from the royal flocks. Smarting at this, Banks would have briefed Bligh about the Australian upstart before he left England. Indeed, Bligh and Macarthur quickly became archrivals. According to Macarthur, when he came to Government House asking Bligh to confirm his land grant, the new governor raged:

> What have I to do with your sheep, sir; what have I to do with your cattle? Are you to have such flocks of sheep and herds of cattle as no man ever heard of before? No, sir! You have got five thousand acres of land in the finest situation in the country; but by God, you shan't keep it!*

Bligh banned the use of rum as currency, a relief for settlers without connections to the corps. He replaced officials, cancelled land grants (ordering that the houses already built on them be demolished) and damned the corps officers as wretches, villains and tremendous buggers.† 'Damn the law: my will is the law, and woe unto the man that dares to disobey it,'‡ was his retort to a judge-advocate who questioned the legality of his reforms. 'I have heard much about Bounty Bligh before I saw him,' wrote the surgeon for the corps

---

* Salmond, *Bligh: William Bligh in the South Seas*, epilogue.
† Salmond, *Bligh: William Bligh in the South Seas*, epilogue.
‡ Salmond, *Bligh: William Bligh in the South Seas*, epilogue.

after Bligh dismissed him from duty, 'but no person could conceive that he could be such a fellow – Caligula himself never reigned with more despotic sway than he does.'[*]

He was Bounty Bligh, Breadfruit Bligh or simply the Bounty Bastard. To be sure, the settlers had political reasons for evoking his command of the *Bounty*, yet his conduct in Australia did follow the same pattern of behaviour. He immediately participated in a corrupt land deal, a clear signal to the settlers that, like the corps, he was not above using government resources for private profit. Before he took the reins from King, he received three illegal land grants totalling more than a thousand acres, and then he made a reciprocal grant, also illegal, of almost eight hundred acres to King.[†] He used convict labour to farm his newly acquired land. Meanwhile, he sent Banks a stream of misleading letters, declaring the colony had 'recovered from a most deplorable state',[‡] even though the political situation was fast unravelling.

In early 1808, a swift sequence of events led to open revolt. Macarthur was committed for trial after flouting costs attached to one of his ships, but the corps officers refused to serve as a jury. Bligh wrote to the commander of the corps, Major George Johnston, asking him to come to Government House to discuss the matter, but Johnston turned him down, saying he was recovering in bed from a carriage accident. (He

---

[*] Salmond, *Bligh: William Bligh in the South Seas*, epilogue.
[†] Preston, *Paradise in Chains*, ch. 21.
[‡] Preston, *Paradise in Chains*, ch. 21.

had drunkenly fallen out of his gig on the way home from seeing his mistress.) When Bligh shot back that he regarded the conduct of the corps officers as treason, Johnston hurried to the corps barracks, where soldiers and settlers were gathered and fearful of being hanged. The men determined to arrest Bligh before he arrested them. Johnston declared himself lieutenant-governor of New South Wales and ordered Macarthur's release.

At dusk, hundreds of soldiers from the corps marched on Government House to arrest Bligh. At their head were Macarthur and Johnston, his face still puffy and bruised from his carriage accident. At the gates to the residence, Bligh's 27-year-old daughter Mary Putland barred the way with her parasol until she was dragged away. Next the rebels began a somewhat drawn-out search for the governor. Bligh had been dining with his followers and, on hearing the troops arrive, left the table and hurried upstairs. He was either found beneath a bed, according to the soldiers, or stooped over beside the bed while destroying official papers, according to his own account. He was dressed in full uniform, his jacket dirty with cobwebs and dust. That night liquor ran freely, bonfires blazed and William Bligh was burnt in effigy. Macarthur rode triumphant through the streets on a lofty chair. No physical harm came to Bligh: he and his daughter were kept under house arrest at Government House.

Fourteen months later, the Sydney mutineers cautiously allowed Bligh to board the warship *Porpoise* in the harbour after he swore 'on his honour as an officer and a gentleman' to sail directly to Britain.* But after a moment of confusion, if not madness, where he unsuccessfully prevailed on the ship's captain to aim a cannon at Sydney, Bligh sailed for the southern coast of Tasmania instead. At the starving and lawless outpost of Hobart, he would attempt to muster support for his reinstatement.

Whether Bligh offended Hobart's lieutenant-governor in his exasperated call for assistance, or the settlement was simply too thinly stretched to help him, his plan was in vain. He remained impotently on board the *Porpoise* in the harbour, and by the time he sailed back to Sydney in 1810, his successor, Lachlan Macquarie, had already arrived from England. Macquarie couldn't muster much sympathy for Bligh either; he described his predecessor as 'certainly a most disagreeable person to have any dealings, or public business to transact with; having no regard whatever to his promise or engagements however sacred, and his natural temper is uncommonly harsh, and tyrannical in the extreme. He is certainly generally detested by high, low, rich and poor.'†

Bligh's daughter Mary had had a miserable time in New South Wales. Her husband had died of tuberculosis soon after they arrived. Now, as Bligh was preparing to depart for Britain, Macquarie's deputy asked him for Mary's hand in marriage. Bligh flatly refused, not aware Mary had already

---

* Preston, *Paradise in Chains*, ch. 21.
† Preston, *Paradise in Chains*, ch. 21.

accepted. After some discussion he assented and embarked alone, leaving New South Wales stripped of his governorship and, it seemed, his own daughter.

In England, Bligh was again court-martialled, acquitted and promoted. His seniority now secured him further, automatic naval promotions up to vice admiral of the blue. But he remained on half-pay, and never again was he given a commanding position. Bounty Bligh was thus allowed to retire with his dignity somewhat intact, though he had clearly exhausted the patience of the naval establishment.

* * *

From the time Captain Cook allowed him to chart his Pacific discoveries at the age of twenty-one, it was clear that William Bligh was a genius. He should have taken his place beside Cook in the pantheon of great navigators, but his naval career unfolded in fits and starts, blotted with the fiascos that became his legacy. It was not in his character to admit wrongdoing, and he seems to have believed himself a victim of chronic bad luck. But if Bligh was an unfortunate man, he was also the author of his misfortunes. Jealous of his authority and his own excellence, he was incapable of recognising initiative or promise in his men. Instead, he was a pedant about their faults, and when officers took exception to his fault-finding he responded with personal antipathy. His deputies, the mediators between himself and his crews, usually suffered most under his withering gaze, men like Fryer, Christian and Bond. He always made himself an island, scribbling righteous letters to his patrons about the incompetents around him.

Though from the gentleman class, Bligh was preoccupied with money for much of his life, especially on his *Bounty* salary. In a letter to Betsy from Timor, in the same breath as relating his loss of the *Bounty* and the open boat voyage, he anxiously talked business: 'I have saved my pursing books so that all my profits hitherto will take place and all will be well.'* On his return to England he asked the Admiralty for almost three hundred pounds for the loss of his personal possessions, including port brandy, a dozen nightcaps and a box of pencils left rattling around in his cabin. Admiralty officials denied his request, which amounted to almost fifty thousand pounds in today's value. His superiors understood he was shrewdly using his position as purser for private profit. On his return from the *Providence* voyage, he found his pay had been docked for that reason, and protested in vain. That grabbing impulse was regarded with disgust among his colleagues, even if it stemmed from a benign desire to provide for his family. As the governor of New South Wales he was not only parsimonious but demonstrably corrupt.

Despite his faults, Bligh loved his wife and daughters. His domestic life seems to have been tranquil and happy. In Betsy he had a lifelong friend, although the couple spent most of

---

* Frost, *Mutiny, Mayhem, Mythology*, ch. 1.

their married lives apart. Betsy was already ill, her 'nerves being very much broke', when Bligh returned to England from New South Wales. She died soon into her husband's retirement, aged fifty-nine, perhaps as a result of the trials she endured as his defender. Bligh sold his London property and moved with his unmarried daughters to a manor house in Kent, south-east England. Five years later he collapsed and died of cancer in London's Bond Street, aged sixty-four. He is buried next to Betsy in Lambeth. His tomb is made of pale stoneware, topped with a classical vase and a bullet-shaped eternal flame that is often mistaken for a breadfruit.

In his later years, Bligh must have thought of the *Bounty* often, pausing to examine the old musket ball that hung on a ribbon around his neck, the same musket ball he once used to measure out rations with his makeshift scale in the open boat. At dinner parties he told stories about the foul innards of birds and fish he was forced to eat. Did he utter the name Fletcher Christian in his house? Did he humour his dinner guests with theories of the pirate's whereabouts? By the time he arrived at Tahiti on his second breadfruit mission in 1792, his former lieutenant had become a phantom. Among the throngs of Tahitians, he looked for skerricks of information about Christian. The Tahitians were now wise to his falsehoods about Captain Cook but nonetheless keen to flatter him. He noted unhappily that their neat bark cloth ponchos had been

---

* Salmond, *Bligh: William Bligh in the South Seas*, epilogue.

replaced with dirty linen shirts and waistcoats: 'they are no longer clean Tahitians, but in appearance a set of ragamuffins with whom it is necessary to have great caution'.*

Teina's wife, 'Itia, told him about the *Bounty*'s final visit to Matavai Bay, before Christian cut the cable and slipped away in the night, leaving an anchor behind on the seafloor. Then Edwards had captured the stragglers, five of whom left behind children born to Tahitian women. With their lighter skin, these children were recognisable to the *Providence* crew as the children of doomed men. Stewart had already drowned in the *Pandora* wreck, while Burkett and Millward would soon be hanged for mutiny. Of the fathers McIntosh alone survived. Whether Bligh ever told him about an encounter with his two-year-old daughter, Elizabeth, is unknown. All that remained of Christian were echoes of his expressed intention to run the *Bounty* before the wind and settle an uninhabited island. It must have galled Bligh that his adversary threatened to take up an enduring place in the culture as a Crusoe-like figure. In 1796, he was furious at a hoax pamphlet purporting to describe Fletcher Christian's travels in South America.

'Is it possible that wretch can be at Cadiz [Spain]?' he fumed in a letter to Banks, 'and that he has intercourse with his brother, that six-penny professor, who has more law about him than honour – my dear sir, I can only say that I heartily despise

---

* Preston, *Paradise in Chains*, ch. 20.

the praise of any of the family of Christian and I hope and trust yet that the mutineer will meet with his desserts [sic]."*

Then there was the strange report about the real fate of Christian and the mutineers. It was published in the *Quarterly Review* in March 1810, the year Bligh arrived home from Australia after the Rum Rebellion. It must have reached his desk at the Georgian Terrace in London where he lived with Betsy, a disquieting reminder of the *Bounty* saga that threatened to define his career. His reaction is not known, but given the report's contents it must have floored him.

---

* Alexander, *The Bounty*, ch. 13.

CHAPTER FOURTEEN

First Contact

Eighteen years passed before the pirate colony on Pitcairn Island had any contact with the outside world. There were close calls in the intervening years. In May 1795, the settlers sighted a ship on the horizon and went into panic and hiding. They later discovered the vessel had sent a small boat ashore to gather coconuts, but the hills reaching up from the island's shoreline were so steep that the shore party didn't stray far from its landing place, and remained completely ignorant of the colony. In December of that year the islanders were again 'greatly alarmed' to see a ship, but there was a heavy surf, and the weather was so threatening that the vessel stood to the south-east and disappeared. The islanders interpreted this as an act of divine intervention, because in the week that followed the sea was the calmest they had ever seen it.

It was not until February 1808, that Captain Mayhew Folger, of the American sealer *Topaz*, discovered the island was populated by the descendants of long-time fugitives. Folger had been at sea for more than a year since leaving Boston, hunting for seals in the Pacific. He was born on Nantucket Island, the whaling settlement off the coast of Massachusetts. He would have spoken with the distinctive 'thee' and 'thou' of a Nantucketer, and followed the pacifist religious sect known as the Quaker movement. On sighting Pitcairn Island, Folger was confused, because he was sailing in a backwater where his charts said there should be nothing but ocean. Yet land bore south-west that afternoon: the island stood more than a thousand feet tall, visible for many miles. Folger regarded it both as a potential hunting ground and an open challenge to the nautical wisdom of the day. He gave orders to steer for the island, and his ship neared it over the next several hours. At two o'clock in the morning he was seven miles away. At sunrise he was putting boats in the water for a closer look.

Like Christian, Folger guessed this was Pitcairn Island, and that it had been charted incorrectly many years earlier. He also noticed that, contrary to Carteret's description of Pitcairn as uninhabited, smoke was rising from the hills, a sure sign of human settlement. As he rowed towards the island in a small boat, a Polynesian-style canoe put off towards him carrying three strongly built, dark-skinned men. Folger was surprised when they hailed him in English, asking him to identify himself. The captain replied that he was the master of the sealing ship *Topaz* and he was from Boston, in America. The islanders had a good command of English and their accents were almost British, suggesting regular contact with passing ships. But they had never heard of the captain's home country, and earnestly asked him if America was a city in Ireland.

According to an account of the discovery, filtered through his friend, Captain Amasa Delano, Folger's vigilance gave way to 'surprise, wonder and pleasure'.[*] The strangers in the canoe were friendly. They claimed they were Englishmen because their father hailed from England.

'Who is your father?' Folger wanted to know.

'Alec,' the men replied.

'Who is Alec?'

'Don't you know Alec?'

'How should I know Alec?'[†]

Folger headed towards shore, the waves carrying him aloft as patches of weed rolled beneath the boat. The men in the canoe guided him through a safe passage. He was on his way to see 'Alec', full name Alexander Smith, who had refused an invitation to board the *Topaz*, and instead, invited the captain to have dinner on the island. The man he found waiting for him on the shore looked harmless enough. Smith was a forty-year-old Englishman, fat and bald, with long locks of white hair at the back of his head. He had the body of an old

---

[*]   Delano, *A Narrative of Voyages and Travels*, p. 139.

[†]   Delano, *A Narrative of Voyages and Travels*, p. 139.

sailor, his skin marked with tattoos and scars from a bout of smallpox. Smith led Folger from the shore, scrambling up the steep rock faces that encircled the island, while the captain struggled up behind him. The hike led to a little village of thatched huts in the hills, occupied by a colony of thirty-five men, women and children. The villagers looked at Folger in disbelief.

Alec was from Hackney in London. He grew up an orphan in a poorhouse after his father drowned in the Thames River. When he was twenty years old, he mustered on the British ship *Bounty* bound for Tahiti, unaware that he would never return to Britain or, indeed, the Western world. His nickname among the sailors was Reckless Jack. Alec claimed he had been forced to take up arms and follow Fletcher Christian's lead in 1789, helping to rebel against Lieutenant Bligh and cast him adrift. He was the only mutineer left alive on Pitcairn Island, as well as the only original male settler.

Since the burning of the *Bounty* eighteen years before, he said, all fourteen of the other men had perished, most of them in a series of murders. But the islanders had enjoyed relative peace for years hence, and the population, consisting of Smith, nine Tahitian women and the children of the mutineers, were living in simple harmony. Smith had turned to the ship's Bible as a guide for setting up his little society. It seemed when the other mutineers were dead, and Smith was drunk on an alcoholic brew made from a tropical plant, he had a terrifying hallucination of the archangel Michael throwing a dart at him. Smith became a God-fearing man, and made sure all the children received reading and writing lessons at the island's makeshift school. The villagers grew yams, coconuts and bananas, and reared pigs and chickens. They made clothes the Polynesian way, hammering out the bark of the paper mulberry tree into *tapa* cloth. They were fit, healthy, and incredibly nimble, able to scale the rocks and cliffs around the island like goats. Everybody had full sets of white teeth.

'I think them a very humane and hospitable people,' wrote Folger about his visit. 'Whatever may have been the errors or crimes of Smith the mutineer in times back, he is at present in my opinion a worthy man.'[*]

Folger was familiar with the mutiny on the *Bounty*, and had often wondered what became of Christian, his ship and his party. It was a tale that embodied all the pathos of life at sea, and the captain could not help but feel sympathy for the mutineers and their permanent exile in the Pacific. He had often discussed the subject with his friend, Captain Delano, when the pair crossed paths in port. As Delano explained: 'We had both suffered many varieties of hardship and privation, and our feelings were perfectly alive to the anxieties and distresses of a mind under the circumstances of Christian, going from all he had known and loved, and seeking as his last refuge a spot unknown and uninhabited.'[†]

---

[*]   Wahlroos, *Mutiny and Romance in the South Seas*, p. 276.
[†]   Delano, *A Narrative of Voyages and Travels*, p. 138.

There were other tales about feats of survival on desert islands, like that of Scottish privateer Alexander Selkirk, which probably inspired the much-celebrated story of Robinson Crusoe. Selkirk spent four years marooned on an island off the coast of Chile, hunting goats and hiding from passing Spanish ships. When he was found, the sailor was almost incoherent with joy, and his ordeal was a public sensation. But the *Bounty* mutineers were a different breed of castaway. Rather than dream of rescue, they had renounced society forever. The appearance of sails on the horizon struck them with panic, not joy.

Smith had been made somewhat eccentric by his isolation. He still spoke with the inflection of a Royal Navy man from twenty years earlier. Folger asked him if he'd heard about the developments in Europe in the nineteenth century. 'How could I,' replied Smith ruefully, 'unless the birds of the air had been the heralds?'[*] Folger gave Smith a summary of recent world events: the French Revolution and the rise of the French Emperor Napoleon Bonaparte. Napoleon had dominated much of continental Europe, but failed to overcome the British fleet at sea. That last detail made Smith throw down his hat and give three 'huzzahs'.

Folger also brought disturbing news. Soon after the mutiny, he told Smith, Britain had dispatched a ship, the *Pandora*, to search for the *Bounty* mutineers in the Pacific. The *Pandora*'s

---

[*] Delano, *A Narrative of Voyages and Travels*, p. 141.

captain, Edward Edwards, succeeded in capturing fourteen of the pirates in Tahiti. The ship was wrecked in the coral mazes of the Great Barrier Reef during its return voyage, and four mutineers drowned in chains. The ten surviving mutineers made a miraculous return to England for trial, and three were hanged for their part in the uprising on the *Bounty*. For Smith, the tale served as a grim reminder of his potential arrest. There was no statute of limitations for mutiny, still a hanging offence; and now the location of his hideout was no longer a secret. Folger's rediscovery of the island meant he had to be ready for more visitors in the future.

Smith's redemption story must have appealed to Folger and his Quaker sensibilities. Pitcairn Island is the most remote inhabited island on earth, and yet in their isolation the Pitcairn Islanders had quietly coalesced into a Christian utopia, or so Smith would have his visitor believe. It must have been something more than divine providence that left him as the island's sole authority, with none of his fellow mutineers left alive to dispute his version of events. Time would reveal that Smith was not the pious teacher he held himself out to be, but an old rogue who never told the same story twice. He cannot have made much progress in teaching his flock to read and write, because at the time of Folger's visit, he was barely literate; when he read books aloud it was thought he was speaking 'out of his own head'.* He had also, reformed

---

*   Frost, *Mutiny, Mayhem, Mythology*, ch. 3.

Christian or no, played a direct role in the island's violent past, murdering one of his shipmates with an axe while a seven-year-old girl looked on in terror.

When it was time for the captain to leave, the islanders crowded around him on the shore, presenting him with rolls of Polynesian cloth. So simple and unaffected was their manner as they prayed for his safe passage that Folger regretted leaving, and thought about Pitcairn Island for years afterwards, conceptualising it as a sort of paradise. He sailed to Juan Fernandez Islands off the coast of Chile. On his arrival, the Spanish governor of the island fired cannon at the *Topaz* and threw the captain and his crew in jail for months. When the Admiralty finally received a report of Folger's discovery a year later, it paid no attention. Britain had been hunting Adams and the mutineers for twenty years, but at that moment she was tied down in a war with France.

* * *

A dumbstruck Captain Folger had departed Pitcairn Island with two generous gifts from Adams: the *Bounty*'s azimuth compass and the K2 chronometer. He promised the islanders he would return in eight months, but they never saw him again. Indeed, six years passed before they had any further contact with outsiders, a surprising lag of time, given the island's incorrect charting was now ostensibly fixed. Then in 1814, two British frigates, the *Briton* and *Tagus*, stumbled across the island much as the *Topaz* had. Britain was now at war with America and France, and the ships were combing the Pacific for an American frigate that had been attacking British shipping. The Admiralty was aware of the situation on Pitcairn Island, thanks to Folger, but the frigate captains had not been informed, nor had their charts been updated. It was as though the island were being discovered all over again.

The captains spied huts and plantations on the island through their looking glasses, and watched as the islanders came down to the shore with canoes on their heads. Soon the boats were darting through the heavy surf towards them. Out of one of these canoes, a young man climbed aboard the *Briton*: Thursday October Christian, twenty-four years old, a son of the pirate captain, Fletcher Christian.

Thursday October's name was a riddle; naming children for the day of their birth was a practice among the African slaves his father would have encountered in the West Indies. He was the first child born on the island, about a year after the mutineers' arrival. Friendly and polite, he looked at the frigates with the fascination of an adult who had never laid eyes on a boat much larger than a canoe. He was tall and tanned, dressed in a bark cloth poncho, a loincloth and a straw hat adorned with black chicken feathers.

The captain of the *Briton*, Thomas Staines, took Thursday October and his teenage companion on a tour below deck. The boys were amazed at the size of the ship, the guns, and the animals in the pens. They were alarmed at the sight of a cow, and wondered whether it was a huge goat or a horned pig. 'What a pretty little thing it is,' said Christian's friend upon seeing the ship's little black terrier. 'I know it is a dog, for I have heard of such an animal.'[*]

The young men offered Staines some of the stories about the colony's founding, but referred the captain to a man on shore for more details. They said his name was John Adams: since Folger's visit the patriarch was no longer going by Alec, or Alexander Smith. Adams had mustered on the *Bounty* under a pseudonym, probably because of desertion from another ship or trouble with the law. For whatever reason he had reverted to his birth name.

The captains managed to get to shore through the waves and rocks in their small boats. When they landed, they were soaked but unhurt. Adams, on seeing the men in their British naval uniforms, was visibly worried they were about to take him prisoner. He nevertheless expressed his willingness to return to England for trial, at which point the young women standing around him burst into tears. Adams was now forty-seven years old, but to the frigate captains he appeared an old man. He showed the captains his library, consisting of William Bligh's books from the *Bounty*; Bligh had written his name on the title page of each volume, and beneath each inscription was the name of their subsequent owner, Fletcher Christian. Adams's visitors decided not to arrest him, a bold

---

[*] Barrow, *The Eventful History of the Mutiny and Piratical Seizure of HMS Bounty*, ch. 8.

decision which, they were aware, might raise the ire of their superiors. Captain Philip Pipon of the *Tagus* explained his reasoning for letting Adams remain on the island:

> Although in the eye of the law they could only consider [Adams] in the light of a criminal of the deepest dye, yet that it would have been an act of the greatest cruelty and inhumanity to have taken him away from his little family, who, in such a case, would have been left to experience the greatest misery and distress, and ultimately, in all probability, would have perished of want.[*]

Pipon further justified his decision, perhaps worried an unfeeling Admiralty would reprimand him for allowing the mutineer to get away. Even if he had wanted to arrest Adams, he claimed, the steep terrain would have made it 'impossible to have conveyed him on board'.[†]

Staines and Pipon assured Adams that, far from coming to the island with the intention of arresting him, they hadn't even been aware of his existence. They gave the colony a kettle, some magazines, and a mirror for Adams to shave with, and sailed for Chile. Again, descriptions of the island and its inhabitants reached the British government, but nothing came of it.

---

[*] Barrow, *The Eventful History of the Mutiny and Piratical Seizure of HMS Bounty*, ch. 8.

[†] Wahlroos, *Mutiny and Romance in the South Seas*, p. 347.

* * *

After the *Tagus* and *Briton*, other ships began appearing off Pitcairn Island once or twice a year. The nineteenth-century demand for whale oil, which lit the streets of Western cities and greased the gears of the Industrial Revolution, drove thousands of American whalers around Cape Horn and into the Pacific. At first, the whaleships kept to the western coast of South America, but soon they were striking off into the great blue they knew as the 'offshore ground', where potential profits rose in proportion to mortal danger.

Pitcairn Island was now charted correctly on the map, and the whalemen called there to resupply their ships and to see Adams and his strange colony in the flesh. The Pitcairn Islanders grew to expect visitors, and stood ready to trade island produce for metal and manufactured goods. Adams accepted his role as a kind of living museum exhibit, humouring the visiting captains with tales of Christian and the mutiny on the *Bounty*, and adding his own creative flourishes.

In October 1817, the American whaleship *Sultan* stopped at the island for provisions, trading a jolly-boat and some iron bars for pigs, yams and copper bolts. In 1819, the British East Indiaman *Hercules* delivered Adams a letter from his brother in East London. The letter included a description of the family Adams had not seen for more than thirty years, and mentioned the death of one of his sisters. 'This affected him much,' wrote Captain James Henderson of the *Hercules*, 'and he often repeated that he never expected to see this day, or indeed one of his countrymen more'.[*] The *Hercules* also brought gifts from Calcutta, including a 22-foot cutter, cutlery, guns, razors and a large British ensign.

As shipping increased in the Pacific, the Pitcairn Islands group was more than a source of fresh vegetables and adventure stories for curious sailors; occasionally it became their lifeline when they met with disaster. On his way to Pitcairn, Captain Henderson had sighted an uninhabited atoll a hundred miles to the north-east and named it Henderson Island. The atoll was larger than Pitcairn, with an area of six square miles, but not nearly as habitable; it was covered in sharp coral pinnacles and a dense scrub forest, and the only freshwater source was a brackish spring below the tideline.

In December 1820, twenty Nantucket whalers stumbled from three whaleboats onto the island's white sand beaches. A bull sperm whale had rammed and sunk their whaleship, *Essex*, more than a thousand miles off the coast of Peru. Easterly trade winds prevented the whalers from running straight for the coast of South America, so they had elected to head 1500 miles south, until they met a band of variable breezes that they could ride to Chile or Peru. But in the subsequent month-long voyage they had exhausted their food provisions, including live tortoises from the Galapagos

---

[*] Ford, *Pitcairn Island as a Port of Call*, p. 10.

Islands, and took to drifting aimlessly. Apathetic from starvation, the whalemen had spent their days lying under sails to escape the rays of the sun, and suffering from dizzying blackouts when they attempted to sit up. Owen Chase, first mate of the *Essex*, described the voyage in his journal: 'In vain was every expedient tried to relieve the raging fever of the throat by drinking saltwater, and holding small quantities of it in the mouth, until, by that means, the thirst was increased by such a degree, as even to drive us to despairing, and vain relief from our own urine.'[*]

When the men from the *Essex* chanced across Henderson Island, they dispersed into ragged groups, hungrily devouring seabirds, eggs and crabs, and finding freshwater below the high-tide mark. But the island was only a barren scrap heap of coral. Within a week, they had eaten most of the crabs and birds and were beginning to starve again. They were unaware that salvation lay just a day's sail away, in the form of Pitcairn Island and its outlaw colony.

'Among the rocks were several caves which afforded shelter from the wind and rain,' recalled crew member Thomas Chappel. 'In one of these caves we found eight human skeletons, in all probability the remains of some poor mariners who had been shipwrecked on the isle, and perished for want of food and water. They were side by side, as if they had lain down and died together.'[†]

---

[*] Heffernan, *Stove by a Whale*, p. 50.
[†] Ford, *Pitcairn Island as a Port of Call*, p. 11.

The crew took stock of their desperate situation. Three men decided to remain behind on Henderson Island, while seventeen got back in the whaleboats and headed east for Easter Island. The men who chose to sail soon exhausted their stockpile of island fare and began to die one after another. The third man to perish was kept aboard and, after some discussion, his shipmates ate his body, gnawing the bones clean. Eventually, the bodies of seven crew members were cannibalised: at one point, the men drew lots to decide who among them would be eaten. Owen Coffin, seventeen years old, drew the black spot; the captain offered to take his place, but he refused. Coffin's young friend drew the second black spot and became his executioner.

In February, the last of the survivors were rescued off the Chilean coast by the crew of a Nantucket whaler, the *Dauphin*. They were so affected by starvation and thirst that the sight of their rescuers terrified them, and they jealously clutched at the human bones that littered the bottom of the boat, refusing to give them up. They had sailed almost four and a half thousand nautical miles across the Pacific. On 8 April 1821, four and a half months after the wreck, the English ship *Surry* rescued the three men who remained on Henderson Island and called at Pitcairn Island, where they were welcomed with warmth and pity, before sailing on to Port Jackson, Australia. Of the twenty men who escaped the *Essex* shipwreck, only eight survived. The *Essex* ordeal inspired Herman Melville to write his 1851 novel, *Moby-Dick*.

Although Pitcairn Island was correctly charted by the mid-nineteenth century, Oeno Island, a barren atoll that lay ninety miles to the north-west, was not, and its circular reef claimed several ships. In March 1858, the merchant clipper *Wild Wave* was sailing from San Francisco to Valparaiso when she ran into Oeno's reef. The island had been charted twenty miles out from its true position, hence the wreck, which left the *Wild Wave* in a tangled and irrecoverable mess. Her crew salvaged their provisions and pitched tents on the island that lay two miles within the circular reef, a 'dreary waste of sand', as Captain Josiah Knowles described it in his diary, 'with hardly enough vegetation to deserve the name'.*

Knowles continued:

I passed the night in sleepless anxiety as to our probable fate, while the continual roar of the surf seemed to remind me constantly of our utter desolation. Our beds were laid on boxes and barrels from the ship, but had any of us been disposed to sleep, the rigorous attacks of the land crabs and rats would have prevented it. You may think it very strange that I found rats on this desert island. On landing I saw some spars and other wrecked stuff, and concluded that at some previous time some other ship had met the fate of ours, and as far as we knew, the rats were sole survivors.†

---

* Hale, *Stories of the Sea Told by Sailors*, p. 198.
† Hale, *Stories of the Sea Told by Sailors*, p. 198.

It was hopeless to wait for rescue. Captain Knowles decided to leave forty-one men on Oeno and strike out with six crew members for Pitcairn Island in one of the ship's small boats. He left his second mate in charge at Oeno, with orders to proceed to Pitcairn with the rest of the crew in the event he did not return in a month. As he left the island, his company gave him three cheers; and he stopped at his battered ship to recover a cargo that had been weighing heavily on his mind: $18,000 in gold, or half a million dollars' worth in today's value.

The captain had been expecting assistance from the *Bounty* settlers, but on landing at Pitcairn two days later he found the island temporarily abandoned. The settlement was a ghost town, with the doors to the cottages standing open and chickens, goats and enormous pigs roaming free. Notices posted about the overgrown buildings announced the British government had relocated the Pitcairn Islanders to Norfolk Island. Soon after Knowles arrived, his moored boat was smashed to pieces in stormy weather, stranding him and his men.

Knowles buried his gold. He converted one of the cottages into a makeshift chicken coop, and kept a sharp lookout for passing ships. His situation on Pitcairn was 'infinitely preferable' to that on Oeno, with an abundance of fruit and livestock, but he could not help thinking of his friends and family who, when his ship failed to call at Valparaiso, would assume he was dead. Knowles struggled with depression in the months that followed, not helped by constant rain. He read a copy of *Jane Eyre* that he had found in one of the homes, hunted goats and wandered around the empty settlement, thinking of his young wife in Massachusetts. On 27 March he expected his second mate to arrive, but there was no sign of him. His sojourn on Pitcairn was such a torment that he had desperately wanted to leave the island in his second mate's boat, even though the island offered his best chance of survival. He wrote that he and his men had eaten nineteen meals of goat that week.

By April, Knowles and his men had decided to build a boat and sail to Tahiti. The party began cutting timber and hewing planks out of logs, which he described as 'very tedious and hard work'. They found axes and planes in the abandoned houses. In the hard labour, the captain's shoes gave out, his clothing became threadbare, and his hands grew calloused from long days swinging an axe. He celebrated his twenty-eighth birthday later that month.

In June, the thirty-foot schooner was finished, a crude bricolage of island materials. Her mast was the village flagstaff; her anchor was an old anvil, and her sails were stitched from rags of every sort. Her American ensign was fashioned from a white shirt, a blue dungaree and red trimming from the settlement's church pulpit. Bracing himself for the voyage to Tahiti, Knowles salted goat meat, gathered charcoal to use as fuel, and left letters recounting his adventures in the cottages. Two dozen chickens were loaded on board, as well as twelve hundred oranges and a stove made from a copper kettle. The vessel was christened the *John Adams*.

As the crew readied the boat for launching, they stove her hull slightly on the rocks; three of Knowles's men took this as a bad omen and refused to go to sea in her. Knowles, happy for the extra space, made no objections. The captain and his other three men set sail in the motley vessel. The boat exceeded expectations, though she had a peculiar, nausea-inducing motion at sea. Knowles had intended to sail to Tahiti, but the wind was against him, so he steered for the Marquesas Islands instead. At Tahuata, Polynesians thronged the boat in canoes and invited Knowles to anchor, but the captain pulled away, regarding his would-be hosts as a 'savage-looking set'.*

At Nuku Hiva, Knowles sailed around the island, searching in vain for a European settlement. He had given up on the Marquesas, and decided to sail to Hawaii, when he rounded the point of the harbour and spotted a lone ship at anchor, the *Vandalia* of the American navy. Knowles hoisted his scrappy ensign and was welcomed aboard. The *Vandalia* had only arrived at Nuku Hiva the day before, and she had been preparing to depart. No American vessel had called at the island for almost five years.

Knowles eventually returned to Massachusetts. In the seven months since he left San Francisco, his wife had given birth to a baby girl. She had believed a newspaper report claiming the *Wild Wave* had gone down with all hands, and was stunned to see her husband alive. The *Vandalia* also

---

* Hale, *Stories of the Sea Told by Sailors*, p. 217.

retrieved the three men left behind on Pitcairn Island, and forty crew members from Oeno, one having died. The men on Oeno had built a boat from pieces of the wrecked ship, but the vessel was so cumbersome they had not been able to launch her. Knowles reported in his diary they had quarrelled among themselves and had 'anything but a pleasant time'.*

---

* Hale, *Stories of the Sea Told by Sailors*, p. 221.

CHAPTER FIFTEEN

An Interview with John Adams

Through the early 1820s, a steady stream of whalers visited Pitcairn, and the islanders, a devout and trusting people, found themselves living at the whims of passing ships much as the Tahitians had. The saltwater and ginger tea they used to treat local ailments could not inoculate them against the disease carried by Western sailors. The frigates had left them with headaches and an invasive population of houseflies. A whaling crew, coming ashore with scurvy patients to practise an old folk remedy, burying them up to their necks in the ground, left the islanders with boils and sores. Later, influenza repeatedly swept through the settlement.

The vulnerability of the Pitcairn Islanders to lawless strangers was made painfully apparent in 1824, when an unnamed British trading brig arrived from Valparaiso. The captain, coincidentally named Bligh, invited Adams and some of the island women aboard, plying them with alcohol. By nightfall one of the girls was fast asleep in the ship's stateroom and couldn't be roused. Bligh was said to have drugged her with laudanum.* The captain persuaded Adams to leave the girl on board and come for her in the morning; as security, he locked the door to the stateroom and gave Adams the key. But in the morning the brig was gone, having sailed during the night, and the Pitcairn Islanders never saw the girl again. Bligh reportedly landed her at Tahiti years later.

Captain Frederick Beechey arrived at Pitcairn Island on board the HMS *Blossom* on Christmas Day in 1825. Twenty-nine years old, with ruddy cheeks, boyish features and a shock of brown hair, Beechey was on a three-year voyage of discovery, during which he explored the coast of Arctic Alaska, travelling further north than any non-Inuit had ever been. Before he headed for the Alaskan coast, he was under orders to take stock of Pitcairn Island and its inhabitants and map the surrounding atolls. When they raised the island, his crew gathered excitedly on the decks of the *Blossom*; anxious, wrote Beechey, to see and partake of the pleasures of the island's

---

* Ford, *Pitcairn Island as a Port of Call*, p. 12.

'little domestic circle'.* They were also eager for fresh pieces of the *Bounty* lore that John Adams so readily dispensed.

Beechey saw a boat under sail coming off the island and assumed it belonged to a visiting whaleship, but as it drew near, he saw it was filled with Adams and ten island men. They were a ragtag group with bare feet, their dress a mishmash of presents from passing ships: coats without shirts, shirts without coats, or waistcoats without either. Before setting off to hail the ship, they must have dressed up for the occasion; usually, the men on Pitcairn went around in a *maro*, or loincloth, and saved their English clothes for Sunday service. Adams, now in his late fifties and somewhat overweight, was dressed in a sailor's shirt and trousers, with a low-crowned hat. He still had his sailor's manners, removing his hat and smoothing down his bald forehead when the officers addressed him.

An awkward scene commenced as Adams suffered 'temporary embarrassment'.† Finding himself on his first British naval ship since the *Bounty*, he was torn between the attitude of common seaman and town dignitary. The men in his entourage were also taken aback by the ship, which they described as 'so rich' compared with others they had seen.‡ Adams must have primed them to be on their best behaviour, because they were so wary of offending the crew that they would not even move without asking permission. Beechey, as

---

* Beechey, *Narrative of a Voyage to the Pacific and Beering's Strait*, p. 66.
† Beechey, *Narrative of a Voyage to the Pacific and Beering's Strait*, p. 67.
‡ Beechey, *Narrative of a Voyage to the Pacific and Beering's Strait*, p. 96.

he led them on an hours-long tour of the ship, was bemused by their constant permission-seeking and their ignorance of how to open doors.

While Adams was aboard Beechey's ship, the islanders watching from the shore were crying bitterly. They had identified the *Blossom* as a British warship and feared their leader was being arrested. But after an agonising wait, they saw boats coming off to the island, and Beechey and Adams were ferried ashore through the gauntlet of heavy surf. Adams's daughter Hannah rushed down the hill and threw her arms around her father, betraying her anxiety about his fate. Hannah had run ahead of her companions, who Beechey saw making their way down the steep path to the shore. The women were wearing bark cloth petticoats and mantles that reached to their ankles. Like the men, they were dressed for the occasion; great morinda and tobacco flowers adorned their freshly oiled hair. Beechey described them as tall and muscular, their skin a 'dark gipsy hue',[*] their eyes 'dark and animated, and each possessed an enviable row of teeth'.[†]

'They are certainly a finer and more athletic race than is usually found among the families of mankind,'[‡] he wrote.

Adams put his daughter at ease and escorted Beechey up the path to the village, through shady stands of coconut trees. The steep ascent, the tropical heat, and the swarms of

---

[*] Beechey, *Narrative of a Voyage to the Pacific and Beering's Strait*, p. 127.
[†] Beechey, *Narrative of a Voyage to the Pacific and Beering's Strait*, p. 99.
[‡] Barrow, *The Eventful History of the Mutiny and Piratical Seizure of HMS Bounty*, ch. 8

flies introduced to the island by previous visitors exhausted the captain and his men. They lagged behind the Pitcairn Islanders and rested on a slab of rock while the women used leaves to fan the flies off them.

When he reached the village in the evening, Beechey found it bustling with a population of sixty-six people, nearly double what it had been when Folger rediscovered the island. Beyond a central hamlet of five cottages were fruit plantations, a cemetery (the grave markers of Fletcher Christian and the other mutineers were conspicuously absent), and Adams's house, further up the hillside, where the patriarch lived with his blind and bedridden wife.

Beechey's men were divided among the cottages in the town centre, where they were served a dinner of baked pork, yams and taro, cooked in a Polynesian-style earth oven. In the Christian household, Beechey was surprised to find a table set with a diverse assortment of plates, knives and forks. The dining table was lit with torches made from candlenuts, which cracked and flared in their tin pots. As was customary in Tahiti, the women didn't eat with the men, instead standing behind the chairs of the visitors and swatting the flies off them. The captain openly criticised that inequity, but the islanders were unapologetic: in the Bible man was made first, they argued, so he should always be first to table.

The islanders had a hybrid culture: their farming, cooking and clothing unmistakably Polynesian, while they adhered to the scriptures, or Adams's interpretation of them, with ardent devotion. They rose early and worked through the day, fishing, tilling their fields and hammering the bark of the mulberry tree into cloth. But they had lost the Tahitian love of dance and music, which they had come to view as a heathen distraction. A few of the older women danced reluctantly when the *Blossom* sailors asked, but only briefly. A violin performance by one of Beechey's men was lost on them; they preferred drumming on a gourd and the *Bounty*'s copper fish-kettle.

They never told jokes, Beechey noticed, and they took everything literally, thinking irony a falsehood. They spoke cautiously, afraid of lying and of being kept to their word. Beechey gave as an example the case of two would-be lovers, Polly and George. Polly had made the mistake of saying she would never give her hand to George, but she later developed romantic feelings for him. Now her earlier vow was the only thing preventing the pair from marrying. (They asked Beechey for a judgement on their case and were relieved when he ruled in favour of marriage, although they couldn't be persuaded to follow through.)

Before Adams's moment of revelation, perhaps Fletcher Christian had already begun nudging his little community in the direction of religious piety. Years earlier, one of the young men who climbed aboard the *Briton* told an officer that Christian had 'caused a prayer to be said every day at noon', a practice the islanders continued. The prayer in question might give an insight into Christian's mental state in the years following the mutiny: 'I will arise and go to my Father, and say unto him, Father, I have sinned against heaven, and before thee, and am no more worthy of being called thy son.'*

In any case, by the time Beechey arrived, Adams could not unfairly be described as a religious fanatic, and his island was like an abbey of monk-like devotees. When Adams dined with the captain, he said grace before and after every mouthful of bread. Sundays on the island were a marathon of worship, with the week's sermon read three times in a row, to make sure the islanders got every word. There are hints in travellers' accounts that the piety of the islanders struck an off-note; they were said to quote from the scriptures 'with a freedom and frequency that rather impair the effect'.† But their morality was also held up as a welcome example for Victorians undergoing a crisis of faith in a rapidly industrialising world.

The Pitcairn Islanders were also seen as a curious link between white and brown people at a time when natural historians hierarchised the races, with the white race at the top and other, dark-skinned races ranged beneath it. Captain Pipon of the *Tagus* said he observed in Christian's son, Thursday October, 'all the features of an honest English face'.‡ In 1834 the whaleship surgeon Frederick Bennett wrote that the islanders 'form an interesting link between the civilised

---

* Alexander, *The Bounty*, ch. 12.
† Bennett, *Narrative of a Whaling Voyage Round the Globe*, p. 34.
‡ Barrow, *The Eventful History of the Mutiny and Piratical Seizure of HMS Bounty*, ch. 8.

European and unsophisticated Polynesian nations … their features, though far from handsome, display many European traits."* These were the beginnings of a pseudoscientific interest that reached its apogee decades later. Arthur Keith, a believer in the crackpot theory that miscegenation produced inferior offspring, measured the islanders' skulls with calipers and decided their brains were smaller than those of Europeans.

After putting out the candles, Beechey's host family gathered in the centre of the house and chanted an evening hymn. The captain listened to the chorus of singing as he settled onto his palm-leaf mattress beneath crackling bark cloth sheets. Beechey and some of his men were sleeping in a spacious, two-storey cottage with a roof of thatched palm leaves. On the upper floor, reached by a ladder and trapdoor, were four beds, one in each corner.

In the morning, Beechey woke to the sound of a morning hymn, and fell back to sleep. When he came to again, he could hear the sound of a hammer at work on a piece of bark cloth nearby. Fresh fruit adorned his bedside and there were flowers in his hat. A group of women were standing in the middle of the room, a delegation sent to bring him water and wash his linen. There were no partitions or screens, so, with some awkwardness, he got dressed in front of them.

* * *

---

* Bennett, *Narrative of a Whaling Voyage Round the Globe*, p. 33.

The problem of the bastard colony in the South Seas had been lost in the bureaucratic churn of the Admiralty for decades. But in the 1820s, the British government suddenly showed an interest in John Adams and his flock. Indeed, it appeared to be sizing up Pitcairn Island as a colonial outpost acquired by accident.

Captain Beechey had been sent to get the lay of the land. He spent a total of nineteen days on Pitcairn Island, eating baked pork, climbing sheer volcanic slopes, and wearing hand-plucked flowers in his hat. His stay allowed enough time for a full interview with Adams about the mutiny on the *Bounty*. Adams, no longer fearing the gallows, talked about the circumstances with new candour. He said in his opinion the 'reason the majority of the crew yielded so easily to the persuasions of Christian was, that the captain stinted them in their allowance'.* He also said tensions had first emerged between Bligh and Christian during the ship's outward voyage, at the Cape of Good Hope.

The *Bounty*, tattered and leaky from her attempt to round Cape Horn, stopped in the mountainous harbour of Simon's Bay for repairs and supplies. It was a dismal Dutch port, where food was scanty and expensive in the wake of a famine. Decomposing bodies hung from gallows along the shore, and slaves staggered to and fro with heavy loads on their backs. While the *Bounty* regrouped, Bligh loaned Christian money,

---

* Alexander, *The Bounty*, ch. 12.

sending the bill back to England to be repaid with interest. As Adams described it, Christian came 'under some obligations to him of a pecuniary nature, of which Bligh frequently reminded him when any difference arose'.[*]

Bligh was known to be a harsh creditor. When he advanced money to his men for their living costs in Batavia after the open boat voyage, he did so on the condition they sign affidavits that the *Bounty* mutiny was unprovoked and not of his making.[†] As the *Bounty*'s surgeon's mate, Thomas Ledward, wrote to his uncle from the Dutch port, he demanded further concessions:

> The captain denied me, as well as the rest of the gentlemen who had not agents, any money unless I would give him my power of attorney and also my will, in which I was to bequeath him all my property; this he called by the name of proper security. This unless I did, I should have got no money, though I showed him a letter of credit from my uncle and offered to give him a bill of exchange upon him. In case of my death I hope this matter will be clearly pointed out to my relations.[‡]

Ledward died en route back to England, probably in a shipwreck. Whether his financial obligations to Bligh were ever settled is not clear. In any case, the fact Christian

---

[*] Beechey, *Narrative of a Voyage to the Pacific and Beering's Strait*, p. 70.
[†] Salmond, *Bligh: William Bligh in the South Seas*, ch. 12.
[‡] Salmond, *Bligh: William Bligh in the South Seas*, ch. 12.

accepted money from Bligh would have added further strain to what was already a beholden relationship, a murky amalgam of personal and professional obligations. Christian was at once Bligh's deputy, protégé and family friend. His life prospects had become dependent on his commander, which must have put him in a state of constant suspense, given Bligh's tendency to treat him as a close friend in one moment and an inept subordinate in the next.

Adams also described how the mutineers set up their society on Pitcairn Island. At first the Polynesian men were seen as friends of the Europeans, but very soon they became their slaves, tilling the soil, building houses and gathering wood and water. The island was divided into nine equal portions, one for each mutineer. If Christian and Young, the only gentlemen on the island, felt their 'degraded situation' more than the seamen, they didn't let on, Beechey wrote.[*]

'Not a single murmur or regret escaped them; on the contrary, Christian was always cheerful, and his example was of the greatest service in exciting his companions to labour. He was naturally of a happy, ingenuous disposition, and won the good opinion and respect of all who served under him.'[†]

The trouble started with the mutineer John Williams, who about a month into the settlement, lost his wife in a fall from a rock while collecting birds' eggs. Williams grew dissatisfied and insisted on having another wife. He threatened to leave

---

[*]   Beechey, *Narrative of a Voyage to the Pacific and Beering's Strait*, p. 93.
[†]   Beechey, *Narrative of a Voyage to the Pacific and Beering's Strait*, p. 93.

the island on the *Bounty*'s small boat. The mutineers were fearful of losing him because he was handy as an armourer, fixing and fashioning metal tools with the *Bounty*'s anvil. So they assented to his demands, forcing one of the Tahitian men to give up his wife to Williams. That planted the seed for a revolt, and on a single bloody day, the Polynesian men moved from one plantation to the next with muskets, killing Williams, Christian and three other mutineers. (As we will see, this account of Christian's death is uncertain.) The white men who heard the sharp reports from the muskets believed the Polynesians were shooting pigs. Adams himself was shot in the attack, a musket ball entering his right shoulder and passing out through his throat. He fell on the ground, bleeding and grovelling, and one of his attackers struck him with the butt of the gun, breaking two of his fingers. He managed to leap to his feet and run clear of them, and finally his pursuers offered him protection in return for surrender.

'Here,' wrote Beechey, 'this day of bloodshed ended, leaving only four Englishmen alive out of nine. It was a day of emancipation for the blacks, who were now masters of the island, and of humiliation and retribution for the whites.'*

The six Polynesian men now got in a fight among themselves over the wives of the murdered Europeans, Adams said. They were all murdered, mostly by the women. For the next five years, life went on again quietly, with the four remaining

---

* Beechey, *Narrative of a Voyage to the Pacific and Beering's Strait*, p. 86.

mutineers occasionally arguing over the Tahitian women. The next violent episode broke out when one of the mutineers, McKoy, a Scot who had once worked in a distillery, managed to make an intoxicating liquor out of the roots of the tropical ti plant. From that point, McKoy was constantly drunk or in fits of delirium. He fell to his death from a clifftop.

In the following year, another mutineer, Quintal, lost his wife to a cliff fall while collecting birds' eggs, and insisted he should take the wife of one of the other whites. Adams seems to ascribe the deaths of women to accidental cliff falls too often; perhaps it was a euphemism for suicide. In any case, Quintal's companions denied his request, and he drunkenly threatened to murder them. Adams and the other remaining mutineer Young responded by dispatching him with a hatchet.

Although these last two mutineers were from different stations – Young was an officer and Adams a seaman – they seem to have formed a strong alliance. Adams claimed that Young taught him to read and write, and the pair turned religious, holding family prayers and church services on Sunday, and devising Bible lessons for the children. By now there were nineteen children living on the island, many aged between seven and nine. Young died of an asthmatic infection about a year after the death of Quintal, leaving Adams as the only surviving Englishman, and the island's de facto leader. Reeling from a divine hallucination induced by the ti plant, Adams renounced liquor, shut down the island's makeshift distillery and devoted himself to the scriptures.

When they first settled on Pitcairn, Christian had found a cave at the highest point of a ridge that ran along the island's north side. He loaded it with ammunition and built a little watchhouse that looked out over the land, apparently in case a warship ever found his colony. Adams led Beechey to the cave; the approach was so difficult that Christian could have used it to hold off an invading force 'as long as his ammunition lasted'.* With his back against the rocks in that dripping grotto, the mutineer had planned to sell his life dearly.

In the hills, Adams showed Beechey where the mutineers had built their summer houses in the cooler air, overlooking plots of yams. He also pointed out the place where 'Christian was first buried'.† The pair saw ancient stone figures, not unlike those on Easter Island, indicating the island had supported Polynesians before the mutineers. The original settlers might have reached Pitcairn as early as the eleventh century and remained for several hundred years. Perhaps the island had been abandoned for one or two centuries before the mutineers arrived. There was evidence the settlers had quarried basalt and volcanic glass from the cliffs to make stone adzes, which they probably traded with the people of Mangareva, an island three hundred and thirty miles to the north-west. It's possible the trade network broke down, forcing them to sail back west. For whatever reason the tendrils of Polynesian society found their impasse at Pitcairn Island and withdrew.

---

* Beechey, *Narrative of a Voyage to the Pacific and Beering's Strait*, p. 109.
† Beechey, *Narrative of a Voyage to the Pacific and Beering's Strait*, p. 108.

* * *

Beechey reported back to King George IV, the son of King George III, and five years later, another British ship arrived with clothes and tools for sixty people: jackets, trousers, shoes, women's dresses, shovels and rakes.

When Adams died in 1829, aged sixty-two, his people were left somewhat lost. Most of them had never travelled beyond the high platform of their two-mile-long island. They spoke English to outsiders, but among themselves they used Pitkern, a creole blend of eighteenth-century English and Tahitian loanwords. They were a brown-skinned, biracial people, and yet at Adams's instruction they had a deep-rooted fear and distrust of 'blacks'; Thursday October Christian had tried to evacuate the *Briton*'s gunroom at the sight of a West Indian servant, even though his mother and wife were Tahitian. Adams also took pains to teach his flock that they were subjects of King George, despite his criminal exile from his homeland. His apparent nostalgia for king and country may have stemmed from the same instinct that led the mutineers to name their Tubuai stronghold 'Fort George', or Captain Cook to christen Australia's eastern coast 'New South Wales'. Like all explorers, the mutineers populated the wilderness with familiar references, naming buildings, peaks and beaches after things they knew at home. Adams never stopped using his Englishness as a bearing, but it can't have been much solace for his children.

In March 1831, Admiralty ships transported the island's entire population of eighty-six people to Tahiti. Adams had begged Beechey to pass on his concerns about overpopulation to the British government, but the relocation went ahead hastily, and the islanders were reluctant to leave. Despite their Polynesian roots, and the fact that four of the original female Tahitian settlers were still alive (one of them was reunited with her sister after forty-two years), the return to their ancestral homeland was a terrible shock.

In the nineteenth century, contact between the Tahitians and the outside world had increased at a rapid pace. Whalers and beachcombers had introduced rowdy saloons, gambling houses and brothels, rife with European diseases to which the Tahitians had no immunity. In the thirty years from 1800, influenza, dysentery and tuberculosis had thinned the island's population from sixteen thousand to some five thousand people. The saloons and brothels appalled the God-fearing Pitcairn Islanders and contact with the diseases they had never known took a heavy toll. Fletcher Christian's first son, Thursday October, was the first to die of a fever, and eleven others soon followed.

William Driver, captain of the trading brig the *Charles Doggett* from Massachusetts, found the survivors huddled together in a large thatched house in Papeete and fearing for their lives. By September 1831, the captain had restored the Pitcairn Islanders to their island, but five died on the return voyage. Driver, famous for nicknaming his American ensign

'Old Glory', was proud of his rescue of the Pitcairn people and had it inscribed on his grave marker.

Pitcairn was now attracting eccentric travellers who fell in with its native population, some with malign intentions. In the months before Adams died, an English missionary, George Nobbs, had begun to take over as the island's chief. But in 1832, a year after the failed relocation to Tahiti, a con man named Joshua Hill arrived on a pearling ship, claiming the British government had sent him to be the island's leader. In the most remote outpost of civilisation on earth, where news arrived in dribs and drabs from passing ships and visitors had to be taken at their word, Hill usurped Nobbs and controlled the island for several years as a self-styled 'President of the Commonwealth'. He ordered public floggings and had islanders locked up in a makeshift jail for minor offences. At one point, he ordered a twelve-year-old girl to be executed for stealing yams, before her father intervened and stopped the sentence from going into effect. Hill claimed to be a close friend of the Duke of Bedford. His falsehoods were found out when the duke's son, Lord Edward Russell, happened to arrive at the island as the commander of the Royal Navy ship *Actaeon*. Hill lived on the island for a further year, powerless and humiliated, until another warship forcibly removed him to Valparaiso.

By 1838, the Pitcairn Islands group was incorporated into the British Empire. Today it forms the sole British Overseas Territory in the Pacific. That year, the Pitcairn Islanders asked a visiting Royal Navy captain, Russell Elliott, to help them establish some semblance of authority over the island. Whalers were running rampant when they called for supplies. The whaleships that raised Pitcairn were often more than a year out from their home ports, their holds creaking with hundreds of barrels of whale oil. The crew members who rowed ashore were crass and unruly. They propositioned the women, threatened to overpower the men, and scoffed when the islanders claimed they were under British protection. Sometimes, the island's men had to personally guard the women from the whalers, spending time away from their all-important crops. 'There have been cases of recent occurrence,' wrote Elliott, 'where half the ruffian crew of a whaleship were on shore for a fortnight, during which time, they offered every insult to the inhabitants … taunting them that they had no laws, no country, no authority that they were to respect.'* Elliott responded by instituting an island magistrate, elected on a yearly basis and answerable to the British government. Pitcairn was now, in effect, a British colony.

In 1856, the island's population had ballooned to almost two hundred people, and the Pitcairn Islanders wrote to their English overseers requesting a solution. Again, Britain sponsored a relocation. This time, they were shipped to Norfolk Island, a former outpost of the penal colony at New South Wales. The Australian colonists had given up on the island's

---

* Ford, *Pitcairn Island as a Port of Call*, p. 18.

flax and pines and left behind a pack of dogs to turn wild and discourage landings by other nations. Norfolk Island was several times larger than Pitcairn, but similarly remote, falling in a barren tract of the Pacific nearly nine hundred miles east of Australia and five hundred miles north of New Zealand.

The Pitcairn Islanders arrived one year after the last of the British convicts had been removed to Tasmania, and occupied the stone buildings that were left standing. They built cattle ranches and hunted whales beyond the island's reefs. In the early twentieth century, the British government handed Norfolk Island over to Australia to be administered as an external territory. The islanders had their own government until recent years. In 2015, despite widespread protest, Australia forced the Norfolk Islanders to dissolve their parliament. The island was brought under the administration of the state of New South Wales, the modern incarnation of the penal colony that overthrew William Bligh as governor two centuries earlier. At the time of writing, the island's residents are still fighting to have their own parliament reinstated. In a strange quirk of fate, the man serving as Prime Minister of Australia during the takeover of Norfolk Island was Malcolm Bligh Turnbull, his middle name a family tradition in honour of the *Bounty* commander.

Pitcairn Island is still inhabited today, sustaining a population of about fifty people, because some of the migrants to Norfolk Island grew homesick and moved back. On their return to Pitcairn in January 1859, they would have found traces of Captain Knowles and the men of the *Wild Wave*, who had found refuge on the island a year earlier. The captain had simply burnt down some of their houses to salvage nails, while the church had been transformed into a boatbuilding workshop. The timing of the islanders' return was fortuitous, because soon afterwards a French warship appeared, her crew hoping to claim Pitcairn Island for France.

* * *

Pitcairn Island wasn't the only territory in the Pacific the French were looking to control. The reign of Tu's family over a unified Tahiti continued into the nineteenth century, the British propping up his dynasty through Christian missionaries. Tu's granddaughter, Pōmare IV, ascended to the throne in 1827 at the age of thirteen. Her royal name was Aimata, Eater of Eyes, recalling the old practice where a priest would tear out the eye of a human sacrifice victim and offer it to a chief for symbolic eating. Aimata lived up to the strength of her name in the face of foreign meddling, but the colonial powers eventually left her overwhelmed and humiliated. In the nineteenth century, Tahiti was becoming a key commercial centre, conveniently located between Valparaiso and New South Wales, as well as a refreshment port for whalers. The French, outmanoeuvred by the British in Australia and New Zealand, set their imperial sights on Tahiti instead.

In 1836, when Aimata was twenty-three years old, a pair of French Catholic missionaries slipped into Tahiti on a schooner, disguised as carpenters and flouting the residence laws of the time. The queen asked them to leave, no doubt influenced by the jealousies of the British Protestant missionaries. When the intruders refused, she had them forcibly removed, an insult France did not forget. Two years later a French warship arrived demanding concessions.

By 1843, France had declared Tahiti a French protectorate and installed a governor on the island. Aimata was heavily pregnant with her sixth child (she had ten children, four of whom died as babies). She opposed the French incursion, and had written to Queen Victoria asking that the island be placed under British protection. The British queen refused, probably to avoid offending the French, and as a consolation sent Aimata a carriage, horses, a crown and a drawing room suite. Aimata, in want of money, sold the carriage to the king of Hawaii.

Once the protectorate treaty was signed, the French moved in. A sense of the spectacle was given by the American novelist Herman Melville, who described the French military presence in the neighbouring Marquesas in 1842. Melville observed hundreds of French troops camping ashore, building fortifications and carrying out conspicuous marches and drills:

The islanders looked upon the people who made this cavalier appropriation of their shores with mingled feelings of fear and detestation. They cordially hated them, but the impulses of their resentment were neutralised by their dread of the floating batteries, which lay with their fatal tubes ostentatiously pointed, not at fortifications and redoubts, but at a handful of bamboo sheds, sheltered in a grove of coconuts!*

The islanders started to carry out night raids on their French occupiers with clubs and spears, and in response, France declared war on the very island Bougainville had praised as 'the true Utopia'. In April 1844, hundreds of French soldiers laid siege to a fortified camp of about a thousand Tahitian rebels. Bitter hand-to-hand combat followed, the Tahitians fighting with their spears against the bayonets of the French soldiers; only half of the islanders had firearms. France suffered fifteen dead, while the Tahitians lost more than a hundred men.

France went on to claim more than a hundred islands in the Pacific, crushing local resistance as in Tahiti. The Tahitians defeated in war, Aimata returned to her throne with her powers greatly diminished. Her son, Pōmare V, was forced to abdicate when the French annexed the island and proclaimed it a colony of France in 1880. Thus terminated the one-hundred-year reign of Tu's dynasty: founded by Cook; flattered and reinforced by captains like Bligh; and defended in battle by the *Bounty* pirates. There have been attempts to

---

* Melville, *Typee: A Romance of the South Seas*, p. 16.

revive the dynasty in defiance of the French state ever since. The most recent claimant to the throne, Athanase Teiri, has spent the past decade in and out of Tahitian jails for, among other things, circulating unofficial currency and ID cards.

CHAPTER SIXTEEN

The Fate of Fletcher Christian

What became of Fletcher Christian? Nothing he wrote down has survived except for his cursive signature on *Bounty* documents. His character has always come to us filtered through the divergent attitudes of the men around him. After the mutiny on the *Bounty*, an event witnessed and recorded by many people, the circle of narrators around Christian begins to thin out. Starved of sources, we are forced to rely on characters like John Adams, whose freewheeling relationship with the truth is a riddle in itself. Thus Christian's life blurs from history into myth.

Adams blithely changed his story about Christian's fate to each successive captain who visited Pitcairn Island. The captains, meanwhile, like the early European visitors to Tahiti, wrote accounts that were riddled with their own ideas and biases. The Tahitians had been held up as Rousseau's natural men. Now the Pitcairn Islanders were served up to readers in different, albeit no less idealistic terms, as models of Christian morality. Adams became a legend of the Protestant faith. His prayer book, ponytail, and even his gravestone were shipped to London and presented in glass cases as national artefacts.

More understandably, Adams was unreliable in describing his own role in the mutiny on the *Bounty*. He told the frigate captains he was sick in his hammock when the rebellion broke out, and was later forced to take up arms against his will. But the court martial testimonies indicate he was an active mutineer, following Christian when he went to the armourer to demand the keys to the arms chest, and standing sentry over Bligh with a loaded musket. When the mutineers dismally cast their votes on Tubuai about how to proceed, Adams voted to remain with Christian, renouncing any chance of returning to England and being exonerated of mutiny. He was part of a hardcore group of mutineers who followed Christian to the end.

Yet he was inconsistent in descriptions of his old shipmate, and almost arbitrary in his contradictions. To Staines and Pipon, he described Christian as a sullen and morose leader who became as cruel and overbearing as William Bligh himself. But to Beechey, eleven years later, Adams remembered Christian as a cheerful man, well liked and respected to the end of his days. All those years after their time aboard the *Bounty*, Beechey noted, Adams still referred to his old shipmate as '*Mr* Christian', not forgetting his officer status.

With all those inconsistencies, the character of Adams, hailed by the captains who met him as a benevolent patriarch, grows ever more ambivalent and perhaps even sinister. He told Captain Pipon it had been Fletcher Christian who, when his wife died, sparked a Tahitian rebellion by seizing another. But Christian's wife was then still living, and in Adams's later accounts the instigator of the rebellion morphed into John Williams. He told Pipon that Christian himself set fire to the *Bounty* on arrival at Pitcairn Island, but he told Beechey that Christian wanted to run the ship aground, and an errant Matthew Quintal set fire to her.

Why did the story keep changing? It's possible Adams spoke poorly of Christian in an attempt at distancing himself from the mutiny. His opinion of his former leader brightened considerably when he no longer feared the gallows. He may also have been in a state of mental decline, his sense of reality blunted from decades in isolation. In his late forties, he already looked like an elderly man and he could not recall the dates of events on the island with any accuracy. Despite his shortcomings, he was the island's sole authority and oral historian for many years, unlikely to be contradicted by his flock. He was persuasive, with a 'sincerity in his speech which I can hardly describe',* recalled Captain Pipon. But there were

---

* Belcher, *The Mutineers of the Bounty*, p. 176.

other survivors of the violence on Pitcairn, never questioned by the captains, who might have proven more reliable: the Tahitian women who settled with the mutineers.

Nobody bothered to interview Christian's partner, Mauatua, who lived to be as old as eighty, only dying of an epidemic brought by a passing ship in 1841. Mauatua could remember Captain Cook's first visit to Tahiti; she must have been in her twenties when the *Bounty* arrived. It is sometimes claimed that Fletcher and Mauatua married when the former returned to Tahiti following the mutiny, but there is no account of a wedding. She also takes the form of a princess or the daughter of a local chief in *Bounty* lore; it's possible she was related to Teina, but there is no evidence for it. Mauatua was likely a font of knowledge about Pitcairn's history. There is a passing glimpse of her in the account of Bennett, the whaleship surgeon, in 1834: 'Her hair is very white, and she bears, generally, an appearance of extreme age, but her mental and bodily powers are yet active.'*

Bennett also met Susan Christian, a small and cheerful woman who presented him with a roll of bark cloth and a lock of her curling hair. Susan was the wife of Thursday October, but she cannot have been much younger than Thursday's mother. Like Mauatua, she was one of the island's original settlers. Bennett does not seem to have delved further into the life of 'Old Susan', other than to mention that she 'arrived on

---

* Bennett, *Narrative of a Whaling Voyage Round the Globe*, p. 32.

the island as the wife of one of the Tahitian settlers, and bears the reputation of having played a conspicuous part when the latter were massacred by their own countrywomen'.*

The women of Pitcairn Island were a potent force in the island's early years, quietly fighting for their own interests, pitting the men against each other and plotting murder. They might also be credited with the colony's survival; it was probably their Polynesian methods of gardening, cooking and cloth-making that carried the settlement, rather than the 'labour and ingenuity of European hands',† as Captain Pipon observed.

In 1817, a Tahitian woman called Teehuteatuaonoa, who had the English name Jenny, left Pitcairn for Tahiti on the American whaling ship *Sultan*. Jenny gave two published interviews in Tahiti. The first appeared in the *Sydney Gazette* in 1819, and the second in the *Bengal Hurkaru*, an English-language newspaper in Calcutta (present-day Kolkata), in 1826 (and was reproduced a few years later in an English periodical, the *United Service Journal*). The inclusion of the word *atua*, or god, in Jenny's name shows she was from one of the elite families in Tahitian society.

She began her odyssey with the Europeans as John Adams's wife, and had the initials of his pseudonym, Alexander Smith, tattooed on her arm, with the date 1789.

---

*   Bennett, *Narrative of a Whaling Voyage Round the Globe*, p. 33.
†   Barrow, *The Eventful History of the Mutiny and Piratical Seizure of HMS Bounty*, ch. 8.

After sailing with the mutineers to Pitcairn Island she became the wife of Isaac Martin up until his murder. Unlike the other women, she never had children. Her life on Pitcairn was unhappy, and after she convinced the crew of the *Sultan* to take her on board, she became the first original settler to permanently leave the island. 'She has been apparently a good looking woman in her time, but now begins to bear the marks of age,' wrote her first interviewer, only adding to his perfunctory description that Jenny's hands were 'hard with work' and she spoke 'neither English nor Tahitian, but a jumble of both'.*

In her own telling of the island's history, Jenny said Christian was killed in the revolt by the Tahitians, along with most of the other mutineers, in a carefully executed series of murders. Neither Jenny nor Adams gave dates for what is known in island tradition as 'Massacre Day', but the *Pitcairn Island Register*, a record compiled by later settlers to the island, gives the date as 1793, three years after the burning of the *Bounty*.

Jenny said several mutineers set fire to the ship against Christian's wishes. The settlers planted sweet potatoes and yams and divided up the land; one lucky mutineer found the paper mulberry tree growing on his lot, and after 'some squabbling' they agreed to divide it equally.† About a year after their arrival, John Williams's wife died of a disease in

---

*   Teehuteatuaonoa (Jenny) interview, *Sydney Gazette and New South Wales Advertiser*, 1819.

†   Teehuteatuaonoa (Jenny) interview, transcription from *United Service Journal*, 1829.

her neck (Adams told Beechey she died in a cliff fall while collecting birds' eggs). The mutineers drew lots to determine who among the wives of the Polynesian men would be 'given' to Williams. The lot fell on the wife of Tararo, the chief from Raiatea. Tararo was humiliated, and exiled himself to the mountains, a place of recurring refuge for Europeans and Polynesians alike during island conflict.

After a few days, Tararo managed to steal his wife and take her into hiding with him. A plot now emerged among Tararo and some other conspirators, with whom he kept in secret contact, to kill the whites. The mutineers learnt about the conspiracy. (Adams said the warning came in the form of an ominous song overheard from one of the Tahitian women, which included the words, 'Why does black man sharpen axe? To kill white man.')* Christian sent one of the Polynesian men who remained with the Europeans into the mountains with a pistol to crush the murder plot. The assassin was successful, killing Tararo and Oha, one of the Tubuaians.

On the dawn of Massacre Day, four Polynesian men had two women to share, and relations with the white men were unravelling again. Manarii, a Tahitian man, had been severely beaten for stealing a pig from McKoy. 'The natives again concerted among themselves to murder the English and went about from day to day with their muskets, on a

---

* Beechey, *Narrative of a Voyage to the Pacific and Beering's Strait*, p. 83.

pretence of shooting wild-fowl,"* said Jenny. She described the purge that followed.

> The mutineers did not suspect their intentions: Williams was the first man shot, while putting up a fence around his garden. The natives next proceeded to shoot Christian: they found him clearing some ground for a garden, and while in the act of carrying away some roots, they went behind him and shot him between the shoulders – he fell. They then disfigured him with an axe about the head, and left him dead on the ground.[†]

According to Jenny, Fletcher Christian's luck had finally run out, and he was gunned down without ceremony in the midst of a domestic scene. He would have been twenty-eight years old, his wife pregnant with their third child.

Jenny said the Tahitians proceeded to another cottage, where they shot down the *Bounty*'s gunner's mate, John Mills. At Isaac Martin's house, they shot Martin twice as he ran away. Martin staggered to the home of his neighbour Brown, the *Bounty*'s former gardening assistant, and collapsed. The Polynesians then 'beat him on the head with a hammer till he was quite dead'.[‡] They then descended on a startled Brown,

---

* Teehuteatuaonoa (Jenny) interview, transcription from *United Service Journal*, 1829.

† Teehuteatuaonoa (Jenny) interview, transcription from *United Service Journal*, 1829.

‡ Teehuteatuaonoa (Jenny) interview, transcription from *United Service Journal*, 1829.

bashing his head with stones and leaving him for dead on the ground.

But the white man sprang up and ran for his life, and one of the rebels quickly gave chase and overtook him. With a musket in his face, Brown begged hard for mercy, asking to see his wife before they killed him. The Polynesians promised to spare his life, but one of their party crept up behind him and shot him dead. The rebels now crept up on Adams's house and fired at him, a musket ball grazing his neck and breaking two of his fingers. The Tahitian women threw themselves on his body and successfully appealed for his life to be spared.

In the confusion of gunfire on that spring afternoon, Quintal and McKoy had managed to flee to the mountains. Only two white men remained in the settlement: Young and Adams. The Polynesians turned their muskets on each other, probably in a fight over the wives of the dead mutineers. Manarii shot Teimura three times, killing him. (In her first interview, Jenny said he was drunk on the new spirit the mutineers had distilled but in her second interview, she said the mutineers began distilling the spirit only after all of the Polynesian men were dead.) Fearing for his own life, Manarii fled to the mountains and joined McKoy and Quintal in hiding. He offered the whites his musket and resolved to live in exile with them. But the Tahitian women knew where the whites were camped and, in a secret meeting, persuaded them to kill Manarii, which they did.

The two remaining Tahitian men went in search of McKoy and Quintal in the mountains. They spotted the whites in the high country and fired at them, believing they had wounded McKoy. The women met secretly with the exiles again, telling them to come into the settlement under the cover of darkness and kill the two Tahitian men who remained there. The whites promised to do this, but didn't keep their word.

Next day the women turned to the mutineers still living in the settlement, Young and Adams, to carry out their plot. The Polynesian men were resting in the mid-afternoon heat, lying on the floor of one of the houses, when Young and a woman attacked them. The woman hit one of them in the head with a hatchet, at the same time calling out to Young to fire his musket, killing the other.

There now remained on the island eleven Tahitian women and four Englishmen: Smith, McKoy, Young and Quintal.

In her interviews, Jenny was recalling chaotic and traumatic events that happened decades earlier. But she seems to have been more reliable than Adams. She was disenchanted with life on Pitcairn Island, had no fear of the gallows, and her story did not change substantially over time. The common ground between the accounts of Jenny and Adams is that the society on Pitcairn was set up with the Polynesians subordinate to the Europeans, and the resulting strain, in particular tensions over women, led to a massacre. A plantation mindset seems to have existed not solely among the mutineers but also among the Tahitian women, who bought into the superior social rank of their European husbands. The Tahitian women defended the mutineers, kept watch over them, begged that their lives be spared, and avenged their deaths with further bloodshed.

Two months after the massacre, Edward Young, the second-to-last surviving mutineer, began keeping a journal. Adams showed the document to Beechey, who copied out some of the entries verbatim, and paraphrased others. After the captain departed on the *Blossom*, the document was lost to posterity. Adams can't have forged it, because his writing ability was poor, as shown by a two-sentence attempt at an autobiography where he referred to his childhood self and three siblings as 'poore orfing' (poor orphans). It's possible Adams edited the journal through omission, but Beechey did not suspect him of doing so. According to Beechey, the document was a spare account of the goings-on in the colony; sometimes the events of a year occupied a single page. But it also gave a compelling insight into life on the island after the massacre and brought to light new details, such as the atmosphere of distrust and paranoia between the surviving mutineers and the Tahitian women.

The entry for 12 March 1794, said: 'Going over to borrow a rake, to rake the dust off my ground, I saw Jenny having a skull in her hand: I asked her whose it was? And was told it was Jack [John] Williams's. I desired it might be buried: the women who were with Jenny gave me for answer, it should not.'*

---

* Beechey, *Narrative of a Voyage to the Pacific and Beering's Strait*, p. 89.

Young wrote that he approached McKoy, Smith (Adams) and Quintal with the skull problem, and told them: 'I thought that if the girls did not agree to give up the skulls of the five white men in a peaceable manner, they ought to be taken by force, and buried.'*

Tahitians sometimes kept skulls as *'oromatua*, the disembodied spirits of their loved ones. Young, the only gentleman left on the island, took exception to the practice as barbarous. The women must have assented to Young's request because, according to his journal, five months later they dug a grave and buried the bones of the murdered people. He did not specify the location of this mass grave.

Young wrote that 'since the massacre, it has been the desire of the greater part of them [the women] to get some conveyance, to enable them to leave the island'.† The mutineers agreed to start building a boat for the women in April 1794; in a desperate attempt to hurry the project along, Jenny tore the boards off her own house. By August, the women were launching the vessel, but 'according to expectation' it capsized,‡ and they swam back to shore in defeat.

The women continued their unhappy lives on Pitcairn. Quintal and McKoy often beat them, and Quintal in particular proposed 'not to laugh, joke, or give any thing to any of the girls'.§ Young described himself as 'bothered

* Beechey, *Narrative of a Voyage to the Pacific and Beering's Strait*, p. 89.
† Beechey, *Narrative of a Voyage to the Pacific and Beering's Strait*, p. 89.
‡ Beechey, *Narrative of a Voyage to the Pacific and Beering's Strait*, p. 89.
§ Beechey, *Narrative of a Voyage to the Pacific and Beering's Strait*, p. 90.

and idle' in November as the men lived in suspense,[*] not knowing whether the women would rise up against them, as they had done against the Polynesian men. Sure enough, a conspiracy to kill the mutineers in their sleep was discovered and foiled. Nineteen days later, the women again collected and attacked the men, but no lives were lost. Sometimes the women abandoned the settlement entirely and hid in other parts of the island with muskets; the men must have spent those nights in watches, fearing for their lives.

In December 1795, everybody scattered in terror at the sight of a ship on the horizon, but the surf was so big and the weather so poor that, to their profound relief, she disappeared. It seems incredible that after the protracted misery of island life, the settlers were still terrified of passing ships.

The next few years were relatively peaceful. The mutineers dined at each other's houses and shared what meat and vegetables they could hunt and farm. There was no further discontent among the women. Then McKoy figured out how to make liquor from the ti plant in 1798.

According to Jenny, in a drunken affray, Quintal's three countrymen killed him. (Adams said he and Young killed Quintal after McKoy had already died.) The murder was witnessed by Elizabeth Mills, a seven-year-old girl who lived to be ninety-three. She was present when Young and Adams got Quintal drunk and killed him with an axe. She

---

[*] Beechey, *Narrative of a Voyage to the Pacific and Beering's Strait*, p. 90.

often recalled the terrible sight of Quintal's lifeless body on the floor and his blood sprayed across the walls.* Around this time, McKoy, in a drunken delirium, leapt into the sea with his hands and feet bound and died.

Young's journal stops around the time of McKoy's purported death. According to Adams, Young lived another two years without writing another entry and died a natural death on Christmas Day.

Twenty-one years old when he signed on the *Bounty*, Young was biracial, from the West Indies. He was the son of a navy officer and educated as a gentleman. Other than Christian, he seems to have been the only officer on the *Bounty* who played an active role in the mutiny; at the court martial, several crew members said they saw him striding the decks with a musket. When Christian called a vote on Tubuai and gave an emotional speech about sailing onward in the *Bounty* until he found an uninhabited island, Young declared: 'We shall never leave you, Mr. Christian, go where you will.'† Bligh's physical description of Young is not at all flattering, but like his description of Christian, it was probably coloured by personal hatred. The lieutenant wrote that Young had a strong build, with a 'dark complexion and rather a bad look'.‡ He had lost several of his front teeth, and 'those that remain are all rotten'.§

---

* Wahlroos, *Mutiny and Romance in the South Seas*, p. 350.
† Christian, *Appendix to Minutes of the Proceedings of the Court-Martial*.
‡ Wahlroos, *Mutiny and Romance in the South Seas*, p. 433.
§ Wahlroos, *Mutiny and Romance in the South Seas*, p. 434.

It's possible that Young had a hand in Christian's death. He was not attacked on Massacre Day, which implies he had prior knowledge of the attack, if he wasn't involved in organising it himself. According to John Buffett, an early immigrant to Pitcairn in the 1820s who became the island's schoolteacher and de facto leader, Adams once hinted that Young had planned the massacre. Buffett said when the Tahitians spared Adams after wounding him, they claimed to have forgotten 'Young told them not to hurt [him]'.* After Fletcher Christian's death, Young went on to have three children with Christian's widow, Mauatua.

It's also possible that Adams killed Christian. Louis Becke, who visited Pitcairn Island in the 1860s, maintained he knew the 'descendants of the *Bounty* mutineers and the *native* story of Christian and his life better than any man living'.† He said Adams shot Christian while the latter was trying to escape the island in a small boat, hoping to flag down a ship in the distance. According to Becke, Adams covered up the murder, claiming Christian had died at the hands of the Polynesian men.

There might be a shade of truth in Becke's account. The mutineer John Williams, when he demanded another wife, was said to have threatened to leave the island in the *Bounty's* small boat; but a few years later, the mutineers had to build a boat from scratch when the Tahitian women wanted to

---

*   Frost, *Mutiny, Mayhem, Mythology*, ch. 3.
†   Frost, *Mutiny, Mayhem, Mythology*, ch. 3.

leave the island. What happened to the boat? Did Fletcher Christian use it to hail a passing ship or make a run for South America? Did the money from the *Bounty* (one hundred ducats, never recovered) disappear along with him? And could Adams have agreed to cover up his departure, hence the confused patchwork of stories?

Adams told Folger, the island's first visitor, that Christian became sick after several years on the island and died a natural death.* Soon afterward, the story went, the Polynesian men killed the other Englishmen in a revolt. Another report, attributed to Folger's second mate, had it that Christian went insane and threw himself off a cliff. Several years later, the story changed again. Adams told the frigate captains, Staines and Pipon, and later Beechey, that Christian was shot and killed during the revolt itself, between eleven months to two years after the island was settled. In any case, Christian's gravesite has never been found. Adams's obfuscation suggests something about Christian's fate was worth concealing, or that he had more of a hand in it than he wanted to admit.

Alan Frost makes a case for Christian's escape, which he says may have taken as long as two years through ports in New England, Macau or South America, until his arrival in England around 1796.

Assuming he reached England, Christian's return must have become a closely guarded family secret, and some

---

* Delano, A *Narrative of Voyages and Travels*, p. 140.

writers point to the family's behaviour in later years in the suggestion they were hiding something. Edward Christian, after his public spat with Bligh, fell oddly silent on the subject of his brother. Neither Ann, Charles nor Edward Christian left a will when they died, unusual for a family in the legal tradition and especially so in the case of Edward, a lawyer and a judge who was survived by his wife at their home in Hoddesdon. Among the possessions handed down to Edward's wife's relatives was a 'strange native hat' from Pitcairn Island,* although this souvenir might have reached him from the crews of the *Tagus* or *Briton*.

Young's journal is an obstacle to Frost's theory. At the time that Young was writing about the skulls of 'five white men', four Europeans remained alive, so by his account the skulls must have included Christian's. That entry alone seems to prove that Christian was dead by 1794, but giving it credence requires faith in Beechey's note-taking, and the integrity of the document he was copying from. I believe Young's journal entry was real, therefore Christian died on Massacre Day. But as Frost points out, either version exists as a possibility: death on Pitcairn Island or return to England.

* * *

---

*   Alexander, *The Bounty*, ch. 13.

Frost thinks the balance of probability tips in favour of Fletcher Christian's return, because Adams's stories vary to a bewildering degree, there is no physical evidence for Christian's death, and there are eyewitness accounts of Christian in England years after the massacre.

In the period when Adams was giving out conflicting tales, rumours were already spreading that the *Bounty* pirate was alive and well in Britain. A circle of 'Lake Poets', named for the Lake District in Christian's native Cumbria, northwest England, are all inextricably tied to Fletcher Christian's return, real or imagined. The poets were Robert Southey, William Wordsworth and Samuel Taylor Coleridge. They were all friends and collaborators, aesthetes of the Romantic school, and radical supporters of the French Revolution (at least initially). Of course, the simplest explanation for their interest in the *Bounty* mutiny is that it served as good creative fodder at a time when they were transfixed by revolution and its attendant moral questions. But at least one of these men genuinely believed Fletcher was in England.

In an 1809 review of an account about Christian missionaries in the South Seas, Southey referred to Bligh as 'notorious'.[*] A friend wrote to him querying the description. In explanation, Southey said he knew a great deal about the *Bounty* mutiny from James Losh, one of the men on the interview panel for Edward Christian's pamphlet.

---

*   Frost, *Mutiny, Mayhem, Mythology*, ch. 3.

He added:

> I know too, or rather have every reason to believe that Fletcher C. was within these few years in England and at his father's house – an interesting circumstance in such a history, and one which I hardly ought to mention – so do not you let it get abroad. For though the Admiralty would be very sorry to hang him, some rascal or other would gladly enough apprehend him for the price of blood, and hung of course he would be, but if every man had his due Bligh would have had the halter instead of the poor fellows who we brought from Tahiti.[*]

When his friend, curiosity piqued, asked for more information, Southey replied that he knew a country gentleman who had attended school with Fletcher Christian, and encountered Christian about five or six years ago. He was walking near his house with his daughter when he saw two gentlemen riding towards him, and recognised one of them enough to say to his daughter, 'Look at this man – it is F.C.'[†] Southey said his friend considered it would be better not to speak with Christian, and they passed each other in silence. There had been a dog with the horsemen, and presently some boys came along who had picked up a collar that bore the name of Christian's father.

James Losh was a Christian family friend, a revolutionary sympathiser (he travelled to Paris in 1792), and a practising

---

[*] Alexander, *The Bounty*, ch. 13.

[†] Frost, *Mutiny, Mayhem, Mythology*, ch. 3.

lawyer in Bristol, a potential first port of call for a returning Fletcher Christian. In an entry in his diary in 1798, Losh confirmed he explained 'the real state of Christian's mutiny' to Southey, who 'seemed much struck by it'.* The entry implies Losh was somehow privy to information that had not reached the public in Bligh's narrative or Edward Christian's pamphlets, but what?

Years earlier, Wordsworth, a close friend of Coleridge and Losh, reacted strangely to the publication of the hoax pamphlet *Letters from Mr. Fletcher Christian* in 1796, writing in a published letter to a magazine editor: 'I think it proper to inform you, that I have the best authority for saying that this publication is spurious.'† It was the only time in Wordsworth's career that he used his real name in a letter to an editor.

Wordsworth and Christian attended the same school, although the poet was four years Fletcher's senior. There were links between the two families; an uncle and a cousin of Wordsworth had been among Edward Christian's panel of respectable gentlemen when he interviewed the *Bounty* crew. The poet's letter to the editor raises several questions: when he said he had the 'best authority' for knowing the *Letters* were fake, did he mean the Christian family had told him so, because they had not heard from the real Fletcher Christian? Or had they informed him of his old schoolmate's secret return to England?

---

* Frost, *Mutiny, Mayhem, Mythology*, ch. 2.
† Frost, *Mutiny, Mayhem, Mythology*, ch. 2.

Lyrical Ballads, a collection of poems published by Wordsworth and Coleridge in 1798, marked the beginning of the Romantic movement in British literature, its soaring verse a departure from the strictures of neoclassical poetry. Coleridge included his famous poem *The Rime of the Ancient Mariner* in the collection, a Gothic tale of a voyage to the Pacific and the return of a lone sailor. There are obvious parallels between the poem and the story of Fletcher Christian, reinforced by a particular entry in Coleridge's notebook, compiled around the time he wrote the poem: 'Adventures of Christian, the mutineer'.* There is no way Coleridge, a lifelong opium addict and a known gossip, could have kept Christian's return to England a secret, but perhaps it was the more circumspect Wordsworth who planted the idea in his friend's head. The idea for the poem was conceived as the pair walked together in England's Quantock Hills.

Thus was born the story of an old mariner with a long grey beard and glittering eye, who stops a wedding guest with his skinny hand, choosing him as the captive audience for his tale. He relates how he shot an albatross during a voyage to the Pacific, invoking a curse that killed his fellow sailors one by one. The ship sank and he returned alone in a small boat to his homeland, where his guilt doomed him to 'pass, like night, from land to land'.† After the mariner concludes his story and disappears, the wedding guest is left a 'sadder and a wiser

---

* Alexander, *The Bounty*, ch. 11.
† Coleridge, *The Rime of the Ancient Mariner*, *Lyrical Ballads*.

man'.* It is hard not to think of Christian, forever doomed to a lonely and marginal existence after one reckless act.

Around this time, Wordsworth was also working on a play, *The Borderers*. Published decades later, the Shakespeare-inspired tragedy was a cultural flop and has since been largely forgotten. But in 1797, Wordsworth made an interesting revision to the play: he added a mutiny to the backstory of one of the characters. And he made the change after a visit to Losh in Bristol; perhaps the lawyer had also revealed the 'real state of Christian's mutiny' to Wordsworth.

In the play, the character Rivers tells another character, Mortimer (who is also a somewhat captive audience), that he led a mutiny in his youth. During a voyage in the Mediterranean, Rivers explains, he left his 'imperious' captain marooned on a desert island.† The crime had the support of the crew ('All hated him, and I was stung to madness'), and as the ship pulled away, some scoffed at the captain with 'hellish mockery', while the captain stretched forth his arms and called for mercy.‡ Arriving at port, Rivers took refuge in a convent and embarked on 'lonely wanderings',§ abandoning regular morals in order to live with his mutinous past. Rivers passes on his moral guilt to Mortimer, deceiving him into leaving an old man to die on the heath. Mortimer then becomes a tormented loner, wandering the earth without rest.

---

* Coleridge, *The Rime of the Ancient Mariner*, *Lyrical Ballads*.

† Wordsworth, *The Borderers*, act 4.

‡ Wordsworth, *The Borderers*, act 4.

§ Wordsworth, *The Borderers*, act 4.

Christian's mother, Ann, lived to be ninety years old and died in 1819. She would have learnt about the colony on Pitcairn Island, and the existence of the three biracial grandchildren she would never meet. She must also have been aware of the accounts of her son's violent death, as well as the rumours he was in fact still alive. In her final years, she shared her house in Douglas with Charles, Fletcher's older brother, now almost fifty. Charles had fallen on hard times. The surgeon was writing an autobiography defending his good character in response to accusations of using forged bank notes around town.

Charles vividly recalled his last meeting with Fletcher. The brothers had spent a night ashore, probably drinking in a tavern, before Fletcher departed Spithead on the *Bounty*. The latter had bared his bicep and said it was the result of 'hard labour'; he prided himself in mixing his officer duties with the work of seamen. Their meeting would have traversed sombre family news, such as Charles's ordeal in a mutiny on the *Middlesex*; the recent death of their only surviving sister, Mary, at the age of twenty-six; and their mother's ongoing financial woes. But in all, Charles remembered Fletcher as 'full of professional ambition and of hope' about the voyage ahead.* He wrote that Fletcher was 'as a boy slow to be moved' but recalled from his own time at sea that when men are cooped up for a long time in a ship, 'it is enough on many

---

*   Preston, *Paradise in Chains*, ch. 7.

occasions ... to change the disposition of a lamb into that of an animal fierce and resentful',[*]

Across the Irish Sea in Cumbria, locals generally believed that Christian was alive and well in the area in the early 1800s.[†] It was said that he made private visits to an aunt who lived there, and was sometimes seen wandering the wooded paths and byways in the Lake District. A fugitive could conceivably vanish at will in that wild country, dissected by valleys, mountains and rainy moors. As Wordsworth wrote of the area: 'So much was this region considered out of the way until a late period that persons who had fled from justice used often to resort thither for concealment, and some were so bold as not infrequently to make excursions from the place of their retreat for the purpose of committing fresh offences.'[‡] Yet another allusion to Christian?

Heywood, the pardoned mutineer, also believed he saw Christian in England years after his purported death.[§] After he escaped the death penalty with the help of his sister Nessy, the tattooed gentleman saw action in the French Revolutionary Wars and surveyed the eastern coasts of Sri Lanka and India. Heywood's star rose in proportion with the Admiralty's disillusionment about Bligh. If there had been

---

[*] Preston, *Paradise in Chains*, ch. 13.

[†] Barrow, *The Eventful History of the Mutiny and Piratical Seizure of HMS Bounty*, endnotes.

[‡] Wordsworth, *The Complete Poetical Works of William Wordsworth*, p. 146.

[§] Barrow, *The Eventful History of the Mutiny and Piratical Seizure of HMS Bounty*, endnotes.

any doubt about his eligibility for promotion in the Royal Navy, it was dispelled when he was promoted to lieutenant without the minimum six years' service. He proceeded to reach the rank of post-captain at age thirty.

As for the other *Bounty* crew members, several had returned to naval service and met unfortunate fates at sea. Morrison, the other mutineer who received the king's pardon, drowned when his ship went down with all hands in a gale off the coast of Madagascar. Thomas Hayward and John Hallett, Bligh's loyal but incompetent midshipmen, both drowned in separate shipwrecks. John Fryer served as sailing master on the British flagship *London* in the Battle of Copenhagen, and lived to retire. The carpenter William Purcell was said to be in a 'madhouse' in 1831.* The physical toll of the open boat voyage did not prevent him from living into his seventies. Indeed he outlived all of his *Bounty* shipmates, including Bligh.

Heywood thought he saw Christian in 1808 or 1809, around the time of Folger's rediscovery of Pitcairn Island. The sighting was related by Sir John Barrow, Second Secretary of the Admiralty, in his 1831 book about the *Bounty* mutiny. Barrow was so convinced of the truth of Heywood's account that he vouched for it personally. It went like this. Now about thirty-six years old, Captain Heywood was running an errand on Fore Street, a wide and bustling highway that terminated at the dockyards of Plymouth. He found himself

---

* Barrow, *The Eventful History of the Mutiny and Piratical Seizure of HMS Bounty*, ch. 4.

walking behind a man whose shape, he noticed, was so much like Christian's that he quickened his pace. The sound of Heywood's steps caught the attention of the stranger, who turned to get a look at Heywood, and immediately ran off. The captain gave chase, convinced he had caught a glimpse of Christian. Both ran as fast as they could, and after making several quick turns, the stranger disappeared.

At the time, no account of Christian had reached Heywood since they parted ways at Tahiti. The resemblance of the stranger, his agitation and his effort to run away, all came together to form a deep impression on his mind. According to Barrow, he thought about it for the rest of his life. Perhaps he half-expected to see it again whenever he rounded a street corner in a strange port, or cast his eyes around a gloomy tavern: the face of Fletcher Christian, his friend the mutineer.

AFTERWORD AND ACKNOWLEDGEMENTS

In early 2020, I found myself unemployed and under lockdown in the United States, which would prove one of the worst-affected countries in the coronavirus pandemic. In the year of isolation that followed, I was able to dedicate myself fully to writing *Men Without Country*, a project I might not otherwise have realised. I'm grateful to my wife for her faith and support, and to my parents for their inspiration and encouragement.

I relied on primary sources as much as possible. The most useful resources were the published journals, narratives and letters of James Cook, William Bligh, James Morrison, Frederick William Beechey, George Hamilton, George Robertson, the Heywood family, and Teehuteatuaonoa. I also relied on Edward Christian's pamphlets and the published minutes from the court martial of the mutineers. Despite his brotherly relation to Fletcher, Edward was able to produce an account of the mutiny that was considered substantially accurate. I hope the same can be said of my account.

Joe Bennett encouraged and coached my writing over many years. My agent Vicki Marsdon was the book's first champion. Careful reading of the manuscript by my editor, Brigid Mullane, and copyeditor, Deonie Fiford, led to major improvements where I could no longer see the wood from the trees. I have also benefited from the published works of many writers and scholars: Dame Anne Salmond, Diana Preston, Caroline Alexander, Herbert Ford, Sven Wahlroos, Sir John Barrow, Douglas L Oliver, Alan Frost, Glynn Christian and Greg Dening.

BIBLIOGRAPHY

Alexander, Caroline, *The Bounty: The True Story of the Mutiny on the Bounty*, Penguin, London, 2004, e-book edition.

Barrow, John, *The Eventful History of the Mutiny and Piratical Seizure of HMS Bounty: Its Cause and Consequences*, John Murray, London, 1831, e-book edition.

Beechey, Captain FW, *Narrative of a Voyage to the Pacific and Beering's Strait, to Cooperate with the Polar Expeditions*, Henry Colburn and Richard Bentley, London, 1831.

Belcher, Lady Diana Jolliffe, *The Mutineers of the Bounty and their Descendants in Pitcairn and Norfolk Islands*, John Murray, London, 1870.

Bennett, Frederick, *Narrative of a Whaling Voyage Round the Globe from the Year 1833 to 1836, Vol. I*, Richard Bentley, London, 1840.

Besant, Walter, *Captain Cook*, Macmillan and Co., London, 1904.

Bligh, William, *A Voyage to the South Sea*, George Nichol, London, 1792, e-book edition.

Bligh, William, *An Answer to Certain Assertions Contained in the Appendix to a Pamphlet*, George Nichol, London, 1793.

Bougainville, Louis Antoine de, *A Voyage Round the World*, translated by John Reinhold Forster, J Nourse, London, 1772.

Coleridge, Samuel Taylor. *The Rime of the Ancient Mariner, Lyrical Ballads*, with a few other poems, J & A Arch, London, 1798.

Cook, James, *A Voyage Towards the South Pole and Round the World* (Vols 1 and 2), W Strahan, London, 1777, e-book edition.

Cook, James, *Captain Cook's Journal During the First Voyage Round the World*, Elliot Stock, London, 1893, e-book edition.

Christian, Edward, *Appendix to Minutes of the Proceedings on the Court-Martial held at Portsmouth, August 12th, 1792, on Ten Persons charged with Mutiny on Board His Majesty's Ship the Bounty*, J Deighton, London, 1794.

Christian, Glynn, *Fragile Paradise*, Little, Brown and Company, 1982.

Delano, Amasa, *A Narrative of Voyages and Travels in the Northern and Southern Hemispheres*, EG House, Boston, 1817.

Dening, Greg, *Mr. Bligh's Bad Language: Passion, Power and Theatre on the Bounty*, Cambridge University Press, Cambridge, 1992.

Dening, Greg, *Performances*, Melbourne University Press, Melbourne, 1996.

Dunmore, John, *French Explorers in the Pacific* (Vol. 1), Clarendon Press, Oxford, 1965.

Edwards, Philip, *The Journals of Captain Cook*, Penguin Books, London, 2003, e-book edition.

Ford, Herbert, *Pitcairn Island as a Port of Call*, McFarland & Company, Inc., North Carolina, 2012.

Forster, Georg, *A Voyage Round the World* (Vol. 2), B. White, London, 1777.

Frost, Alan, *Mutiny, Mayhem, Mythology: Bounty's Enigmatic Voyage*, Sydney University Press, Sydney, 2018, e-book edition.

Hale, Edward Everett, *Stories of the Sea Told by Sailors*, Little, Brown and Company, Boston, 1909.

Hamilton, George, *Voyage of HMS Pandora*, Francis Edwards, London, 1915, e-book edition.

Heffernan, Thomas Farel, *Stove by a Whale: Owen Chase and the Essex*, Wesleyan University Press, Connecticut, 1990.

Heywood, Peter and Nessy (edited by Donald A Maxton and Rolf E Du Rietz), *Innocent on the Bounty: The Court-Martial and Pardon of Midshipman Peter Heywood, in Letters*, McFarland & Company, Jefferson, 2013.

Hobbes, Thomas, *Leviathan*, Andrew Crooke, London, 1651, e-book edition.

Hughes, Robert, *The Fatal Shore*, Vintage Books, New York, 1988, e-book edition.

Linder, Professor Douglas O, Transcript of the Court-Martial of the Bounty Mutineers, UMKC School of Law, https://www.famous-trials.com/bounty/399-transcript. Retrieved from URL.

Melville, Herman, *Typee: A Romance of the South Seas*, John Murray, London, 1847.

Morrison, James, *Journal on HMS Bounty and at Tahiti*, 1787–1781, Mitchell Library, State Library of New South Wales, http://acms.sl.nsw.gov.au/_transcript/2015/D33357/a1221.html. Retrieved from URL.

Oliver, Douglas L, *Ancient Tahitian Society*, University Press of Hawaii, Honolulu, 1974.

Preston, Diana, *Paradise in Chains*, Bloomsbury USA, New York, 2017, e-book edition.

Robertson, George (edited with introduction by Oliver Warner), *The Discovery of Tahiti*, The Folio Society, London, 1955.

Salmond, Anne, *Bligh: William Bligh in the South Seas*, Penguin Viking, 2016, e-book edition.

Scott, Ernest, *The Life of Captain Matthew Flinders*, Angus & Robertson Ltd, Sydney, 1914.

Teehuteatuaonoa (Jenny) interview, transcription from *United Service Journal*, 1829, Herbert Ford, Pitcairn Islands Study Center, https://library.puc.edu/pitcairn/pitcairn/jenny.shtml. Retrieved from URL.

Teehuteatuaonoa (Jenny) interview, *Sydney Gazette and New South Wales Advertiser*, 1819, National Library of Australia, Trove Service, https://trove.nla.gov.au/newspaper/article/656630. Retrieved from URL.

Wahlroos, Sven, *Mutiny and Romance in the South Seas*, Salem House Publishers, Topsfield, 1989.

Wordsworth, William, *The Complete Poetical Works of William Wordsworth with an introduction by John Morley*, Thomas Y Crowell & Co., New York, 1892.

Wordsworth, William, *The Borderers*, Copyright Group, 2015, e-book edition.